Sheila Macqueen's
ENCYCLOPAEDIA OF FLOWER ARRANGING

by the same author

★

FLOWER DECORATION IN CHURCHES

SHEILA MACQUEEN'S

Encyclopædia of
Flower Arranging

with illustrations by
YVONNE SKARGON
and a chapter on Ikebana
The Art of Japanese Flower Arranging
by NORMAN SPARNON

FABER AND FABER
London

First published in 1967
by Faber and Faber Limited
3 Queen Square London WC1
First published in this edition 1971
Printed in Great Britain by
Robert MacLehose and Co. Ltd,
The University Press, Glasgow
All rights reserved

ISBN 0 571 09598 4 (Faber Paper Covered Edition)
ISBN 0 571 08567 9 (Hard Bound Edition)

TO
SANDY AND JANE

Contents

Illustrations

Acknowledgements

———————⋯⋯≪⊙≫⋯⋯———————

I am greatly indebted to Mr Norman Sparnon for his valuable and interesting contribution on Ikebana; in addition to the text Mr Sparnon very kindly provided me with photographs of some of his own Japanese flower arrangements.

I would like to thank Miss Walsh of *Housewife* magazine for allowing me to use the colour photographs in this book; and Tom Belshaw for his care and help in taking them. Also my thanks go to Mr and Mrs Luff for all their help in compiling the encyclopaedia section; Mr Downward and Ernest for their infinite patience in taking the black and white photographs and Miss Yvonne Skargon for her beautiful line drawings.

I owe particular thanks to Mrs Audrey Parker: without her help this book would never have been completed. Finally I would like to thank my publishers for their patience and co-operation.

Introduction

The idea for this book originated many years ago when Miss Chase, then editor of *Housewife*, suggested that I should write a series of articles for the magazine on various flowers and how to arrange them. The flowers were listed alphabetically, and under each entry I gave a short description of the flower concerned and suggested how it could best be used to make the most effective arrangement — whether it should, for instance, be mixed with other flowers (and, if so, which ones), arranged en masse, or left as a single bloom.

The series proved so popular and brought in so many letters that I felt a book on similar lines might help and interest the modern flower arranger. It is designed primarily for those who have had some experience, although I hope beginners will also find it useful. My basic aim is to show you how to make the most of whatever flowers you may have, either growing in your garden, or bought from a shop, and to encourage you to experiment with different varieties. The Encyclopaedia section will tell you, quickly and without fuss, the best ways of arranging any given flower, how to make it last as long as possible and, if practicable, how to preserve the leaf, flower, or seed head. The general chapters set out the principles of flower arranging, give details about equipment, methods, conditioning and drying, and make suggestions about flowers for special occasions.

I hope that you will not find that I have failed to mention your favourite flower. With such a big subject it is impossible to cover everything and, inevitably, much has had to be missed out. I have, however, tried to include most of the flowers I grow myself, as well as those I would very much like to grow, given the right conditions. I have deliberately said little about culture, since this varies so much throughout the country.

Flower arranging changes all the time and I find that, although I have done it for more years than I like to mention, I never stop learning. I must confess that I know little about Japanese flower arrangement which is now becoming more and more popular, and I was particularly glad when Mr Norman Sparnon said he would write a chapter on the subject for me. Mr Sparnon's fame has spread from his native Australia to America and Great Britain, and he is of course well-known

I. This group of small rock and alpine plants makes an interesting and attractive arrangement that looks well on either a mantelpiece or coffee table. Though the flowers look fragile, they last surprisingly well in water. The few split leaves of *Tiarella cordifolia* and the ivy help to show off the small flowers and add weight to the base of the vase. Proportion is important and flowers should be approximately one and a half to twice the height of the vase. The small vase in this case is metal and was probably designed as a candle holder. It has been converted by removing the spike and fixing in its place a bowl for water.

A   Dwarf tulip, *T. clusiana*
B   *Fritillaria pyrenaica*
C   *Narcissus* 'Silver Chimes'
D   Dwarf tulip species *T. hageri*
E   *Fritillaria meleagris*
F   *Narcissus triandrus* hybrid
G   *Muscari* (Grape Hyacinths)
H   *Polyanthus*
I   Leaf of *Arum italicum pictum*
J   *Hacquetia epipactis* (Syn. *Dondia epipactis*)
K   *Primula auricula*
L   Leaves of *Tiarella cordifolia*
M   Leaf of the common ivy, *Hedera helix*
N   Dwarf tulip, *T. linifolia*
O   *Fritillaria meleagris alba*

1. A mixture of June glory: peonies, canterbury bells, delphiniums, foxgloves, hydrangea and escallonia, which shows how to choose the right flowers for the right container. On the left is a spray of brilliant blue, a hybrid of 'Blue Butterfly' miniature delphinium, unique because it first appeared in my grandmother's garden.

in Japan where he is a frequent visitor. His demonstrations and lectures are a delight to watch and his personal charm has won him a large international following.

This has been a highly enjoyable book to write and I very much hope that it may add to the pleasure you take in making your own flower arrangements.

CHAPTER ONE

The Principles of Flower Arranging

To take a bunch of flowers and arrange them well to suit your own surroundings, to enjoy the blending of colours and the mixture of textures, to make the most of light and shade and depth and quality, is something that we can learn about today. The art of flower arrangement is of great interest to so many people and, time absorbing as it may be, it is at least a form of relaxation that for many of us severs the tension of this rather hectic world we live in. It takes us a step further with our other interests. The desire to have the unusual to pick gives gardeners an additional motive. Then fresh interest is taken in colour, and in furnishings and backgrounds, a change of scheme whereby one flower arrangement looks better than another, and so a more critical eye is developed about the house. The choice of curtains and covers becomes more positive, instead of the casual approach that anything, preferably something that wears, will do. Extra thought goes into any changes in decorating: a new paint or paper which can make flowers look more attractive, the use of softer, blending colours, perhaps trying out subtle and off-beat colourings, so that one has more scope for using a wide range of flowers throughout the year. Ferreting around the antique shops looking for old or unusual containers, makes a shopping expedition exciting. Holidays abroad bring chances of searching markets and shops for unusual baskets or glass-ware that can be used for flowers on return.

Flower arranging has become a national hobby, with flourishing Flower Clubs in every town. These claim a membership of over fifty thousand, which is quite an achievement in not much more than ten years. People wishing to learn about flower arrangement should contact the secretary of their local club, but — a word of warning—there could be a waiting list owing to increasing popularity. On the other hand, many people feel that flowers arrange themselves; although they like to see a well-arranged vase, they have no desire to learn. Many more have other activities and little time, and some prefer not to learn in case of becoming a copyist and losing their own way of expressing themselves. All I would like to say is that the approach does not matter one bit, as long as you enjoy flowers for their own sake and like to see them growing and to have them about you indoors; how you arrange them is of course your own affair.

Personally I still feel very strongly that one must consider surroundings first and always arrange the flowers to fit in with them, picking up colours and textures. Today there is a tendency to work for a perfect vase regardless as to whether this will look right in your home. It is so much nicer, though, if someone says how lovely your flowers look with your curtains, carpet or chair-covers than how clever you have been to do a vase of such-and-such a shape. Also, however gratifying it may be to have your work admired, rooms quickly become 'over-flowered', giving a tiresome sense of one group after another. I often think one really good vase in a room is all that is needed, or perhaps a large one and a really small one. Over-elaborate flowers seem very self-conscious.

I love to grow my own flowers to arrange. There is an enormous satisfaction in picking a collection of bits from the garden on a winter's day, creating a flower arrangement without buying anything at all.

I like to pick a bunch and start arranging it in my hand as I go round the garden. Usually it is quite easy to decide what vase to use before you begin. This kind of collecting can be dictated by some special flower that is out at that particular moment. You might feel that three apricot tulips could be spared from a bed of a dozen; knowing that none would be more than nine inches, after picking to allow the lower leaves and a small part of the stem to go back into the bulb for next year, gives the idea that, say, a twelve-inch gold urn could well be a suitable container — and you pick accordingly, remembering that the outline material usually requires something light and feathery for a backing; this could be a blossom of some sort, or a branch of foliage in good contrast and just tall enough to be an inch or so above the main flower. Then you decide on additional flowers or foliage: perhaps a stem of rhubarb in flower or the dark leaves of begonia or tiarella, and so you build up your picture.

The proportion of container to flowers is important, yet there can be no standard rule. It is a matter of trial and error. Of course, it is obvious that delphiniums four feet long look wrong in a tiny vase, also that long-stemmed flowers cut down to fit a particular vase can often look unhappy and out of place. Never cut a stem more than is necessary, but by the same token never feel restricted about removing pieces once the flower has been picked. The moment to consider the length you would like is before you actually cut from the plant or shrub; this is not such a problem with herbaceous plants or annuals: it applies mainly to shrubs and trees. I find then that picking, from young bushes especially, becomes a major decision and a lot of time can be spent on trying to choose which branch can be taken, so as not to spoil the shape of the tree but as far as possible to improve it.

Furniture and personal treasures — photographs, china and ornaments — all

II. Springtime: a shallow picking basket in which I have placed a bowl to hold water; in this a few layers of crushed wire netting are tied securely in position and covered with fresh green moss. (Moss, incidentally, can be kept beautifully fresh for many weeks if it is just left until required in a polythene bag.) The flowers are inserted in bunches: I sometimes find that for an arrangement of this kind I tuck in bought primroses as a whole bunch, just loosening the raffia or elastic band. The best effect is achieved by keeping the bunches in self colour, even though the flowers may not all be of the same type. This is well illustrated by the bunch of blue, which gets its brilliant colour from three different kinds of flowers. Daffodils, having rather stiff stems, seem to look more attractive when placed in small clumps together, two or three of the same variety. The background in this arrangement is just a little piece of flowering cherry, but can be varied by using stems of catkin, pussy willow or any blossom available.

A   Flowering cherry, *Prunus serrulata* 'Kanzan'
B   The pink daffodil *Narcissus* 'Rosy Sunrise'
C   *Narcissus* 'Sempre Avanti'
D   *Hyacinthus* 'Pink Roman'
E   *Muscari* (Grape Hyacinths)
F   *Myosotis* (Forget-me-not)
G   *Primula vulgaris* (Primrose)
H   *Primula polyantha* (Polyanthus)
I   Siberian wallflowers, *Cheiranthus allionii* Sutton's 'Orange Bedder'

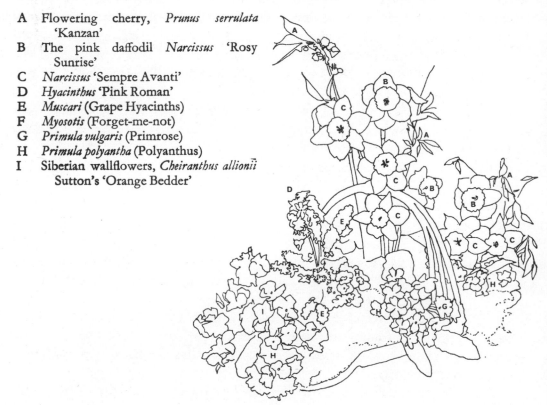

need to be considered when you are deciding how many flowers you can put in a room. The placing of flowers in each room includes practical problems: not in direct sunlight or over central heating; out of a draught, and away from a door or window or other danger spot where a vase could easily be knocked over or spilled. Then come questions of background — a plain wall for preference. If you have flowers against a patterned wall-paper, especially if the pattern is fussy, the effect looks confused: you get neither a good outline nor any feeling of colour. Against the window is another place to avoid if possible, as flowers seen against the light lose all their colour-value and just take on an outline or silhouette. This difficulty can be met, with a good deal of thought about the right choice of flowers and container; the flowers that look best are those with an airy effect — old man's beard, gypsophila — anything feathery or light.

Good lighting is very important. If artificial light is required, it should preferably come from above. Nothing but outline shows if light shines on to the flowers from below; again colour-values are lost and only a silhouette is obtained. Of course, for hotels or shops, this can be an advantage and a few flowers, even though half dead, can look quite attractive in a subdued light shining up from a lower level; but this gives a false effect and should be avoided, I feel, in your own home. If you have panelled walls in dark wood, you must use flowers in pale shades. Yellows, whites or pale pinks show up best of all. Try to avoid deep reds or blues; blues have a nasty habit of turning black by artificial light, but will show up if used with another colour, such as pale pink or white.

Vases arranged all the way round I personally avoid, except for a small one now and again, perhaps on a coffee table. I would always move furniture to try to avoid having a large 'all-round' vase, because I find this takes so many flowers and needs constant attention. Of course, there are times when it cannot be helped, and then a suitable vase must be chosen and one which will not hold too much; I feel the bowl type of container on a pedestal stand is perhaps the most generally useful.

The value of flowers in any house or flat is surely the fact that they make it seem lived-in and give a feeling of welcome or home-coming. I like, if possible, to have a vase that gives an evident welcome and can be noticed immediately by anyone entering the room. For this reason a mantelpiece is a good place for flowers: a small vase for everyday and a large long one, if you can, for a party. A vase here is an excellent focal point.

One of the nicest ideas for linking flowers with your room is to arrange them under a picture to pick up all its colourings. This adds so much to the general effect and draws attention to the painting as well as to the flowers.

Flowers in the hall give a welcome as soon as the door is open — on a pedestal, for example, or if space is precious then on the wall. A wall vase is most helpful in a small narrow hall, perhaps in a flat or a cottage. A trough of house plants can be attractive and needs little attention; it can be watered and cared for once a week except in very hot weather. In modern flats it is possible to have them built in, and the plants can be quite happy over a radiator although they will need more watering because of the heat.

The dining-room needs table flowers and these are often quite enough, depending on the size of the room and the amount of furniture. Table flowers are usually better matched to the colouring of china or table linen, rather than to the general room-colouring by linking up with carpets and so on. A scheme to incorporate the dinner service always looks attractive, and it is sometimes possible to use part of the service for flowers — a vegetable dish or a soup tureen, gravy boats or a meat dish, according to the time of year and whether the flowers are long-stemmed or short.

For a party, of course, any amount of flowers can be used, either in vases or hung on the walls to save space. Hanging balls of fresh flowers from electric light fittings, or a wall vase or basket hung for the evening, all look very festive.

Flowers in the guest's room are especially welcoming and pleasure-giving and usually I try to choose something fragrant. I have stayed in only one house where I had the luxury of flowers on the breakfast tray, but I still remember the pleasure it gave me.

I love flowers in my own room and usually manage to get a few all the year round, but I think best of all are the sweetly scented ones: honeysuckle, pinks and jasmine. I picked ginger lilies in Honolulu and they were almost over-powering, but I can't smell one now without thinking of the surf and golden sands of that enchanting island.

The bathroom triumphs in this era of house plants. Ivies, begonias and others enjoy the warm steamy atmosphere and they can look charming. Many of the variegated ivies are very decorative and can easily be trained to grow up trellis work, or just to cascade from a hanging container.

The sun-room or loggia is another place where house plants look happy and thrive in the warmth and sunlight. Simple line arrangements are also suitable and flowers in shallow bowls of water are very effective. Dried flowers in winter harmonize well with the fawns and browns of wickerwork and cane furniture.

CHAPTER TWO

Equipment and Methods

Every flower arranger needs a certain amount of equipment, and I think the amount really depends on how much one is concerned with the subject, and, of course, how much time one can give to it. To many people in recent years it is not only a hobby but a part-time job; but like cooking or dress-making it is so much quicker and easier if you have the right tools. I find it is so easy to collect a lot of bits and pieces, and so a small room or even a cupboard is essential. My small room for this is the one room in the whole house that I have to tidy and spring-clean entirely by myself, as the amount of what must appear to be absolute rubbish to the uninitiated is in point of fact quite essential. Apart from vases, which take up a lot of room, there are so many odd things, such as wire netting, string, scissors, that all need a special place so that one has them immediately to hand.

The first thing I would suggest is to make a collection of varying-sized polythene bags. Besides all their other uses, these are invaluable just for keeping your vases in. Every now and then I have a big tidy-up and pack vases into these bags as it really saves so much time. Silver kept from the air in this way stays clean for a long time, as does ormolu. Once the vase has been well washed and the netting scalded under hot water, the netting can be put back and the vase is all ready for the next occasion. It is so much simpler to go on using a vase when it has the wire ready in place beforehand. If you have several vases, it is natural that you will use some of them only at special times of the year, so that there will be many months when these sit about and get dusty. If they are in a cupboard, the packing in polythene is not so important, but it is most helpful if they are on an open shelf.

Next we come to the rest of the equipment, used as follows for various purposes.

Cutting

The small stub scissors that are used by florists are a 'must'. They cut not only stems but wire as well. They are easy to handle, can be slipped into a pocket or handbag and, apart from thick branches, will cut just about everything. As I have a habit of losing scissors, I have to have several pairs to hand, but that is just me! Fortunately, they are exceedingly reasonable in price.

Secateurs are most useful. The small ones brought out by Wilkinson, called Flower Cutters, are excellent and I can thoroughly recommend these; they are compact and light, they will cut the thickest stems, and I carry mine about everywhere, especially in the car for picking the odd branch as I go about the countryside. There is a long-arm kind made by the French firm Talabot Pradines; this they name Cueille-Fleurs. It has a light clipper on a two-foot handle — so convenient for the odd high spray and good for dead-heading roses, as you can use it with one hand and it saves treading all over the beds. This firm make excellent pruning knives and lopping shears. The French are renowned for their knives and I always look for these when I have the chance.

Carrying

A trug basket or shallow flower basket that will hold flowers quite flat is the ideal for picking. If you can pick a lot of flowers straight into a basket, it saves a great deal of time and many trips to the garden.

For carrying flowers to a friend, or to where you have the job of arranging them, a really large polythene bag is invaluable. I keep a large stock in varying sizes and can never have enough. It is best to give the flowers several hours in water, and to de-thorn roses and others, before packing them in. Always put the flowers in head first and of course the tallest material first. A word of warning — white flowers and all those with delicate petals should never be kept in polythene for too long; whereas tougher material such as decorative cabbage and so on, I have had in a bag for a week and it came out looking as good as new. Bluebells and any wild flowers carry extremely well if put head first into a polythene bag as soon as they are picked. Otherwise, wild flowers always seem to wilt very quickly. Wilted flowers take a long time to recover, and sometimes never do. If you have no polythene bag handy, always wrap the flowers in a sheet of newspaper — or anything that keeps their heads out of the air. Good florists always wrap flowers so that the heads are not exposed to the air, and this is a great help, particularly in very hot or very cold weather.

Dust sheets for use when removing old flowers are most helpful, and some enterprising person devised the idea of sewing two long canes one on each side of a sheet of thick polythene so that this is quickly spread out on the floor and easy to roll up and store. However, any old sheet is really all that is needed. Remove all the dead flowers from the vase, put in the clean water, and throw away the old flowers before bringing in the new. I much prefer to do a vase in the position in which it is going to stay. It is surprising how the height of even similar pieces of furniture can vary, and the way the light falls from a window can completely alter the effect of the colour of the flowers, so that often one needs extra foliage for backing or finds no need for quite so much after all. So, whenever possible, spread out your dust sheet and work in the room where the vase is going to remain.

Watering

A watering can or bucket is needed if you are doing flowers away from home. It often saves many valuable minutes if you don't have to search round a strange church or house for a can. The vases are easier to arrange with the water in, as this gives them more balance. I like to fill them three-quarters of the way, and top them up at the end. For topping up you need a small can with a long spout, or often a milk bottle is ideal.

Positioning

The method used for holding flower stems in position varies with everyone, and I often find that the first instruction they had on this is the one that most people follow. Some think wire netting the ideal, others, pin-holders and so on. No matter what it is, use what you personally find the quickest and easiest.

WIRE NETTING. I have got accustomed to two-inch mesh wire netting, and this I would recommend. So often one starts with smaller mesh, only to find that once it is crumpled it does not allow enough space for the stems. Well-galvanized wire will not rust so quickly, and it is often possible to buy odd lengths from your local ironmonger. A guide as to how much you want is twice the size of the aperture at the top of the vase. For very small-stemmed flowers you will need a little more, and for large stems, such as delphiniums, less. Large mesh is advisable in every way, and is much more pliable and easier to handle. Plastic-covered wire netting is excellent for precious vases, but they seem to have a much better version of this in Australia than we have here.

PIN-HOLDERS. These are a series of small upright pins on a heavy base, which impale any flower stem pressed on to them. Always buy the most expensive pin-holder as it is an economy in the long run. This usually just means that it is heavier and made in copper, which doesn't rust — and the heavier the holder, the easier to use. To hold the pin-holder firm, if you are using it alone, roll a piece of plasticine or Bostik no. 5 into a circle and fix it on to the base of the holder before placing it in the vase, making quite sure that the surface is dry. The Japanese have marvellous 'well' pin-holders — rather like a small pot made in metal with the needle-point pins in the bottom. I find these extremely useful,

III. Rich and rare — in the lead urn opposite a collection of beautiful and exotic lilies, *Hippeastrum puniceum* and *Lilium longiflorum*, surrounded by a background of prunus 'Kanzan' and wild cherry. The few solid leaves at the base add weight to balance the large and beautiful heads of the Barbados lilies. Nothing is overcrowded, for I have tried to show each individual flower to its best advantage. I feel one would consider this a party piece or a vase suitable for the Easter church services.

A   'White Heart' cherry buds
B   Wild cherry
C   Leaves of *Sansevieria trifasciata laurentii*
D   *Lilium longifolium*
E   Barbados lilies, hybrids of *Hippeastrum puniceum*
F   *Prunus serrulata* 'Kanzan'
G   Back of the leaves of a hybrid rhododendron
H   Leaf from *Fatsia japonica*
I   *Acer pseudo-platanus brilliantissimum*

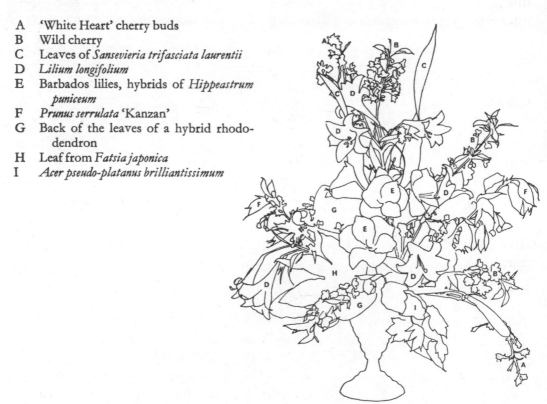

and perfect for using a spliced piece of wood or board. I like to use an ordinary pin-holder at the bottom of a large vase, and then several layers of crushed-up wire netting. In this way, one seems to have the best of both worlds; the weight of the pin-holder secures heavy background branches, and the wire netting allows for easy placing of the smaller and horizontal stems.

FLORAPACK, MOSSETTE and OASIS. These are synthetic bricks that need soaking well for several hours, before you can press the flower stems into the brick.

OASIS. This is my own favourite: it is green in colour and seems to remain firmer than the others. Take the brick and cut out a piece to fit the size of the vase, soak this really well and after that you can use it and have no worry about the flowers lasting for at least twelve hours without additional water. Flowers stand in it easily and it is a joy to the demonstrator, who once having placed a stem can be certain that it will not move. I like to use it in deep water, and with a piece of wire netting over the top to ensure that it will not break up easily. When it is under water, one knows that the flowers will last really well.

MOSSETTE and FLORAPACK. These are better if they are crumbled first, then placed in a jug full of water with a weight on top, to get really soaked. After that put them in a polythene bag, fill it with water and immerse the whole in the vase. You may find it advisable to puncture the bag, and then secure it with a piece of wire netting over the top.

All these are useful in vases sent on board ship or to a nursing home, where flowers may well stand out of water for some time. They are quite expensive and I rarely use them in my own home, because I can fill up the vases, but for a wedding or flowers for a special occasion then I think they are worth every penny. The American idea of covering Oasis with a piece of foil paper is a good one, and this method used in a high shallow container that does not hold very much water is ideal.

CONES or TUBES. These green, cone-like tin holders can be bought from your local flower club, should you need them for any large vases. They are invaluable for raising a few short-stemmed flowers to give additional height and colour to a group. Using silver wire or Sellotape, attach each cone to a cane or stick at the height you require; push a small piece of wire-netting into the cone itself to prevent the stems from slipping about; secure the netting and fill the cones with water — they should hold enough to keep the flowers fresh for several hours. As it is difficult to fill them with water once the vase is crowded with flowers, remember to do this first. When the cones have been filled place the whole device in the vase, pushing the canes through the wire netting in the vase so that they go right to the bottom. I find this method useful for really large groups but I try to avoid using cones too often as they tend to give a slightly artificial effect. Heads of, say, short-stemmed hyacinths right up at the top of a vase of spring flowers can certainly look very odd! But they are invaluable sometimes for foliage, or some lilies perhaps, that you don't want to cut on too long a stem from the garden.

STRING. Handy at any time and useful to tie round a vase to keep the wire netting in securely. Once the flowers are in place, they are balanced and the string can be cut; however, I never bother to do this unless the string actually shows in the finished arrangement.

SILVER WIRE. Even more useful, as it never shows. If you only want a little, then a card of fuse wire is all that you require, but the reels that are obtainable from a florist or local flower club are a good investment for a few shillings.

SELLOTAPE. Again something that can be used to hold the wire netting securely in the vase. It hardly shows and can be placed either just over the sides or right over the whole vase. Roll the Sellotape that goes over the top of the vase, as it is inclined to take up too much stem space.

ELASTIC BANDS. Also useful for keeping wire netting in place.

FLORIST'S WIRES. These are handy to have in the house and though I never advocate wiring any flower that goes into a vase, a broken stem can be splinted with a wire run up the inside. It can be quickly attached to a stem to keep it in position. Try to avoid wiring flowers that are in an arrangement as they immediately assume an unnatural angle. Only wire such flowers as are to be worn or carried. Bundles of wires can be bought from an ironmonger, or from a flower club, in mixed gauges and lengths.

Balancing

Strips of PLUMBER'S LEAD can be used instead of string for securing wire netting in a vase. Make a loop round the wire netting with one end of the strip and let the other hang over the back of the vase; this helps to balance the weight of the flowers in the front. They can also be used to keep a heavy stem or branch in place. Take a strip of lead about nine inches long, cut it along the middle to about half way down, so that you have two arms and a trunk; insert the trunk part in the vase and wind the two arms round the branch; this will ensure that the stem is really steady — most important, as the stem carries most of the weight.

GRAVEL and SAND are a help for weighing down an otherwise rather light vase or tin.

STONES of attractive colour or shape, are good for weighting or for concealing a pin-holder, and can also add charm to an arrangement. I collect pretty pebbles and chunks of stone from streams and sea shore. Scotland is a wonderful hunting ground.

Small WINDOW-WEDGES are most useful for propping under a sloping vase. These are particularly good for a sloping window-ledge in a church. The thickness of the wedge depends on the slope you need to counteract. A shallow ovenware dish can be used on a sill with quite a steep slope and still be kept firm, and the water kept level, with one of these wedges.

One other small gadget I have found most useful is a STRIPPER. It is shaped like a pair of sugar tongs, with a V cut out of each end. You place it two or three inches up the stem, depending on the amount of green you want to remove, and pressing both ends together, pull firmly downwards. This removes any surplus leaves and thorns from the bottom of the stem. Most useful in the summer, and especially for prickly thistles or roses.

Methods of Arrangement

As I mentioned earlier, the aids that you use to hold your flower stems in place are a matter of personal choice. I think I use wire netting more generally, simply because it is what I started with, because pin-holders really only came in after the war; but I have no fixed ideas on this subject, and like to use pin-holders for shallow vases, and with wire netting as well for large groups.

Once you have decided where you are placing your vase, and which shape and size of vase is right for the amount and height of your flowers, the next thing is to fill it three-quarters of the way up with water, and spread your dust sheet, ready for all the pieces.

Starting with a basic urn which calls for a fan-shaped arrangement. . . . take your tallest stem and fix this firmly in the wire netting. This stem is of paramount importance, as if it starts to slip or move it can disarrange the whole vase and often end in tipping it over. In short, fix the main stems firmly. Then get your general outline shape. For a fan-shaped arrangement this should be approximately one and a half to twice the height of the vase, and the overall width about

IV. Three beautiful and unusual arum lilies inspired this arrangement: I find it is often the flower which will give me the idea and desire to do a vase. The next step is to decide on the container, in this case a home-made dish of builders' lead, cut to a shape with a tapering end with the edges folded up about an inch and a half, so that it held enough water for the flowers. A piece of rolled plasticine is pressed round the outside of a pinholder, and secured onto the bottom of the dish before the water is added (it is most important that the pinholder is fixed onto a *dry* surface). The three stems of Solomon's Seal give the desired width to the arrangement, as they come out to the end of the dish. The sansevieria leaves form the height, and the broad leaves of hosta give additional colour value and solidity at the base. A collection of wide-shaped and prominent leaves add under-shadow and distinction to the shortest bloom, and here the three marvellously-veined leaves of *Arum italicum pictum* complete the picture. These leaves first appear in mid-winter in the open, so you will realize the value of growing them.

A   Leaves of *Sansevieria trifasciata laurentii*
B   Solomon's Seal, *Polygonatum multiflorum*
C   Yellow arum lilies— *Zantedeschia elliottiana*
D   *Hosta fortunei albo-picta* leaves
E   Leaves of *Arum italicum pictum*

the same. These are just guides, and not rules. Use the lighter and more delicate spray-like material for the outline. Having placed the central piece to give you the height, take two stems that are slightly shorter and place them one on either side; these should not be of identical height, or the whole vase will look too symmetrical. The next stems on either side can be shorter still; the next, almost the same height as the first, but placed at a slight angle to the horizontal to give you the fan shape; the next should be threaded through the wire netting horizontally, to curve over the sides of the bowl. Then carefully choose slightly curving pieces, to hang over the front. In order to get these to fall gracefully, again the stems should be threaded through the netting almost horizontally. To ensure that these stems are well in water, it is essential to fill the vase right up to the top. Now fill in this outline with flowers: say, one or two stems of delphiniums, and larkspurs, gradually coming to the more solid flower heads. For the actual centre use the boldest and best flowers with a 'face', as we call them — flat-headed of many petals, such as an open rose, dahlias or, chrysanthemums. Use an uneven number in the centre; this prevents forming straight lines. So take two or three roses for instance, and let these hang about six inches to a foot over the front of the vase; then recess or tuck in one or two more right in the centre, and these will give the impact of colour to the arrangement. It is interesting to note that these central flowers dominate the colour of the vase, and if in a mixed vase you want blue to predominate, then the blue must go right in the centre. Recessing one or two flowers deep in the centre of the vase may seem a bit of a waste, but they are most valuable for this intensifying of the colour effect. Study the stems and the angle at which they have grown, so that you find a piece that will curve naturally to the right and one that will curve to the left. This can be achieved more easily with stems that fall gracefully, with a natural tendency to bend slightly in one direction or another. Stems of ivy, old man's beard, *Alchemilla mollis*, periwinkle, and so on, all give a natural down-sweeping effect. There is no need to push every flower stem right down to the bottom of the vase; some can well be tucked in horizontally provided a good part is under water and not exposed to the air. The one stem that must always be upright and firmly fixed through the layers of wire netting, and then impaled on the pin-holder if you use one, is the upright stem with which it is easiest to start all flower arrangements. It is better not to shorten any stems until you are certain that this is essential. Before cutting the stem, hold your flower against the arrangement to get an idea where you are going to place it. If it seems a little too long always first try pushing it down well into the vase, then take it out again and cut it if necessary. Try to keep all stems as long as possible, as this takes away from an over-stiff and too formal effect. A natural effect is very often hard to achieve. You can never add a piece on! — in the final adjustment to the vase a stem is often better pulled forward a little, and this might not be possible if the stems have been cut too short. For large groups the conical tubes mentioned earlier can help to give added colour and height to bridge the gap between tall foliages and short flowers. The use of foliage is something that we have learnt a great deal about in these last few years, and the use of several large leaves tucked in at the base of the vase helps to add under-shadow and has the effect of 'cleaning up' the whole vase. A good example is shown in the illustration on page 141 with hostas in the cupid vase, and also on Plate 19, of leaves of *Begonia rex* with viburnum and hyacinths.

Next, the method for a shallow dish as on Plate 2 of the white martagon lilies. Here I have used a pewter collecting plate. The hollow in the centre holds just enough water for a few flowers: three stems of lilies and the pin-holder concealed with leaves of hosta. Fix the pin-holder firmly with a strip of plasticine. Roll the plasticine between your hands into a sausage, fit this round the base of the pin-holder and press down on a dry surface. Take the tallest stem and fix it firmly on the pin points, allowing the beauty of the lily stem to show to advantage, as befits any perfect flower, and trying to arrange the next two so that none of this beauty is concealed. This oriental type of vase is so peaceful-looking and pleasant to have about. Because of the simplicity, I have grown increasingly fond of this sort of arrangement. Many people find that they are easier to arrange than a mixed mass group, and I think this may be true; but you must be quite certain of having the right materials.

The arrangement in the tin (shown on Plate 3) is another example of simple grouping; and for these it is so important to choose your curving branch with great care, and if necessary to prune it to get the shape you want.

The method for making a moss garden, as in the illustration of the basket of mixed spring flowers (Colour Plate II), is one that I use with various flowers all through the early spring. Take your vase or bowl and firmly tie in the wire netting, using a pin-holder as well as the wire if you find it easier. Then spread a layer of green moss over the whole. It is sometimes a good idea to raise the wire a little higher than you usually would, to prevent the moss from coming in contact with the water. Finally, making small holes in the moss with the tip of your finger, pop in the small bunches of primroses, scillas, polyanthus, and so on. A few twigs of catkins or flowering viburnum will give the otherwise rather flat vase a little height. I like to keep the small bunches in one colour if I can as even if the flowers are not all the same, they give a better concentrated effect if they are tucked into clumps of blues, pinks, yellows. This is the way I like best of all to arrange daffodils, in either a bowl or a basket with a layer of moss over the

2. The elegance of flowers. The white martagon lilies stand alone in a pewter collecting plate, with three hosta leaves at the base. It would have been a pity to obscure their form in a crowded arrangement.

3. A blue-grey Japanese vase with sprays of the escallonia 'Donard Seedling' and three blending pink roses.

wire. I take the daffodils two or three at a time, with a few of their leaf-spikes, and allow them to fall into place quite naturally as if they were growing.

For massed arrangements of all one kind of flower and its own foliage, choose a box with a lid, or an oblong china dish or a copper trough, depending on the length of stem of the flowers you are using. Fix in the wire netting firmly, then take your well-soaked flowers — whether honeysuckle, bluebells, jasmine, old-fashioned roses, or wallflowers — and with small bunches of a few stems together arrange them in a flowing and unrestricted way. The flowers that are chosen for such arrangements are generally the ones that smell sweet and are perhaps not very long-lasting in water, but closely packed like this they seem to live longer. Or it could be that because of the mass of flowers, the fallen petals are not so conspicuous. Massed arrangements like this are illustrated on page 99 by the box of anemones and by the polyanthus and roses on Plates 4 and 20.

Foliage arrangements, or 'mixed greens' as they have come to be known, are more widely used and enjoyed than ever before. They can be done at all times of the year and for me anyway are a constant delight. They last well and one can rely on at least one vase looking fresh at almost any hour of the day — and this for a flower arranger is a big thing, as one feels that one should never be caught out without a flower in the house! I love a background of lichened branches to a winter group of ivies, ferns and perhaps a stem of variegated camellia foliage. A vase of grey greens and a vase of yellow greens both make interesting subjects. When I set out to do mixed foliages, I like to avoid the rules and mix in seed pods in all the shades of green, and perhaps a few green flowers. These make really unusual vases. Of course if you are showing a group and the class says mixed foliage, then one cannot put in any flower or seed head, however green it may be. By the same token, one cannot put in yellow or greys for a class of green foliage. These variations are much more fun to do at home. Try to find unusual and varying shapes and forms: leaves that are stiff and upright, such as iris; feathery foliage, such as ferns; leaves and sprays that hang easily. All these make for more interest than leaves of just one shape. Although these foliage groups last longer than flower groups, they often take a little longer to arrange and pick for and need a lot of thought beforehand.

Having dealt with vases of flowers on their own, and then foliage alone, we come to the mixing of both, using flowers and unrelated foliage — such as sprays of reddish berberis with flowers in all the shades and tones of reds; pieces of different-coloured autumn foliage with orange-yellow dahlias or roses; grey foliages with pinks or mauves. Pink carnations are excellent mixed with greys, and, as seen in the illustration on page 137, a few tulips make an attractive group with a mixture of greens and dried seed heads. So many combinations to choose

c

V. The value of lime green and yellow is well shown here, in this mass group arranged in May. The maroon red introduced by the peonies, *P. delavayi*, and the *Tulipa viridiflora* 'Artist' add a touch of the unusual. I like to put a flash of a different colour through the centre of the vase, and it is this colour in the centre which dominates the whole. The vase is part of an old epergne with delightful ormolu figures reaching upwards as if holding up the world. It was bought during the war at a Red Cross sale at what seemed then a vast extravagance — but how different today.

A   Wild grasses
B   *Enkianthus campanulatus*
C   *Tulipa viridiflora* 'Artist'
D   *Azalea mollis* 'Spek's Brilliant'
E   *Tellima grandiflora*
F   Leaves of variegated balm, *Melissa officinalis variegata*
G   *Paeonia delavayi*
H   Double Ghent azalea 'Phidias'
I   *Clematis armandii*
J   Leaves of *Hosta fortunei albo-picta*
K   *Begonia rex* leaf
L   *Rhododendron cinnabarinum*

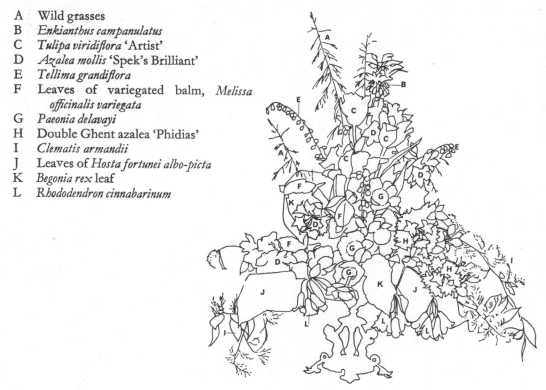

from! — and living as we do with such changing seasons, we have really more choice here than anywhere else in the world.

Although a great many flowers are required for a big group, they should not be overcrowded. This perhaps makes the big group one of the most difficult forms of arrangement, though nowadays, with the interest in flower festivals, they are being done more than ever before by a wider range of people. If you are doing flowers for a wedding or some important occasion, then a pedestal vase is the very thing — and aim to make this as bold and important as you can. Choose good backing: flowering branches of cherry, stripped lime, autumn-coloured leaves. . . . Next well-grown stems of gladioli, delphiniums, acanthus, lupins, and any flower that has a good flower spike. Lilies not only add quality to a big group, but have such good 'faces' that they show up well from any distance. Then concentrate on the focal point, with heads of hydrangeas, dahlias, roses, peonies or rhododendrons in the centre. I think it is a good maxim to go for quality rather than quantity, especially when you are working on a big vase. This prevents overcrowding, which can be caused by trying to create a startling effect, and in so doing, it is easy to lose the personality of each flower. Try to let each flower play its part and be seen as a whole flower, not overshadowed by another. Try to place each flower so that it is not obscured in any way. This is essential for flowers that form the focal point in the centre, for once this becomes overcrowded and messy the whole group is spoiled. Some of these central stems should be recessed to give a three-dimensional effect. Large groups that are seen from a distance need to be clear-cut with a tailored look. Bold leaves of arums, or saxifrage, and of course hosta, all play an important part at the base of a big group. They help to give it a feeling of tranquillity. These groups need design, and to be more than just the harmonious massing of colour.

I find flower arranging horribly contradictory, but perhaps because of this the interest never flags. For instance, it is so easy to say that delicate flowers need delicate containers — and basically I feel this, thinking of cosmos and columbines in dainty glass or porcelain vases. Sweet peas surely come into this category, yet what could be more lovely than an enormous earthenware bowl arranged with a mass of sweet peas in groups of individual colours? So at all times let common sense prevail, and avoid too many rigid rules that may stifle your imagination and initiative.

CHAPTER THREE

Containers and Vases

The vase or container plays such a very important part in modern flower arrangement. Container seems the word now generally used for a vessel into which flowers can be put, but which has not really been designed as a flower vase. It is these that I think we all search for, and buy if we can, for some special kind of arrangement. An old copper kettle, a mixing bowl, preserving pan, tea-urn, and so on, are some of my most cherished flower holders. To have a range is the ideal, as so often there is only one month in the year in which you can use, for instance, a really bright blue glass goblet, for the side shoots of delphiniums, or some stems of gentian; then such a vase suddenly becomes of paramount importance for emphasizing the brilliance of the blue flowers — and in the same way, a pewter jug filled with red roses, an earthenware pot holding the heads of cow parsley and grasses picked by the road side, an elegant gold vase of lilies. . . . It is of course not always desirable to show the container, and if you have a garden to pick from you may find you have plenty of summer flowers, and suddenly the vase itself is of no matter and you can use an ovenware dish and get a wonderful effect.

On the other hand, if you live in town and have no garden to pick from, then the choice of container becomes so very important; a small delicate piece of china can hold a bunch of primroses, or a spray of roses, which will look pretty just as it is and no unrelated foliage will be needed. Should the room require a large vase, then it is often possible to buy one with a lid so that it can hold flowers when they are plentiful, or when they are scarce and expensive, you can always pop on the lid! The vase plays a far greater part in the house of the non-garden-owner than for the plant-grower.

If you are buying a vase that is going to be used nearly all the time, then get one in a neutral colour, say in white or grey, or a dusky pink, so that nearly all mixtures of colourings can be used in it. If you have a container of strong colour, it is very much more restricting, and you will find that you really only enjoy using it at certain times of the year and with flowers of a certain colour. So buy a vase with care, though gradually as you become a flower arranger you will spend a lot of time (and possibly too much money!) in the constant search for others.

4. A mass arrangement of polyanthus in an old papier-mâché box. This makes a welcome change from the perpetual mixed-flower groups.

5. Lichened branches give the outline for this grey arrangement, dominated by the silvery *Begonia rex* leaves and the grey cotton-wool-like leaves of the thistle *Onopordon acanthium*.

I spend many happy hours browsing around the antique shops, and in shops and markets at home and abroad, in search of something unusual; though naturally I still have my favourites, and these are used over and over again. Using a different vase in the same place in your room will change the whole effect, and the more often you can do this the better, and so much more interesting.

Some even quite small rooms can take a pedestal arrangement well. The deciding factor is the amount of space you can allow for flowers. A large arrangement can take the place of a piece of furniture, and this is helpful for the young who are starting up a home, with perhaps not a great deal of money to spend on furnishing for the first years of their married life; also perhaps not quite knowing the type of thing that they are always going to like to live with. So a really large group which can be arranged with dried seed heads and preserved flowers in winter, and perhaps mixed foliage in the summer, will effectively tide one over this time. A pedestal and vase are lovely for a party, showing up well and easily seen, even in a crowded room of guests. This takes a lot of flowers, although good use can be made of inexpensive material. A good idea is to have a lamp, or decorative ornament, that can be placed on the top of the pedestal for everyday use or when there is not enough time for arranging flowers. These pedestals fill many a corner most effectively and, if used in a room with a very high ceiling, help to fill the gap between floor and ceiling, having the effect of making the ceiling seem lower. They are of course ideal for using in a church, for a wedding, or in a hall or ballroom for a dance.

Wall vases were more popular several years ago than they are today, but they are still ideal in a restaurant, so that flowers can be seen and admired without being at all an encumbrance. They are also effective in the hall of a small flat or house, as they give a marvellous welcome, yet are well out of the way, taking up no floor space. As they look very cheerless when empty, it is as well to have a picture handy, so that when flowers are scarce, it can be hung up as a change. Because of their good plain background, they are easy to arrange and you can achieve some lovely effects, with a well-shaped branch and good design, without too many flowers.

Nearly everyone likes to have some flowers on the table, and here the choice of vase can easily be a mistake. With the modern interest in flower arrangement, this is improving all the time, but in the past I felt that starting off with a very large container meant having to use many more flowers than was really necessary. Again, one must be guided by the amount of space that is to be used for the flowers themselves, remembering everything else that may have to go on the table, including fruit and candles and other decorative effects. Often a small rose on a shell, or a few flowers tucked into a bowl of fruit will give you the best results. Otherwise, my advice is take a smaller vase than you feel you will need and spread the flowers out well from the edge of the bowl. View from all sides, and keep the arrangement fairly low, or have it in a very tall vase, so that it will not obstruct the line of vision. When it is completed, always sit down and look at it, to make certain that no wire shows and that the rim of the vase is well concealed. There is of course a wide choice of containers, but sometimes it is nice to put the flowers in part of the dinner service, using perhaps a vegetable dish or sauce boat. Generally speaking, flower arrangements for the table must be all-round, or oval. Of course, if the table stands against the wall, the vase can be placed at the back, to face in one direction only — so much easier to arrange and requiring half the amount of flowers.

Flowers are always welcoming in the guest's bedroom — preferably just a posy of something fragrant, placed on the dressing table or by the bed-side. Some of the pretty little Italian figurine vases are ideal; or one of the old-fashioned china hands, or other small pretty piece of china. Flowers on the breakfast tray, as a special luxury, could well be done in an egg cup.

When placing your vases, take care that the one in the hall is solid, firm on its base and not likely to fall or get knocked over. With the front door constantly being opened, a vase could easily be caught by a gust of wind; so be sure to use a good solid one. As I always emphasize, avoid using too many flower vases in one room; a tall vase perhaps, and something low, and a pretty little vase on a coffee table, is really all that you need. It is so much better to do one really attractive arrangement than trying to rush through too many.

A jardiniere is now very popular, with the ever-increasing interest in house plants. It is much more effective to collect several pots and put them together, rather than having pot plants in odd corners round the house. These indoor gardens are particularly suitable in a sun-room, or in the hall, and are a constant stand-by, giving so little trouble.

For everyday use, I would advise a vase that holds plenty of water. The shallow bowl-type ones that I love to use do need constant filling up, and are often better kept for a special occasion.

Here is a list of various kinds of vases and vase materials that are all good to use at one time of the year or another.

ALABASTER. I have collected alabaster vases for more years than 1 care to mention. The delicate creamy colouring blends so well with all kinds of different colour combinations, from creams and yellows to brilliant reds; and almost all kinds of flowers are suitable, though I feel that some flowers look even better in it than others. I love roses in alabaster as much as I like a collection of cream and brown seed heads. It needs rather special care. Water roughens the surface after a time, and it is better to line the vase with a bowl to prevent this from happening. The acid from flower stems leaves deep marks, and if alabaster is left near constant heat it loses a great deal of its translucence and becomes opaque. It should be treated with olive oil.

BASKETS. These are useful all the year round — a garden basket, baby trug, cornucopia — but avoid the gilded long-handled types. They can be bought quite inexpensively in every shape and size. If they are specially made to take flowers, they are supplied with a liner to hold the water; but should you see some other one that you like, it is quite easy to find a bowl or tin that will hold enough water for the flowers; pack this firmly round with newspaper to stop it moving about. If you want to make your own, Dryads of Bloomsbury Street, London, W.C.1 sell all the necessary materials. The trugs can be bought from Hurstmonceaux, Sussex, and many other sorts from your local basket shop, the Lord Roberts Workshops, or the Basket Shop, Hemel Hempstead.

BRASS. This lacks the warm look of copper, but gives good highlights and is lovely with soft yellows, lime greens, and autumn colourings. It is possible to find very nice brass bowls and boxes, though urns are a little more rare. Brass and copper both go so well with dark oak furniture, and make a nice container for the hall. Flowers last well in the coolness of metal containers.

BRONZE has been used for many centuries for making beautiful vases. Chinese and Japanese flower arrangers use it with exquisite effect, and I can think of no better container than a really well-shaped bronze urn. As these vases are metal, flowers last so well in them and their dark colour will set off very varied material — for instance, the dramatic effect of a black and white group, done with perhaps black grapes or privet berries, and white dahlias or roses . . . but there are endless possibilities. If you are ever lucky enough to find a copy of the Warwick cup in bronze, it is one of the loveliest vases of all for a large, handsome arrangement.

CHINA urns are becoming more popular all the time, for all types of flower arrangement. It is possible to buy them in different colours, and greys and mauvey pink can make a pleasant change from the usual white, which I feel has become rather ordinary. However, as you can put almost any material into a white vase, this would be a good choice if you are going to use it continually.

COPPER. This is ideal for so many types of arrangements, especially for those that have all the golds and reds of the autumn. Copper jugs, bowls and tea-urns all make good containers. If you are frequently using a tea-urn, it is a good idea to have the tap expertly removed to be sure that it does not leak. The glow of a highly-polished copper surface will add warmth and reflections to any dark corner. The problem of constant cleaning has been greatly eased these days with 'long life' cleaner; or you can lacquer the surface, but be sure to remove all really bad stains beforehand — this can be done by rubbing on lemon and salt, or vinegar and salt, with a coarse cloth, and rinsing well with cold water before using a good metal polish.

FIBRE GLASS. Verine Products have been very clever and copied some of the beautiful old lead vases, in pewter-grey fibre glass. The copies are extremely well finished and at first glance one could be taken in by them. They are, however, as light as a feather. Even when they are filled with water, I think it is advisable to add additional weight, with a brick or a piece of lead, if you are going to use them to hold large branches.

GLASS. The traditional glass vases are not as popular as they were, though no doubt they will come back into favour. Their greatest disadvantages are that the wire netting shows, and that the water must be kept scrupulously clean; a glass vase with dirty water looks really sordid. They should be washed with soap and water as soon as they have been used. If they are in constant use, wash them as often as possible, as it becomes progressively more difficult to remove the water mark which forms on the rim. A piece of lemon dipped in salt or Milton will help to remove the stains and sediment from the base. Hydrochloric acid, supplied by a chemist, is a stronger but more drastic remedy which should be used with the greatest care as it can burn hands and clothes badly. Some modern vases are made in mottled glass which obscures the wire netting. I like to use glass when the vase is to stand against the light, giving a silhouette effect.

MARBLE. Old marble is hard to find, but is lovely to use if you can get it, and much more durable than alabaster. It will hold water with no serious effects. A marble urn or bowl for summer flowers is ideal. The modern Italian marble, in various shapes and sizes, successfully reproduces some of the old designs, and though expensive can look enchanting in the right surroundings. Sometimes old-fashioned light-shades — the marble-bowl kind to hang from the ceiling on chains — are to be found and, once the chains are removed, are effective as a table bowl or to stand on a pedestal.

ORMOLU. This is generally made in France for compotes for fruit and flower vases. It is a mixture of metals: tin, copper and brass, with either a bronze or gold finish. The ormolu vases and candlesticks that I have are some of my favourite flower containers. You will see them in some of the photographs throughout this book. Their elegance and colour make them ideal for even a few flowers at any time of the year. A small bunch of grapes, and a few clematis or passion flowers, seem perfect in what is for some people a rather ornate vase. If it is ever your luck to buy one at a reasonable price, then I feel sure it would give you lasting pleasure as mine have to me.

PEWTER. When well polished, pewter reflects the light well, though I am quite happy to have dull pewter to fill with lilacs and mauves, or even brilliant reds. My mind turns to mugs the moment pewter is mentioned, but there are of course many different pieces that are nice for flowers: tea pots, bowls, shallow collecting-plates (see the one that holds the martagon lilies on Plate 2). A shallow pewter plate, with a pin-holder to support the flowers, can make a useful change for the dinner table. A full-blown rose on a shallow plate is another idea.

PORCELAIN. Continental china or porcelains often take the form of a pretty little basket decorated with raised bunches of flowers, and when these are filled with either a few spring flowers or something sweet-smelling, they are ideal for a coffee table or the guest's bedroom. Delicate porcelain wall vases were very popular some years ago; when filled with trails of old fashioned roses, or honeysuckle, they are always so pretty. One house that I visit has beautiful Dresden china figures and these are grouped with a small vase hidden behind, in which a few sprays of flowers according to the season are placed so that they draw attention to the china and in no way obscure it. I was enchanted by the effect that this gave. Porcelain is usually precious and of course needs very careful handling; the wire netting, if used, wants to be cut and shaped all ready before being put in the vase. Never press wire into the vases as it is so easy to break them. Wash carefully and store in a very safe place. Because of the delicate nature of all porcelain containers, the flowers should be just as pretty and light as you can contrive: jasmine, sweet peas, roses, forget-me-nots, and any other pretty little bits. If the vase has a flower design on it, as they so often have, then try picking up the colours of the flowers, or possibly matching up the flowers themselves.

POTTERY. Many pottery urns and bowls are made today for flower arrangement. There is a wide range to choose from, including a great deal of Italian china in

VI. A buffet table for June — a glass chalice-type vase filled with a combination of early summer flowers, pink, mauve and grey monochrome, the whole effect being aimed at keeping the colouring to tone with the grey-blue band on the china. The flowers at the base of the arrangement are placed to lean slightly forward dipping out over the rim of the vase with uneven stem lengths to give a feeling of depth to the composition. Bearing in mind that flowers to stand on a buffet are more effective if displayed carefully, have one or two bold arrangements rather than a lot of small containers which tend to get in the way of the servers and do little but add confusion to the general effect.

A   Russell lupins
B   Leaves of *Thalictrum glaucum*
C   A giant form of the sea pink, *Armeria*
D   Hybrid tea rose 'Sterling Silver'
E   *Stachys lanata* leaves
F   Freesia
G   Columbines — *Aquilegia* long-spurred
        hybrids
H   Honeysuckle — *Lonicera*
I   Hybrid tea rose 'Pink Chiffon'
J   *Hosta undulata* leaves
K   *Artemisia pedemontana*
L   Myosotis (Forget-me-not)
M   *Helleborus corsicus* seed heads
N   Ivy-leaved *pelargonium*

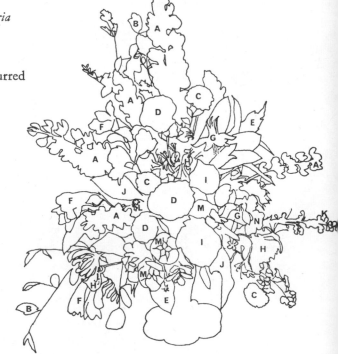

some of the prettiest designs and soft colours. Many of these are white or grey with a pink or blue lining; the inside is so attractive that it is a pity to hide it, and so I often do an arrangement that takes up only half the vase so that the delicate colour of the lining is revealed. Constance Spry of South Audley Street have a lovely range of Scilly Isles pottery vases; these are in the most beautiful colours and very good designs, the pottery is well glazed and has a good finish. I well remember the early days when I was first in the shop; in the early 1930's there were no white vases available at all and we spent hours painting brown earthenware vases with flat white paint. They were sold almost before they were dry. Nowadays one can choose from a range of white vases in every imaginable shape and size. Most of them are fairly well proportioned and so are generally good to use for church flowers, but I find pure white often distracting with the golds and wood of many churches, and I try to avoid it for this purpose. If necessary, the vase can be painted. Black paint mixed with silver gives a good 'pewter' finish. Gold paint with a little brown is also effective, and both of these seem to suit church decoration very much better than dazzling white. Pottery, unlike porcelain, is always replaceable, and so it generally makes the most practical of all the breakable vases.

SILVER. Perhaps this is not used quite so much these days as a few years ago, when it was very much the fashion to have a silver rose bowl on the dining-room table. Generally speaking, these bowls were very large and needed a great deal of material to make a really good show. A smaller bowl can give as good an effect at very much less expense. A second consideration is of course the cleaning of silver, which takes trouble and much valuable time. However, I still feel a really lovely silver bowl filled to overflowing with roses looks delightful. Silver flower vases are often in rather difficult shapes. A cone-shaped trumpet vase may look quite well when filled with gypsophila and sweet peas, but can be a headache to the modern flower arranger. The epergne, so spurned only a few years ago, is becoming widely popular again and I used one myself only recently, filling the silver vases with old-fashioned roses to good effect. The best silver 'vases' are of course the cups, entree dishes, soup tureens, wine coolers, and any well-shaped cake basket, which make superb flower containers and fit into almost any home. But of course these were never intended or bought for flowers until quite recently. Silver has the asset of highlights and looks best, I think, used with a profusion of flowers in high summer. I am never very fond of using it in the spring and prefer daffodils in something else. Silver vases need cleaning inside and out, as both flower stems and water leave a deposit which becomes most difficult to clear if left too long. I have found that continental silver marks very much more quickly. Clean all silver well and store in polythene bags, and this keeps it beautifully for weeks. The new 'long life' cleaner is a great help for any silver that is out and in constant use. Plastic-coated wire netting is excellent to use in a silver container, as it prevents any possible chance of scratching. In the days before this was available I always used to line the bowls with either oiled paper or newspaper. Try to avoid leaving metal pin-holders in silver vases for very long as this tends to stain them badly. A pin-holder used to hold a few stems of flowers in a shallow silver bowl, allowing the water to become part of the arrangement, is very effective and can make a charming table display.

TIN. Ornamental Mexican tin is very decorative and there are some lovely flower vases made of this, but they are scarce here and hard to find. So are some of the early French jardinieres, which are usually hand-painted and can be found in charming soft colours — olive greens, pale blues and dull reds. They very often have a floral design on one side, either in gold or in mixed colours. Oblong or oval shapes make them easy to arrange and most useful, but like all beautiful things they are expensive and hard to come by. The French use them for plants or for a mixture of plants and cut flowers. I love them used for a mixture like this, or just for cut flowers alone. Everyday kitchen tins have many very good uses. As a lining to hold water in a vase or basket, a baking tin or bread tin is excellent. Or the tins can be painted with a coat or two of flat paint; in stone, white, cream or green they are unobtrusive and easy to camouflage with flowers or leaves — ideal for a party, for putting flowers on the mantlepiece, top of a cupboard, or window sill. It is advisable to paint them inside and out to prevent rusting, and this will also act as a sealer for the joins. As tin is in itself very light, it is always advisable to weight it down with either a strip of lead or some clean pebbles or stones. I have seen round tin washing-up bowls effectively covered with a coat of plaster, roughed up and painted, and this makes a good pedestal vase.

WOOD. There are few wooden flower vases, but many good wooden containers that are both attractive and useful for flowers. Wooden tea caddies or boxes, with a tin inside to hold the water, are most effective; these look lovely filled with simple marigolds, or daisies, or with a mixture of oranges and reds in the autumn, or daffodils in a bed of moss in spring. Knife boxes with their fittings removed, old salt boxes that will hang well on the wall, are other ideas for unusual vases. Wooden milk bowls (like the one I have used on page 130) are ideal for making the most of homely flowers — nasturtiums, or daisies. The top of a carved pillar, or any decorative piece of wood, that can be hollowed out

6. A late summer pedestal group standing in the corner of a room for a party, kept high and well out of the way yet visible to all. The background is acanthus, gladioli, phlox, leek seed-heads; and in the centre is a decorative cabbage with roses, hosta leaves and two or three *Galtonia candicans*.

7. A small decorative white candlestick with a holder containing a midsummer posy. The central rose is 'Mme Pierre Oger', known as the Shell Rose. With it are sprays of philadelphus, *Alchemilla mollis, Astrantia major,* the escallonia 'Donard Seedling' and at the top Catmint *Nepeta* 'Six Hills' Giant'.

enough to hold a container for water is unusual, again, and handsome. Pieces like this look very nice if the wood is bleached; this can be done by using parazone and water and leaving out in the sun. If the wood has been painted, then of course the paint must be removed with some form of paint stripper before the bleaching. Lumps of driftwood, and twisted and gnarled roots or branches, are in great demand and much sought after today. They can be used to very good effect to house a small jar or bowl, which is then filled with some wild or simple flowers, and this also makes a very suitable container for some dried arrangements. Wooden platters and bases are part of the general pattern of modern flower decoration; I think this has stemmed from the Japanese, who use a base as part of the whole flower arrangement. I find them extremely useful — perhaps not quite as the Japanese use them, though I like them for certain types of arrangements, but they are also a great help for preserving the furniture. On page 137 a slice of Japanese walnut is used with a concealed 'well' pin-holder, forming an easy and economical type of flower vase. The old bible boxes were a great favourite with Constance Spry. These are difficult to find but it is quite a good idea to make a wooden box that will hold a large roasting-tin; place it on a cheap white-wood stool and paint them both a pretty shade of green, and you will be able to have a large arrangement at knee-height, which makes a most welcome change. Shallow wooden boxes, either painted, or decorated with bark or shells, make an agreeable change for a dried group, and wonderful employment for the young on a wet day. A good use for all those buckets of shells! I have had a large wooden box made to hold my collection of house plants which decorate my sun-room; although I had every intention of lining it with lead or zinc, its lining so far is just two layers of thick polythene and it is serving its purpose very well at quarter the cost. Always well sandpaper any wood before painting — and flat paint is so much nicer (see Plate 21).

PEDESTAL VASES. These can be used in the home, or in a hall for a wedding or party, or in church, to raise the flowers up to or well above eye-level. The type of pedestal should be entirely a matter of personal choice, and so should the vase or container that is used on it, provided that both are in proportion; a small urn on a tall pedestal looks quite out of place. Some people used to cling to the notion that pedestals should carry only unseen containers; but the Georgian mahogany pedestal vases and other lovely examples should dissuade anyone who still holds to this. Large urns of suitable material such as stone, lead, fibre glass, alabaster, bronze, copper, china, are satisfactory provided that they are the right size and hold plenty of water, and that they will stand the weight of heavy and often cascading flowers and foliage. Of course, vases on pedestals in your own home can be smaller and of more delicate material than those you would use in a church or hall. So be guided in your choice by how and where they are to be used. The use of pedestals has become much more general, and they are now considered the ideal answer for keeping flowers well out of the way and showing them off to the best advantage. I well remember the days when it was quite unheard-of to use flowers on a pedestal in a church, and only banks of pot plants and palms were the vogue. I use an old-fashioned wash-hand bowl on my church pedestal more often than not. These bowls are deep enough to hold plenty of water and shallow enough for the bowl itself to be easily concealed from view, with foliage or leaves.

PEDESTALS. These can be bought, or they can be made from a wide choice of materials by a local craftsman. I am lucky in that I have a very beautiful pair — made for me in wood, and painted cream with a little gold decoration. They can be in alabaster, though these are expensive and rare. Pedestals from plywood nailed on to a framework of battens are simple to make and inexpensive, also light and easy to move about. It is best to make these straight-sided, or slightly tapered, but they can be in varying heights, and finished with flat paint, or rough cast distemper. The decorators of Winchester Cathedral finished theirs most effectively; to make them look like stone, they painted them and then covered them with coarse sand. Marble pedestals were used a great deal some years ago and are still to be found. You get such lovely colours in old marble — soft greens, creams, grey — and it is much more durable than alabaster. However, if you are doing a lot of church work or decorating for various functions, I feel it is more practical to have pedestals made in a light material, easier to handle. It is quite possible to have wood painted to look like marble, and very effective it is. There is also a marble Fablon, which is simplicity itself to stick on. Stone pedestals as a rule are really only suitable for churches, or perhaps for use in a garden room. As they are so heavy, it is better to have these only if they can remain in one position. Many of the old pedestals were made of wood, some very ornate and others severely plain. They come in all kinds of woods, from oak to mahogany, some painted and others stripped and the wood bleached, which can look very pleasing. It is quite simple to paint them the colour of the walls of the room. Should you want to strip off any old paint to get a limed effect, use any paint stripper and then paint the surface with parazone; finish by covering with lime and water and brush it off when it is dry. In this way some of the white stays in the cracks and looks very effective. Old wrought iron standard lamps can sometimes be converted to use as pedestals, though many blacksmiths can make wrought iron pedestals to order. If you are having one made, be sure that the container on the top is large enough to hold plenty of water; a small one is often a disadvantage. They can be designed in many ways and be painted in any colours, though they are usually black or white.

As for paints, I personally prefer to use dull finishes on both vases and pedestals, so a matt paint is what I would recommend. Gold paint mixed with a little brown gives a good effect. The new aerosol sprays in gold and silver are quick and easy to use, and a combination of both gives an unusual and attractive finish to plinth or vase. A mixture of black and aluminium gives a pewter finish, and this surprisingly enough is one of the best for a base, to show off flowers really well.

Home-made Containers

As at least three of the photographs in the book have arrangements in home-made containers, I feel these are worth a mention. The first is Plate 8 which is a water-biscuit tin covered with a piece of Japanese rush wall-paper. I stuck it on to the tin with adhesive, leaving a strip of Sellotape down the seam until it had really set. It is possible to do this with strands of plaited raffia sewn together, and stuck on in the same way, or even a rush table mat could be used. To seal the tin, a melted candle run round all the seams prevents it from leaking for a short space of time.

The second one, on page 99, is a cardboard fig-box used after Christmas. This was covered with scarlet ribbon to add brilliance to one inexpensive bunch of anemones. The velvet was stuck on with Copydex and a small bowl was placed in the box to hold the water.

Thirdly, a piece of sheet lead was cut and moulded to make the container on page 161. This has been delightful to use for purple and mauve flowers in summer, as well as for the moss garden of early spring flowers as you can see from Colour Plate IV.

I have also used coconut shells, and various other shells, made into vases. Altogether, there are many ideas that can be easily carried out.

CHAPTER FOUR

Conditioning and Maintaining

The treatment of flowers after picking is of paramount importance. There are different theories about the best time of day to pick. Gardeners, by and large, feel the morning is best as the flowers have regained overnight the moisture that they lose during the day. I agree with this theory, though I do not necessarily keep to it: partly because I find that blooms removed from the plant with the dew still on them are inclined to wilt more quickly; and also because the flowers last much better if they have several hours in deep water, so that I prefer to pick at night and then leave them in deep water till next day when they are all ready for placing in the vase.

Avoid picking in full sun (except for flowers like arctotis and gentian which close up easily) and get all stems into water as quickly as possible; once a stem flags, it takes a long time to stiffen up again. On a very hot summer's day I often take a jug of water round the garden with me to prevent this from happening. As you pick the flowers from the garden, remove all the bottom leaves, especially any that go under the water-line. This prevents the water from becoming stagnant too quickly. It also saves a confusion at the top of the vase, which makes it difficult to see where you are placing the next stems, and in this way you can ensure that they really are under water. Even if you do not give any of the special treatments I suggest, remember it is most important to cut all soft stems and hammer hard any woody ones. Then give them several hours in deep water — up to twelve hours is the ideal.

If you are buying flowers, then it is of course much more difficult to know how fresh they really are; but most shops will never wittingly sell good customers old stock, and flowers more often die from being too fresh and not having had a really good drink than because of being too old. As soon as you get them home, put them as quickly as possible into water, first just snipping the ends as this enables them to take up water more quickly since the ends will have become dry. Try to get them wrapped so that the heads are out of the air; this is as important in the heat of a summer's day as it is if it is intensely cold.

A quick look at the stems will give you a guide as to how long they have been in water. If the stems look dark in colour and at all slimy, then I advise you not

48

8. The home-made container: a biscuit tin covered with Japanese wallpaper gives a simple Oriental effect. Three branches of cherry, three striped aspidistra leaves and two leaves of wild arum set off five narcissi.

9. A mass of colour is produced by this mixture of gay summer flowers: dahlias, roses, heads of hydrangea, kniphofia, phlox and a few stems of hardy fuschia.

10. Our inheritance: wild flowers from the hedgerows.

to buy. With such flowers as lilies and daffodils it is quite easy to see how fresh they are by the amount of pollen that is on the stamens. When a lily bud first opens, the pollen is hardly noticeable. Often the stamens are removed altogether before the pollen can stain the flower, but if by gently tapping a bunch of daffodils you shake off any pollen then it is better not to buy! Nearly all fresh flowers such as daffodils and chrysanthemums have a definite sheen on a newly-opened flower. Naturally with roses and tulips, and so on, the first glance will show you a closed bud or a fully-blown flower. As one gets far more effect from a really open flower, I usually like to buy two or more bunches in various stages — some in tight bud and some in full bloom. You of course will be guided by how you are intending to use the flowers.

Nowadays I am becoming more and more interested in learning various ways of making cut flowers last better, by experimenting with some of the ideas which I am suggesting here and which you may also like to try. We are learning more all the time about the movement of sap, and cell structure, and an outcome of this is the boiling water treatment — one of the discoveries that has enabled me to use many different kinds of foliages that previously seemed to wilt as soon as removed from the plant.

Here are some of my methods of conditioning:

Hammering and Peeling

With really woody stems of shrubs such as lilac and laburnum, either hammer the bottom two inches of the stem; or scrape off the outside bark, leaving the white under-stem showing for at least two or three inches, but be very careful that the whole of the white part goes well under the water-line or the stem will not last. Then remove any foliage that will go below water, to prevent dis-colouration of water, clogging of the cells in the stems so that they cannot drink freely, and bad odour. Also remove heavy or unwanted leaves that may obscure flower heads or berries. This will reduce the transpiration as well.

Boiling Water Treatment

Again, the stems of woody plants can be treated in this way. I find it good for roses and the leaves of many hothouse plants, such as *Begonia rex* and caladium. Place the stem ends in a jug with an inch of really boiling water for about a minute, then fill up the jug with cold water and leave the stems in it for several hours. To prevent the flower heads from getting scorched by the steam, put a towel round the top of the jug, or, as in the case of very delicate flowers such as clematis, cover the flower head itself in tissue paper.

D

VII. A small arrangement that gave me a lot of pleasure, partly because it is unpretentious and uncontrived. I must frankly admit that I don't really think I had anything special in mind when I walked into the garden that day. I was anxious to use the *Arctotis grandis*, and somehow it seemed to build up around them. The soft colourings appealed to me, especially the touch of lime green which seems to do so much for any vase it is put into. I placed the herbaceous clematis on the outside so that the outline of this enchanting little flower shows well. If it were used in the middle of the vase it would be completely lost. Always study the flower and the most advantageous position from which to see it as a whole, keeping the rounded heads and flowers with a flat head (or face as we call it) for the centre of the vase. A few grey leaves are all the foliage that is required. Try not to over-foliage a vase, as it very often spoils all the delicate colour, and green in excess can be overpowering and heavy.

A   Flowers of *Hosta undulata*
B   *Nicotiana alata* 'Limelight'
C   *Clematis fremontii*
D   Candytuft — *Iberis umbellata* 'Rich Purple'
E   *Santolina pectinata*
F   Poppy seed head
G   *Arctotis grandis*
H   *Viola* hybrid — Pansy
I   Laced pink (*Dianthus* hybrid)
J   Leaf of *Cineraria maritima* (*Senecio cineraria*)
K   Rose 'Magenta'
L   *Anaphalis margaritacea*
M   *Tradescantia fluminensis*
N   *Sedum spurium coccineum*

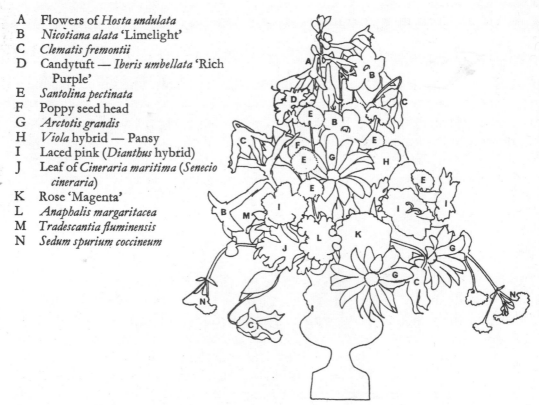

Searing

Hold the stem ends in a gas flame or burn with a match. This has the same effect as the boiling water, but is very much easier when you are taking odd leaves from a stem of, say, spurge or poinsettia, which will result in the bleeding of the white rubbery substance known as latex. Searing stops this bleeding at once. It is also suitable for poppies and hollyhocks, though generally I find it easier to place the ends in boiling water — and very much quicker. However, it can be useful if you are recutting the ends of, say, poppies that have already been boiled, if you want to shorten the stem a little; it is then often easier just to hold the stem under the flame of a lighted match for a few seconds as a precaution.

Floating

Leaves such as arum, and all kinds of ferns, should be floated or submerged for twelve hours if possible. Fill a bath or sink with tepid or cold water, but avoid hot water as it will scald and completely ruin any delicate leaf. Also never submerge completely any grey foliages as this spoils the silvery-grey effect. I think this is because the silver effect is usually created by a coating of very fine hairs on the leaves, and once these get really wet they take a long time to dry and the leaves look quite green until then. Heads of hydrangea, which will wilt quickly, recover overnight if submerged in warm water. Because leaves are soaking wet after this treatment always leave them on a piece of dry newspaper to drain off.

Starching

A weak solution of starch water is useful for submerging arum leaves and ferns. One suitable for most purposes can be made by dissolving 2 teaspoonsful of instant starch in $1\frac{1}{2}$ pints of water. Left in it overnight, they stiffen slightly and this makes them last much longer. It is also good for bracken before pressing and using for winter decoration. This method is one that I am experimenting with all the time.

Boiling Vinegar

A tip I heard in America, where it is used for such subjects as bamboo. Put an inch of boiling vinegar into a jug and insert the stems for five minutes, then allow them to have a long drink of water.

Cutting the Stems Under Water

This is a method used by the Dutch growers, and their stand at the Chelsea Flower Show seems to stay fresh almost better than any other. The idea is to stop any air entering the stem and forming an air bubble which would prevent the assimilation of water. Our use of wire netting makes it difficult to accomplish. It is best to cut the stems in this way in a bucket of water and then to let them stay there to have a drink, afterwards taking care to keep your finger over the end of the stem until you get it into the vase.

Spraying

This is difficult to do in a furnished room, but if you can remove the vase into the kitchen and spray well overhead it does help enormously. It is particularly helpful where there is central heating. It increases the moisture content in the air and so reduces transpiration from the leaves, in this way prolonging their life. It is excellent for hydrangeas, which seem to drink through their heads, and also woody-stemmed flowers such as rhododendrons, which absorb moisture more slowly. Overhead spraying as soon as these two flowers are picked and are enjoying their long drink will, I find, help them to last very much longer.

Filling the Hollow Stems with Water

Hold the hollow stems of such flowers as lupins and delphiniums upside down, fill them with water and plug them with cotton wool, or Oasis. This takes quite a lot of time, but is well worth while if you are doing flowers for some very special occasion.

Breaking Stems

There is divided opinion about this. However, I constantly break, both for speed and lasting; I find it has much the same effect as hammering and the flowers last extremely well.

Retaining the Roots

Occasionally when I have a very large group of flowers to arrange, I find it most helpful to use a whole pot plant — many of which, such as *Begonia rex*, when cut, do not stand well in water without special treatment. If you remove the plant from the pot and wash the soil from the roots, it can be put straight into the vase; or if extra height is needed, insert the roots in a polythene bag and tie on to a cane at the height required.

Warm Water

By warm, I mean the temperature at which you can comfortably insert your hand. All cut flowers revive well in warm water, and I usually fill up my vases

11. The complete arrangement stands less than a foot high. The swirl of grass takes up the line of the silver container, and with it I have used sedum, sprays of cherry tomatoes, lime-green *Nicotiana alata* and three 'Iceberg' roses.

12. A beautiful head of decorative green-and-white cabbage inspired this group. With it are the pale yellow kniphofia 'Maid of Orleans', the seed-heads of martagon lilies, a small piece of the variegated phlox 'Norah Leigh' on the right, and some superbly shiny leaves of giant green ivy.

with warm water if this is available. If flowers arrive limp, cut the stems and then place them in warm water and they will revive almost immediately.

Aspirin and Other Aids

Many people believe that aspirin helps flowers to last, and I personally find it especially good for tulips. On very good authority I have been told that sugar feeds the flowers and that a teaspoonful of sugar and one aspirin is the ideal combination. The aspirin keeps the water clear, as sugar — although flowers like it — does tend to clog the cells and gradually defeats its aim, by not letting the stems take up water. Charcoal is excellent for keeping the water clear, and in Australia they often use allum. The new Dutch product, *Chrysal*, has very good lasting properties, and I can thoroughly recommend it. Read the instructions carefully, as if you can put the flowers into it straight away for a drink and then tip the Chrysal water into the vase, this is far the best way. However, I have used it just in the flower vase, the flowers having had their preparatory drink in cold water only, and I still think it is worth using like this for a special occasion. Milton is good in a vase which has either onion or cabbage, and prevents any odour. Gregory's make a rose powder that I understand is helpful. Anything that may help to give the flowers longer life is worth trying.

Alcohol

To use this for flowers may seem strange to some of us, but nevertheless, it has been used in Japan for very many years, as a method of preserving very special subjects. Having put clematis into champagne after a dinner in Sydney, and literally watched the miraculous way in which they revived, I am now converted to making other tests of this idea. Many of the Japanese studios keep a small bottle of pure alcohol for putting such stems as wisteria, clematis and water lilies into for several minutes; I cannot say that I have had any experience with this, but I did come home and try my hellebores in gin! Though they appeared at first to hang over the vase, I must admit that after a long drink they really lasted extremely well. I understand that the Japanese also inject alcohol into the stems of water lilies and they stay open even at night, although the only method that I find really satisfactory with water lilies has been to put melted wax between the petals which of course forcibly prevents them from closing. It sounds somewhat cruel, but it really does the trick — so it's up to you.

Cotton Wool

Putting cotton wool into a bowl and then filling it with water, is the ideal way for keeping small almost stemless flowers: stephanotis, orchids, and gardenias.

Tissue

A similar idea is to stretch a piece of tissue paper over a bowl of water and fix with an elastic band. Puncture holes in the paper and slip the stem ends into the water. In this way the flowers can drink but the petals remain unspoilt.

Pricking the Stems

Take a needle and prick right through the stem at intervals of about an inch, from the head right down the stem of tulips and hellebores. This prevents an air bubble forming and allows the flower to drink more freely. Another method is to use a needle or sharp pin to scratch from the head to the base of the stem, making a fine cut right down the stalk. I have found this the best treatment of all for hellebores.

Filling the Vases

The filling up of vases, once they have been arranged, is important. I like to fill the vase three-quarters full before I start the arrangement; somehow it always feels easier to put the stems straight into water. Also having the water adds weight and the vase is not so likely to overbalance. When the flowers are arranged and the vase has been moved to where it is finally going to stand, you can fill it up right to the top. If it is difficult to judge this just put your finger over the edge of the vase, so that you can feel the water coming up.

After Care

For ease and quickness in keeping the vase renewed I try to cut out any dead stems and replace them with a fresh bloom. It is so much better to cut out the stem than to risk pulling it out and perhaps dislodging the whole arrangement. Keep constantly filling up. It is surprising how a few minutes each day spent in tidying, removing dead heads and leaves, will save hours of work. I personally never re-do the vase until I simply have to, as once you take everything out there always seems so little worth putting back. Once again, the use of a dust sheet is very helpful, both for putting the fresh flowers on to, ready for use, and for collecting up the old ones for throwing away.

A small glass mat that is unobtrusive can be placed under the vase to save the furniture. Always make quite certain that no water gets spilled underneath, as it can mark very badly. Should you get water stains on the furniture, there are two ways that I find helpful for removing them. The simpler one is to mix a little coarse salt and olive oil together and with your finger gently rub the water stain; it will leave a slightly oily mark, but this soon disappears after a day or so. The second way, which needs great care but is very effective, is to put a little methylated spirit on a soft cloth, cover this carefully with linseed oil, and rub until the stain is removed. This will remove older and more lasting stains.

When you have finished with a flower arrangement, remove the wire netting and wash the vase thoroughly; take the netting and pour some boiling water over it — this will remove any dirt or slime — then tie it back ready for the next time. I find that unless you do this carefully every time, the vases soon become stained and often the water mark is impossible to remove.

CHAPTER FIVE

Preservation and Drying

———————·《》《》《》·———————

This is done with a view to the sparse winter months, when flowers are scarce and expensive. The whole subject appeals to me very much because it is experimental, and it is exciting to try new ideas and methods, to keep flowers for their colour value, or seed heads and leaves in tones of fawns and browns, all the muted shades that blend well with chrysanthemums, and the bronzy shades of autumn and winter. Through the years we have learned more and more about methods of preservation — something that is tried out not only in our small island but in almost every country in the world. The Japanese have had a start on us of hundreds of years, though they are perhaps not so interested in preserving as say the Australians or the Americans. This is possibly because their climate is not so extreme. The heat in Australia and the cold in America make both these countries interested in trying to keep flowers under difficult conditions. Western Australia has a wonderful collection of native material which dries easily with natural colour and beauty, and we are lucky in being able to buy this in many London shops. The Americans, on the other hand, dry flowers in their full natural colour almost better than anywhere else in the world. This, I think, is partly due to a hot, dry climate; one thing that dried flowers will not tolerate is damp, and this makes drying here so much more difficult.

However, from both these countries I have learned a great deal, and some of the American books on the subject are most interesting. *The Dried-Flower Book* by Nita Cox Carico and Jane Calvert Guynn, is particularly good, and a small paperback with the delightful title *Winter Bouquets* by Alice Burt McIlvain has a lot of helpful information. Their methods are very like ours though they dry for colour by the hot sand method, which I will describe later on, but of which I have had very little experience.

I started making arrangements using dried flowers and seed pods many years ago. Working with Constance Spry in London, we had the fun of doing flowers in many lovely houses and shops. As the autumn came, we used berries and seed heads of all kinds. These gradually dried off in water, and were preserved for winter and used then with chrysanthemums until nearly Christmas time. Then, as you can understand, many of the flat-dwellers were loath to part with these backgrounds of seed heads, and asked that they should remain and be added to — and so, many times, I would go back and re-do the vase, taking perhaps some coloured heads of dried hydrangea and achillea to add colour to a vase that was going to remain — and at a reasonable price — until the early spring flowers arrived. For me this was the birth of really 'dried' vases, with no fresh flowers at all. Nowadays, in my own home, I find it most useful to start again at the end of January and put fresh flowers and leaves into the winter dried group. Some stems of hellebore at once bring a vase alive, and the combination of textures is always pleasing.

Searching for dried materials is most rewarding, and the roadsides and fields and river banks all take on a new beauty and interest. Even common grasses have a use, and you look at them with fresh eyes. Drying should be done all through the year because if you dry at different stages of development, you get a change of colourings. If you pick a few stems of wheat or barley when green, then when turning yellow, and when fully ripe and deep gold, drying at these various times gives much more interesting colour value. So with putting beech leaves into glycerine at different times; the leaves will vary in size — small ones in the early sprays and larger ones as they develop — and also vary in colour. For pressing the same applies. Bracken can be pressed when green, then a few fronds as they turn pale cream, and some later still when a deep rich brown. It is quite easy in the autumn to gather seed heads and some foliages that have dried off naturally by themselves. The only difficulty here is to pick them at just the right stage as they 'weather' quickly and become very brittle. Seed heads that have been hung upside down — hence allowing the sap to run into the head — seem to handle much more easily and are not nearly so fragile. With the increase in motor cars nearly everyone has the chance of a run in the country, so there is little excuse for lack of material. If you are interested enough to want to collect dried material, it is within the reach of everyone, even if you have no garden. One thing I would strongly advise is to remove a vase of dried flowers as soon as you feel these have served their purpose, and store them carefully away, so that the best can be used again another year.

Having collected what you can, even if it may not appear very exciting, then look in the shops. It is often so worth while to buy a few of the interesting drieds that are imported: wood roses from Honolulu, banksia from Australia, lotus seed pods from the East . . . so many lovely things that will give your vase character and attractiveness.

VIII. Fruit and flowers — a combination of materials which is of constant interest throughout the year, although I always feel that they look their best in autumn, this being a natural time for coloured foliages and fruits and berries in our gardens. Fruits seem to be best mixed with a few rather exotic flowers — red roses, hippeastrum and even an orchid or two adding elegance and quality to the simplest fruits such as apples and grapes. Green grapes and white gardenias make a lovely table arrangement. Lemons, branches of ilex and paper-white narcissus give a feeling of lemon flower and are effective in January, inexpensive but pretty. There is a variety of effects to be gained by combining these two different materials.

A Gladiolus
B Leaves of the golden privet,
    Ligustrum ovalifolium aureum
C Leaf of *Mahonia japonica*
D *Gerbera jamesonii*
E Hybrid tea rose 'Baccara'
F Leaf of *Bergenia cordifolia*
G *Sedum spectabile* 'Autumn Joy'
H Pineapple
I *Hippeastrum puniceum* hybrid
    (Barbados Lily)
J *Hydrangea macrophylla hortensis*
K Regal pelargoniums
L Quince
M Grapes
N Floribunda rose 'Frensham'
O Variegated kale leaf
P Leaf of *Codiaeum* (Croton)
Q Seed head of *Magnolia grandiflora*
R *Amaranthus caudatus* — Love-lies-
    bleeding
S Gourds
T Pomegranate

Drying by Hanging

This method is used for all seed heads and some flower spikes. It is still the most general method and the easiest. The important thing is to find a suitable place where you can hang up your bunches to dry. Although a garage or tool shed may be quite all right in a good summer, such places are often too damp. It is essential that you should preserve your material in a really dry, airy atmosphere so that it dries off as quickly as possible. Remove all the leaves from your stems as soon as you pick them. This is most important for two reasons. Firstly, it is important to assist dehydration as much as you can — and leaves kept on the stems retain the moisture in the stem, and so prolong the drying period. Secondly, the leaves quickly shrivel and die, and then have to be removed, and this is much easier to do when the stems are stiff and fresh; once they are dry they become brittle and are more likely to crack and break. Hang the seed heads in bunches, tying them with string, elastic bands, or pipe cleaners. Make the bunches small to avoid overcrowding; in fact, I very often prefer to tie each stem individually, as this can give you a more perfect specimen in the end. If they are bunched too closely together, one head can get caught in another, and as you pull these apart when they are dry, they often get damaged. Heads of yellow achillea damage very easily and if all the heads are tied together the stems press into the heads, leaving a hole in the finished specimen. I usually stand these in a flower vase, so that the heads remain perfect while they are drying. This takes up a lot of space however, and the hanging method is the more useful. If drying in a shed, place the nails so that there is plenty of room between each bundle, allowing plenty of air to circulate round them. Light material, such as grasses, takes about a week to dry and heavier material up to three weeks, depending greatly on the warmth of the air. The quicker the subjects dry, the better colour they keep. Watch them every now and again: stems, as they dehydrate, tend to shrivel and to slip out of their string. Either re-tie, or remove them if they are ready, and store in cardboard boxes, being careful to put the lids on and keep them away from the light. I dry all my seed heads by this method: hollyhocks, verbascum, cardoons . . . and also some flower heads such as delphiniums, but these need to be tied individually or as soon as you pull them apart they will shed their petals. Helichrysums — or straw flowers as they are sometimes called — must be dried head hanging down so that the sap runs into the head. I find it best to insert a florist's wire right down the middle of the head, through the calyx, otherwise the flower head flops over. Remove all the leaves and hang the stems carefully so that each bloom has room to open as it dries. Having the wire already in the stem, you can add other wires to it later to lengthen the stem.

Statice, and any other similar flower, is best treated in this way. Although I hang all the larger material outside in the garage, the smaller and more precious things I hang, a few branches at a time, over the warmth of the boiler. In your anxiety to pick for drying, be sure that you leave the flower heads on the plant until they are really fully open up to the tops of the stem, in the case of acanthus, or larkspur and delphiniums; otherwise, the tips with the unopened buds will hang over.

Drying in Water

Extraordinary as it sounds, this is the best way to dry the heads of hydrangeas and other difficult flower heads. Cut the hydrangeas when the flowers are well out — when they have been in bloom on the plant for several weeks and the heads are changing colour from pink to red and blue to green. Remove all the leaves and stand the stems in a vase with a small amount of water. Keep them over the boiler or in the linen cupboard, in as much warmth as you can. The quicker they dry, the better colour they keep. Molucella or Bells of Ireland, with delightful stems of bell-shaped flowers, dry either green or a lovely shade of creamy-parchment. Stand the stems on a pin-holder in shallow water, so that they take on charming natural curves; and then stand them in a jam jar, still with a small amount of water, until they dry off completely. The seed heads of hostas I also like to dry in this way, picking the heads when they are green and watching them open out until all the seeds are showing — again, with a delicate bell-like effect.

Glycerine

Preservation by this method is long-lasting and the stems keep their natural shape and form, just deepening in colour as they absorb the glycerine. Leaves and branches make the best subjects. Mix the solution with one part glycerine and two parts hot water and place this in a narrow vase or jar so that the solution goes as far up the stem as possible. Hammer the woody stems well, two or three inches up the stem, and allow them a deep drink of water for several hours, especially if they have been picked and carried for some time and may have flagged. Then put them into the glycerine and leave them for about ten days, or until the stems have changed colour. Green leaves gradually turn brown as the solution creeps up the stems. It is quite a good idea to coat the leaves with a little of the mixture dipped in cotton wool; this prevents them from curling, and can be repeated as often as you think they need it. Prune the branches before you start, or you may waste the glycerine on a poor branch, or

13. A change of form. The head of *Zea mays* dominates the vase, balanced by spikes of *Molucella laevis*, peony foliage and the beautifully coloured leaves of the handsome vine *Vitis coignetiae*.

14. A candle holder with crystal drops in a silver candlestick contains one stem of single white spray chrysanthemum 'Coronado' with aquilegia, flowering brussels sprouts and the blue feather hyacinth *Muscari comosum monstrosum*.

one where the leaves are imperfect. This is one reason why I like to do my beech leaves early in the season before the leaves get damaged by insects. Take out the branches before the mixture drips off the ends of the leaves, and store them in a box. Beech leaves are generally the most popular, but I have had a lot of fun experimenting with other things and have found that sprays of lime flowers picked just before they are fully open, and with all the leaves removed, provide lovely sprays of delicate flowers that make a nice light background for other dried flowers. Sprays of hips and cotoneaster berries also take up glycerine very well. So does Old Man's Beard — the sprays acquire a pink glow, and although after some weeks in a hot room the flower heads do go more fluffy, they stay on the stems very well and do not shed. The leaves turn a delightful bronze and although they curl after a time, they can be cut off later.

Laurel (*Prunus lauracerasus*) and *Magnolia grandiflora* are of course both ever-green, and so it may seem a waste of time to preserve them. If you do so, how-ever, you will have an upright stem of bronzy, leathery leaves with a wonderful texture — such a help to use either as individual leaves or in a spray, to mix with the lighter and more delicate seed heads. The bold leaves of *Bergenia cordifolia* and *B. crassifolia*, and the keys of hornbeam, also add interest and different form to a dried group. Separate leaves of ivy and whitebeam can be preserved by submerg-ing them in the solution. This is something I have tried only lately, and it is well worth experimenting.

Skeletonizing

This is a difficult process and needs endless patience, but it is most rewarding if you are successful. Large leaves of *Magnolia grandiflora* and some of the hybrid rhododendrons can be skeletonized by soaking the leaves in a strong solution of soda and water and allowing them to decay. This they do more rapidly if they are kept in a place where the heat is constant; on the side of a solid-fuel boiler is ideal. When the green matter has decayed, remove it very carefully, so that you are left with the skeleton. Be very careful not to break the mid-rib — this is the most difficult part of the operation. It is possible to pick up skeletonized rotting leaves off the ground under the trees of the hybrid rhododendrons, and magnolias and hollies; these are small, but delightful painted with gum and glittered for Christmas. Failing doing it yourself, it is possible to buy skeletonized leaves, processed in eastern Europe. How they do it remains a secret, but these leaves have been on sale in Covent Garden for the last twenty-five years at least, and we have used them in bridesmaids' bouquets and mounted on bare branches of beech or oak. Each leaf fixed to the branch with a piece of silver wire, they make ethereal sprays that are a marvellous background for a winter group.

Pressing

This is for flat sprays of beech branches, ferns of all kinds, bracken, and all sorts of autumn-tinted single leaves. Sprays of leaves can only be pressed if their natural habit of growth is flat. It is best to lay out the material on a thick layer of newspaper, cover with another layer and put them under heavy books or some weight — though I find under the carpet best of all. It is important that leaves do not overlap, and take care to see that they are not curled or folded as once they are dry they cannot be straightened, and this may spoil the shape of the frond or leaf. The advantage of pressing sprays of beech is that they retain their lovely colours, whereas when they are preserved in glycerine they become a copper colour. Bracken presses extremely well and by using it in all its shades you can have a wide range of colours, from green to cream and brown. The green hedgerow ferns also press well, and the royal fern *Osmunda regalis* gives tall delicate fronds of autumn colours which are most useful for tall vases. It is sometimes necessary to put a florist's wire up the back of the leaf, once it is pressed, to give it support. A thick wire caught in several places will keep it upright and firm. Smaller leaves need to have a false stem added: put a wire up the back and attach it with Sellotape, then use an additional wire to provide a stem. Stems of anything that is pressed always break off so easily. Single leaves of sweet chestnut or acer give a lovely bit of colour when placed at the base of a dried group. I was given the tip of submerging bracken and ferns in weak starch water for several hours before pressing, and I must say this makes the sprays remain much firmer — a great help if the ferns are to be treated or perhaps painted for using at Christmas-time. Spikes of montbretia leaves press well and keep a good autumn colour. It is always helpful to have spiky leaves to give different form. Of course all pressed material takes on a very flat look, but it mixes well with spiky and rounded seed and flower heads.

Preserving in Sand

This is an American method that I know very little about from experience, but I have seen some remarkable results. In this way, it is possible to dry to keep the colour of the actual flowers, and they keep their true colour very well indeed. For the best results you need to select straight-petalled and light-coloured blooms, but I have seen good results with roses, sprays of ivy, sunflowers, dahlias, marigolds, zinnias and Bells of Ireland — mostly in not too dark colours. Get a box for the sand — one that will allow you to cover the whole flower completely. Shake in a layer of dry fine sand and place in the flower head. The stems of roses should be removed and replaced by a wire, and the rose then laid in so that the sand can be sifted over it. Placing the rose-flower head up, take a handful of sand and carefully let it sift round the outer petals, circling the sand stream round each layer of petals until the whole head is completely covered. Leave the flower for about four days and then scrape away a little of the sand and test the petals to see if they are crisp and dry; they can then be removed and stored in boxes in a warm place for the winter. Zinnias are better dried face downwards, and the sand sifted over in the same way as for roses; the stems stick straight up and will dry off quite well in the air; if they seem brittle when they are removed, then an additional wire stem must be made. For the drying of larkspur and delphiniums slightly longer boxes are needed so that the whole stem can be laid on the bed of sand, and, again, sift it over so that you submerge the entire spike. It is always better to take the smaller stems and side shoots of the delphiniums, as these dry very much more quickly; naturally anything that is very fleshy takes a considerable time to dehydrate. Small flowers such as pansies and Love-in-a-mist all dry well, and these are most attractive if they are used to line a glass bowl to hold pot-pourri.

The dried arrangements throughout the pages of this book are all arranged for different settings. The all-dried group of natural dried material will last without further worry for months, being usually thrown out in the end because one is tired of it, rather than for any other reason. As I have often said, I think I really prefer a background of drieds and something fresh to go with it. The two stems of monkey puzzle with the three yellow chrysanthemums (page 110) is the kind of winter group that I never tire of. Dried flowers look well with a wooden base or separate piece of wood to conceal the container for water, as in the illustration on page 158. This beautiful lump of driftwood, found for me in Ireland, is bleached by the sun and weather to a lovely grey colour and is a wonderful background for grey-green lichen and the creamy dried bells of molucella. This is ideal for showing off just a few shapely seed heads. In all, the cost is almost nothing, yet the effect is pleasing and interesting to create, and something that one can live with and enjoy for many months.

The cone of dried materials shown on page 144 is both interesting and effective. The cone itself is made out of plastic-covered wire netting filled with Oasis. As this is entirely a dried group the Oasis is kept dry. The seed heads of poppies and achillea, fir cones and odd pieces of dried this and that, are stuck into the wire and this pyramid will last for weeks. It is an idea that I saw in America and thought well worth copying.

Lastly, the collection of drieds on the Spanish basket, Colour Plate IX, is something that could be hung in either the sun-room or the kitchen. To make this I tied a piece of Oasis covered in polythene on to the centre of the basket with florist's wire and stuck in the pieces of dried seed heads and fruits, with garlic for its shape and berries to give added colour. As the fruits became squashy, I replaced them, and this decoration lasted for a long time.

You can try many ways of doing dried groups — always remembering that they will not look suitable in every room, and special care should be taken to see that they look in keeping.

15. A simple arrangement of three 'Nellie Moser' clematis, three dark purple dracaena leaves and three of a regelio-cyclus iris.

16. A white and pale pink arrangement of 'Constance Spry' roses, single and double philadelphus and two white delphiniums.

CHAPTER SIX

Flowers for Special Occasions

Flowers play a very special part all through life, especially on the really important occasions; from the flowers at a christening to the sentimental thrill of a spray at a first dance, for confirmation, birthdays and weddings and all really big events. So I thought a few ideas on these lines might help when such occasions come your way.

One of the essential things to remember for these times is to make quite sure that the flowers will be seen by everyone. Often flowers placed on a small table in the sitting-room look very well, but as soon as you get a crowd of people, then they are quickly obscured, so — as a guide — try to raise the flowers above eye-level; in this way they can be easily seen, however crowded the room or hall may become. Large groups can be placed on pedestals, or mantelpieces, on the tops of cupboards or bookshelves — anywhere so long as they are easily visible but not in the way and are not likely to be knocked over or spilt. A few vases are much more worth while than too many small ones. Concentrate on bold flowers and clear colours, and leave the delicate and fussy for the smaller and more intimate vases that are seen close at hand.

To be sure that all the material you use is going to last really well, condition it with extra special care. If you do nothing else, be sure to hammer the hard and woody stems and cut the soft, and then put them into deep water for at least twelve hours. The preparation is the most time-absorbing part of all, but saves endless time in the long run. For large groups the background material is often the most difficult to get hold of. You need really large branches of foliage or berries and, as far as I am concerned, once I have got this, half the battle is over. Get the vases all prepared beforehand, as this saves precious time. Tie in the wire netting with either silver wire or string so that it is really firm. Have the dust sheets, cones, scissors, extra string and odd florist's wires ready in a box or basket. I often find that it is easier to take along a dust-pan and brush and watering can as well, to save time looking round a strange church or hall. The next thing is to be sure and find out if the church or hall is free at the time you want to do the job; and if this is a job in a strange church, to be sure that the vicar or clergy are quite agreeable that you should do it then. It is just politeness to find

E

IX. A basket to hang on the kitchen wall **or for the** sun room and which will last for many weeks. This was an idea that I first saw **arran**ged by a great friend in Nottingham and it is something that I have copied over and over again. I added a lot of fresh fruit — apples, fresh berries, and sometimes plums and grapes — and as these fade or rot I replace them with gourds, dried cones or seed heads so that they continue right through the winter. The shiny brown mahogany-coloured leaves are ordinary laurel preserved in glycerine and water. See the chapter on Drying for instructions on how to make up the whole arrangement. The basket is Spanish, but of course it could be equally well arranged on a decorative tray or any type of flat container provided it is possible to hang it.

A   Dried flower heads of *Sisyrinchium striatum*
B   Leaves of the common laurel, *Prunus laurocerasus*, preserved in glycerine
C   Fading rhododendron leaves
D   Wheat
E   *Physalis franchetii*
F   *Lagurus ovatus* (Hare's Tail Grass)
G   *Sorbus hupehensis* berries
H   *Skimmia japonica* (female)
I   Pine cones
J   Apples
K   Garlic
L   Gourd
M   Onion
N   Poppy seed head
O   Grapes
P   Quince
Q   Artichoke
R   Pomegranate

out if this is convenient, and may save you from clashing with a service or meeting. Nothing could be more frustrating than waiting for this to be over, and it may cause you a lot of unnecessary anxiety wondering if you are going to be ready in time. Always give yourself plenty of time. Doing flowers against the clock is one of the most exhausting tasks that I know of. Another tip is to be prepared for all weathers. Churches on the day of preparation are rarely heated; so in cold weather go with plenty of warm clothes on, and especially something warm on your feet. Also take a thermos of coffee or tea, so that you can slip out and have it in the car perhaps. This gives one a fresh start, and it takes so little time and gives one added strength to cope with the clearing up!

Christenings

If you are allowed, it is nice to put some flowers on the top of the font itself, and the prettiest idea that I know is to make a garland to lay round the top of the font, of any suitable flowers in season. In the spring you can do this with a bed of moss and into it put small bunches of primroses, scilla, grape hyacinths, polyanthus and small sprays of blossom. Later in the year you can use daisies or narcissi — any flower that is childlike and simple. I find the best method is to make a ring of rolled-up wire netting and at intervals put in small paste pots or tiny jam jars, and then cover the whole with a layer of moss, leaving just enough space round each jar so that you can easily pop in a small bunch of flowers, keeping each small pot with flowers in one colour even if the flowers are not all the same; this prevents the effect from looking messy. Bunches of primroses and their own leaves, and violets in the same way, look more as if they were growing, which is the result you want to achieve. Leave a large gap where the vicar is going to stand, as it can be so uncomfortable watching him trying to keep the sleeves of his vestments out of the flowers — so in fact what you are really doing is making a horse-shoe effect. If you can do this, it is ideal, as the flowers can be seen and enjoyed by everyone. However, if it is not possible for some reason, then it is a good idea to place the flowers in a vase nearby, either on a pedestal or raised in some way so that they stand at the back out of the way and yet are seen to advantage. Flowers are so often placed at the foot of the font and this is nice for the ordinary church services, but when you have a gathering of people round the font, then the flowers are immediately obscured. Any florists will make a small garland if they are told exactly what is required; so if you cannot undertake to do it yourself, it can be made up on a moss frame (rather like a wreath) and the flowers wired into it. Choose delicate flowers: single American spray chrysanthemums are one of the best flowers to use for this, and as they are now available nearly all the year round there should be no difficulty in getting them.

Often people like to have pale pink or blue, and I think white takes a lot of beating — it is so fresh and innocent-looking. When you are decorating the church for a christening, and are not just decorating the top of the font, try to find out where the relatives and friends are going to stand or sit, according to where the font is situated; then you can get an idea of exactly where it is best to place the flowers so that they can be well in view. Decorating the font at any other time does not present the same problems; if you can stand a vase either in the font or on the edge of it, this should show up well and help to add colour and life to the west end of the church. Small oblong bread tins painted and well weighted make excellent containers for the narrow edge of a font. As the service for a christening is not very long it is possible to lay flowers round the edge of the font out of water, but I am never very happy about this.

Confirmation

Sometimes flowers are specially arranged for this service, which may take place in a school chapel, and on many of these occasions I have been impressed by the results I have seen. One of the loveliest colour schemes, I thought, was in all shades of apricots and creams. White, again, always looks right, and has a quality that shows up well, especially if the church is at all dark. For dark corners — either panelled or just dark from lack of light — try to use light colours, either pale pink, yellow or white, and avoid blue or purple. For many confirmation services, only the altar is decorated; but if it is possible to have a large group near the steps where the candidates are to kneel, this is quite the best place.

Birthdays

A birthday most years is a cause for a celebration, but there are of course special birthdays, such as twenty-firsts, and naturally they invariably call for a party. If it should be a dinner, then the table is very important. Table flowers must be kept low or really high, and should in no way detract from an easy flow of conversation; it is most distracting if you have to talk round the flowers. For a girl, especially, the flowers are best kept in soft colours, unless those of her college, or sports club, or other particular colours are chosen. We have done a table in racing colours on one occasion. Deep reds are good and suitable for a young man, and I saw a lovely twenty-first table done in pewter and shades of lilac through to deep red which looked extremely handsome for such an occasion. If the flowers are for a dance, then the surroundings should really dictate what is best, and try above all to keep the decorations well out of the way. Buffet flowers, though so nice to have, are better concentrated in perhaps just one spectacular vase, as many caterers find that they can be rather a nuisance.

17. Hanging basket of viburnums: *V. opulus sterile* (Snowball Tree) and *V. tomentosum,* which makes a very effective party decoration.

18. A brass candle wall sconce with a delicate collection of yellow and cream flowers, trollius and maidenhair fern.

19. Grey *Begonia rex* leaves, pale blue hyacinths, pink chestnut flowers, two blush-centred roses and the sweet scented *Viburnum carlesii* are arranged in a bronze urn on a Japanese black wood base.

If the party is to be held in a marquee, decorations that hang will give a far better effect than anything else. Tent poles are always a problem and are better covered. If you can get them just bound round with some of the lining of the marquee, they will fade gently into the background — whereas so often if they are decorated with either green or garlands, they stand out and are more of an eyesore than ever. Tins, or Oasis in foil can be fixed round the poles and filled with flowers; in this way the pole becomes part of the decoration, which is especially effective if the flowers are so placed that they cascade gracefully downwards. The hanging baskets shown on Plates 17 and 18 are an idea that I find suitable for a marquee, and two of these seem to decorate the whole of a large tent. Again, it is the old maxim — raise them high. Flower balls — with a base of Oasis covered in wire netting and foil, and then the stems of some tough sort of flower such as spray chrysanthemums, dahlias, hydrangeas — make a quick and easy decoration. Tie the top of the ball with ribbons and let these ends fall. It is important that the flower balls are as large as possible, as once you raise them in a big space they are quickly dwarfed. Pedestals can be used, but so often the sloping sides of the marquee prevent adequate height and they can look out of proportion. Also, the floor may have been laid on uneven ground, and this can make them unstable. Garlands hung round the walls, made out of either evergreens or suitable flowers look most effective, but these take a lot of making and unless you can get plenty of help I would not really advise doing this. (See under *Christmas Decorations*, page 73, for the method of making garlands.)

In our family we have a tradition that has gone on for many generations. We make a posy and put it on the back of their chair when the 'birthday person' comes down for breakfast. It is such a small thing, but immediately gives a feeling of it being rather a special day.

Weddings

My first feeling when a wedding is being discussed is what does the bride really want? So often it seems that everyone else in the family has ideas about what she should have, and she herself hardly gets a chance to express any ideas of her own. Of course a bride is sometimes quite happy for her mother or some other member of the family to take over the flowers and make all the decisions for her. In that case — fine; but always give her the chance to say what she would like. She may have a fixed idea from childhood that she would like to carry red roses, and it is nice that she should have her wish, despite any opposition! Ideally, the whole wedding should be carried out as a scheme, so that the colourings for the bridesmaids and pages link up with the general effect, both in the church and at the reception. The result is so pretty if the colourings can be carried through, but of course this may not be possible for one reason or another; perhaps the difficulty in getting, say, red flowers in winter; or some unavoidably dominant colour in the church. White is always a safe choice; it looks as lovely as anything can look for either church or reception, and makes a traditional link with the bride. In any case, decide first what the bride will carry, and if this involves any colour then this may decide many other details. Then consider the colourings for the bridesmaids and their flowers. Having arranged all this, visit the church to think out what would be best. This depends so much on what the church is like, and whether it is large or small, and also the number of guests. The flowers may need to be spread out through the church if there are to be a lot of people. If, on the other hand, only half the church will be in use, then just decide to decorate the most important places: the altar, chancel steps, window-sills, and so on. Before the war, we tried to have at least four large groups: two at the altar and two on the chancel steps where the bride is actually married. Nowadays I find that in a small church one large group at the side of the lectern or pulpit is quite enough. Decoration of the altar depends on whether the flowers are to be placed on the altar itself, or whether there is to be a pedestal vase on one side, or a pair of vases, one on each side. If a pair is called for, then a low bowl on a stool on either side may be all that is wanted. Window-sills are a good place for flowers, as they help to spread the concentration of colour right to the back of the church and give it a really flowery look. I did a small posy on the pew ends the other day — something I don't do very often, but the effect was so pretty and gave a feeling that the whole church was filled with flowers. I think it is only a good idea if the posies can be easily attached. In this case I had the old umbrella-stand fittings to attach them to. Tie the posies with a ribbon bow with long ends, and this just finishes them off. There are many other ideas. For instance, you may have the opportunity of hanging something. This can be done from the screen if it allows, or occasionally from the light fittings. If the church is narrow and is to hold a lot of people then something that will hang, and perhaps something for the window-sills, may be all that is required, and you can cut out the idea of a large group altogether. The flowers that you use are important. They should be as bold as possible. Choose some light background-material — branches of flowering shrubs, or blossom in the spring, delicate sprays of beech, or branches of stripped lime flowers. Then try four good, well-grown and solid flowers. This is the time when really large heads of delphiniums, lupins, large dahlias, chrysanthemums, hydrangeas, and lilies, all make ideal materials. Get everything collected and put into water the day before, so that it is as fresh as possible. Long sprays of berries in the autumn are excellent. Pressed bracken, branches of lichen, and preserved beech branches are all worth while to use as background, and much lighter and more interesting than heavy winter foliage of say laurel or rhododendrons.

Next, the hall, house, or marquee, for the reception. Many people feel that this is the more important place to concentrate on, but I don't really think this is so. Although the reception lasts longer, everyone is busy meeting people and talking and eating, so that flowers quickly get forgotten; whereas in the church, before the bride arrives, there is time to sit and look at the flowers and so I think they are much more important there. However, the one place where they are really essential is to give a welcome at the reception. A vase to greet the guests at the entrance to the hall or marquee is in the most important place of all. The colourings here depend on the surroundings: if the hall is light or dark; if in a marquee, the colour of the lining and so on. Again, raise the flowers well up as although they may be seen by the first arrivals wherever they are placed, once you have a crowd of people then naturally they may never get the chance to see them. The table where the cake is to stand is a good focal point, and a white cloth caught up with posies of flowers is one of the best ways of decorating it. For the cake itself the usual small silver vases are now more often replaced by a low mound of flowers that are wired into a moss pad or stuck into a mound of Oasis lined with silver foil. This is much more satisfactory from every point of view, and there is no worry about the water spilling. A garland of matching flowers round the base of the cake is the nicest way of finishing it off. The buffet is another place for flowers and here I think it should be left to the discretion of the caterers as to where they can go, so that they will not hamper the service. If the cake is on a separate table, as I suggested above, then a vase in the middle of the buffet is the best place — and one really important vase is better than anything else. Candelabra, often lent by the caterers, can be fitted with candle-cups, and as these are well out of the way, and because of their height, they are one of the most effective and economical ways of doing a buffet table. A pyramid of roses, as on Plate 20, can look very well. These pyramids can be arranged with various sorts of flowers: peonies, camellias, green grapes, gardenias. . . . If you are really going to town on the buffet, a petticoat of fine material such as muslin or nylon can be made to fit the trestles, hanging loosely so that it can be caught up in loops and finished with posies of flowers. Years ago this was done with green smilax ferns. For one of the loveliest weddings I remember, we did the whole marquee in hydrangea colourings: a soft pink buffet cloth caught with posies of hydrangeas and ribbons; and round the sides large posies of hydrangeas, with ribbons looped from posy to posy all round the marquee.

Other wedding celebrations include ruby, silver, gold and diamond. All of these call for different ideas and give one plenty of scope. For a ruby wedding, the colouring must, I think, be reds; and groups of red flowers on a white or soft pink cloth can be effectively arranged in gold or silver containers. The nicest silver wedding decorations that I have arranged were done with plastic fronds of fern, sprayed with white paint and heavily glittered with a mixture of glass glitter and a little silver, and put into one of the long mirror-troughs so that the flowers stretched well down the table. Then I used white full-blown roses, pure white stocks and white dahlias, having first removed all the green foliage, and added silver ribbon bows with the ends trailing down the table. This gave a glittering silvery-white effect, and on such an occasion as this I feel it is permissible to mix fresh and artificial, even though it is something to be avoided in the general run of flower arrangement.

Golden weddings are a very special occasion. The colouring is easily decided of course, and one has a wide range with all the yellow and gold colourings. Usually it is a dinner table that one is planning for, though my parents had a garden party and I did all the flowers in the marquee in golds and creams, as well as one or two vases in the house. If you want to make an inexpensive gold buffet cloth, this was done most effectively by Constance Spry at the time of the Queen's Coronation, by painting the cloths. These were plastic and painted gold, so that from the distance they looked exactly like rich gold velvet. Vases are easily sprayed with gold aerosol paint for a quick and inexpensive result, though a mixture of gold and silver is prettier.

I have only once had the fun of doing a diamond wedding. We arranged the table with large rocks of pavement glass, that looked as much like diamonds as one could get, then tucked in white gardenias, camellias, and lily of the valley, and the whole took on a sparkling, glassy and — we hoped — diamond-like shimmer.

Wine and Cheese Parties and Cocktail Parties

The wine and cheese party has become very popular and gives the flower arranger lots of scope. A large arrangement on the table where the food is displayed is ideal. Fruit and flowers can be arranged together on a flat plate of wood or pewter, and on to this you can pile up colourful apples, lemons, plums, peaches and bunches of grapes — in fact, almost any fruit in season, though I am never very happy about either oranges (as I find their colour rather strong) or bananas (as they don't seem to lend themselves), though this is purely a personal prejudice. I find that a well pin-holder is the easiest thing to use for putting the fresh flowers into, as it holds just enough water and can be easily disguised. Place the pin-holder at the back of the plate and pile the fruit round about it; then put in some coloured foliage or berries, and one or two rather special flowers, such as carnations, nerines, a stem of lilies, a spray of orchid, or a few full-blown red or orange roses — this all depends on the time of year. Early spring flowers somehow never seem quite right for fruit arrangements. Late spring, summer and autumn are the most suitable times: partly because this sort of arrangement should give the feeling of plenty, as with harvest thanksgiving, when the mixtures of fruits and flowers, and all the plenty on earth, gives the same idea. The fruit and flower arrangement, shown on Colour Plate VIII, which is raised in a high vase, and not kept low on a flat plate, is also effective and can look well on a buffet table, to add height among the food and wines that you may be using. It is not necessary always to use a flat plate.

Other flowers that are arranged about the rooms can be of your own choice. As for a cocktail party, where you have a lot of people in a small space, be sure to raise the flowers so that they are seen by everyone. Mixed reds are always popular, and are arresting and exciting, and add to the party spirit. Bold colourings seem better than the whites and greens, but again it depends so much on what the room colourings are.

Christmas Decorations

Throughout the ages we have concentrated on decorating our homes at Christmas-time and the traditional Christmas tree is a 'must' in many homes. I am delighted that this custom has crept into our churches, and nowadays many churches have a big Christmas tree as the major part of the Christmas decorations. In Westminster Abbey they have had Christmas trees for some years, and these are decorated with a different colour scheme each year, usually two-tone — perhaps one year red and gold, another, silver and white, or silver and gold, blue and silver, and so on. This is so very much more effective than if all the colours are mixed up. Fairy lights that can be bought in many new forms add so much to the decoration; and the small sprays of holly with a light in the berries, and many other new ideas, are well worth considering as these help to lighten the dark green tree and are one of the quickest ways of decorating it. Home-made ornaments from milk-bottle tops and cardboard are always enjoyed, and keep the young amused and employed for many hours. Let them decorate the tree themselves just as soon as they are old enough to do this; and be sure to put the tree in the most convenient place for yourself as, once placed, it will have to stay in that position for every year thereafter!

Garlands are decorative and effective. They can be made out of any evergreen but are best made from conifers: box, yew, holly, both green and variegated, but avoid ivy and bay as they tend to curl rather quickly when left out of water. Make your garland on string or fine reel wire. Cut pieces of evergreen about

X. Candle light and flowers for a winter dinner party: an air of elegance, but when you study it closely not extravagant. Carnations give a feeling of luxury, yet they last well and I consider them a good investment. The background is of materials gathered and preserved during the summer; the brown shades blend well with the elaborate gilt candlesticks and the cream freesias and carnations. If, as in this case, the dinner service is a strong colour then try not to add very much additional colour in the flower arrangements. Garden ivy with berries takes the mixture of glycerine and water very well; beech nuts treated in the same way add the soft buff-toned background. The preserved material was of course used over and over again with a varied collection of flowers. The all-cream ivy leaves are to be found every now and again amongst the variegated foliage of *Hedera canariensis foliis variegatus*, and the individual leaves seem to last very much better than if they are picked on a spray.

A *Dianthus caryophyllus* — cream carnation
B Common garden ivy, *Hedera helix*,
      preserved in glycerine
C Freesia
D Cream leaves of *Hedera canariensis foliis
      variegatus*
E *Fagus sylvatica* — beech nuts preserved
      in glycerine

74

three and four inches in length, and make piles of different varieties, so that you can put your hands quickly on each different kind. Berries add colour and if it is a bad berry year, there are many good artificial ones and these rarely show. Bind each piece of evergreen one at a time on to the string with a figure of eight — once over the stem and once under. In this way, they stay firm. You can do the binding with either wire or string, but I find that wire holds best. Garlands can be made equally well on rolled newspaper, and if they are to be used on stone pillars this is the best method because the newspaper sticks well on the stone; made in short lengths they can then be attached together with wire. If you have a lot of garlanding to do, try to get one or two people to help and then put the lengths of garlands together. Hanging the garlands from one corner of a room to a central light or another corner is the quickest way of decorating a room. On the other hand, they can be hung in loops on the staircase, or placed round a mirror or picture frame. These can be easily attached with Sellotape. A garland is also effective round the lintel of the front door, instead of having a wreath.

The broom-stick tree is an idea that is good either outside or in. Get a broom handle, cover it with ribbon or paint, and wedge on to the top a lump of Oasis covered with wire netting. Cover the whole with silver tin foil. You can omit the foil, but it is very much better if the Oasis is wet, and naturally when damp it keeps the foliage much fresher. Then stick in sprays of holly and pine, and attach some iridescent coloured balls. Attach each ball through its loop to a long florist's wire, and the end of the wire will then go into the Oasis. Or use red or silver ribbons, making bows and streamer ends. Fix the end of the broom-stick into a large flower pot painted white or red. This is effective fixed to the newel post at the bottom of the stairs, or outside the front door as a welcome.

The Christmas table is always a place for flowers or some decoration. I like to make a table centre, to place the flowers on, with some inexpensive material; tarlatan — the material used for ballet skirts — is ideal. On to this you can stick small motifs and make a design as you go along, with silver holly or ivy leaves that can be bought in packets, or cut-out shapes from silver or gold doilies. Stick them with transparent gum. Placed on this, whatever decoration you put on the table looks Christmassy even if it is only a bowl of fruit. Years ago we used to make a whole table cloth, but I find this alternative just as effective and takes much less time. A piece of tarlatan edged with nylon ribbon or velvet will give a very pleasing effect. For the centre piece itself I like candles. The large church-candles that can be bought from the church shop in Vauxhall Bridge Road, Victoria, are lovely. Pressed into the centre of one of the small Oasis holders and surrounded with berried and variegated holly, then finished off with ribbons, they make the quickest and easiest decoration I know.

If you can get plenty of fresh evergreens, there is nothing prettier. On the other hand, it is the one time of year when you can use a mixture of plastic, dried, and fresh materials all mixed up together. With the new aerosol sprays in attractive colours you can get a wide range of colours and effects. The gold is particularly good, as is the bluey-green used with silver. White plastic ferns sprayed with aerosol clear gum and then sprinkled with glitter make a nice table centre used with either white or red fresh flowers. Gilded they are effective used with fresh fruits, and flowers, and if you remove the sprayed paint with turpentine as soon as you have finished with them, you can repaint them in another colour for the next year. If you want to glitter these leaves, you can sprinkle them with glitter while the paint or gum is still tacky. Glitters are available in many colours, but if you can get glass glitter this is quite the most natural-looking on fresh holly and conifers, as it looks just like frost. A table centre arranged with glass-glittered ivy, and fresh or artificial Christmas roses, is one of the prettiest of all. With the quantity of beautiful crackers and Christmas decorations available you can make a pretty table with little effort at all, but it will cost a great deal more money, and to make something yourself is much more rewarding.

Something to hang can be made so easily these days with the use of Oasis. Cover half a brick with kitchen foil and a layer of wire netting. Then fix a wire through the centre, pressing back the end like a hair-pin so that it will hang easily. Stick in short pieces of holly and mistletoe and finish off with ribbon bows on top.

The North American custom of hanging a wreath on the front door to give a welcome is one of the most charming ideas. Even if you don't want to make a wreath, just a bunch of evergreens tied with a ribbon bow is sufficient. You can use a metal coat-hanger made into a round; or buy a lamp-shade ring, bind it with ribbon and put clusters of evergreens attached with wire round the circle. The traditional form is a circular evergreen wreath with a bow of red ribbon at the top, with the ends hanging down. However, it can be varied in any way you like.

When I was doing Christmas decorations in Australia recently, I thought up all the cool-looking but Christmassy ideas I could think of: lots of silver, silver and blue, and so on, knowing how hot it can be out there at that time of year. However, it was a complete waste of time as all that was really wanted was reds and golds, and reds and greens, something that seems, as it does for us, really traditionally Christmas.

When Christmas comes you may find that you are tired of a lot of the dried material that you still have in reserve, so get it out and spray it gold, or gold and silver mixed; then arranged with some stems of variegated holly and one or two

20. 'Constance Spry' roses, remarkable for their musky perfume, their profusion of bloom and pale pink heart-shaped petals deepening towards the centre, are arranged in an alabaster box with a rose lid.

21. My sun room, in which house plants thrive. A rough wooden box, built on top of bookshelves, holds *Begonia rex, Jasminum polyanthum, Adiantum* (maidenhair fern) and *Monstera deliciosa*.

fresh golden chrysanthemums, it will make an attractive vase that has the feeling of Christmas but can well stay long after and still look quite suitable.

As I have dealt with all the important and festive occasions which are celebrated during the Church year in *Flower Decorations in Churches* I feel it is not the moment to say very much more about this subject. Nevertheless, these occasions are all very important and church flowers need extra special care. Try to make them bold and uncluttered: careful choice of materials is the most important aspect of all. Choose flowers with bold outline and a clear flat 'face'. These show up so well from a distance, and few of the flowers that are arranged to decorate a church are seen very close at hand.

Flowers that you send, perhaps to someone in hospital or on board ship, should be arranged in either Oasis or Florapack so that they last really well. If this is well soaked before the flowers leave your hands, then no more filling-up will be needed until they reach their destination — and in fact for twenty-four hours afterwards. There are many light and unbreakable small vases on the market in a papier mâché type of material, and these are ideal for arranging and sending through the post. A vase that is already arranged is so very much appreciated, especially by hospital staff who have more than enough to do these days without the extra work of flower arranging — much as many of them would love to do it.

Flowers that are to be worn or carried for a wedding or dance must be wired and, as this is a very specialized art, I think it is always advisable to employ a florist to do this for you.

CHAPTER SEVEN

House Plants, Bulbs and Foliages

Over the last few years house plants have become increasingly popular. Already widely appreciated in Scandinavia they are being grown here in much larger quantities now, and, thanks to Mr. Thomas Rochford, in many more interesting varieties and of a better quality than ever before. Having built on a sun-room a few years ago I felt it needed growing plants and since I had only limited means for a container, I settled for a local handyman to make me a wooden trough to hold the plants. This had a couple of shelves at the bottom for all my flower books which, with so many new and interesting productions, seem to increase every year. So the trough acquired a dual purpose and, as you will see from Plate 21, is not very beautiful but extremely useful. It was lined with stiff sheets of polythene with the idea that one day I would have a good lead or zinc liner made, but so far that day has not arrived! The plants have a little warmth from an electric bar under the box that just prevents frost worries in an otherwise unheated room. The plants themselves are not very exciting, but the *Begonia rex* is a particular favourite of mine; it is attractive all the year round with little or no attention except for watering and an occasional plantoid. The trough also contains maidenhair ferns, *Monstera deliciosa*, with their broad serrated leaves, tradescantia, and *Jasminum polyanthum*, whose white flowers in early spring scent the whole house. I am gradually training this last plant over the whole side of the wall and can hardly wait for the final result! All the ivies are effective: *Hedera hibernica maculata* is very striking and with support of a cane will grow up to eight feet in height. *Hedera canariensis*, the variegated ivy, is also well worth having, as are some of the smaller-leaved varieties. Sansevierias, with their dramatic pointed leaves edged with cream, last for years and provide a lively contrast in shape. These leaves are wonderful for cutting, though it is difficult to bring oneself to do this; they are most attractive in a foliage arrangement and last for several weeks in water. *Cissus antarctica*, or Kangaroo Plant or Vine, as it is sometimes called, grows quickly and climbs with little effort once you have given it an initial start on canes. The large leaves of philodendron make an excellent spreading plant, as do the fatshederas; the variegated one 'Silver Prince' I find extremely useful as a house plant and for odd leaves for cutting. The smaller

78

plants such as peperomia and chlorophytum are useful for putting in the front of the trough.

House plants

House plants need little attention, but correct watering is very important. Press the tips of your fingers on the top of the soil. When the soil is too dry it is greyish in colour. If it is too wet, which can be bad for the plant, it is soggy and black. The soil should always be moist but firm. During the summer, plants dry out much more quickly and I find that every ten days or so I need to take them out and submerge the whole pot in a bucket of warm water, leaving it until all the air is out and the plant has stopped bubbling. Then I dry it off on sheets of newspaper and return it to the trough. In the late autumn and winter the growth of the plant slows down and outside conditions are much colder, so watering is much reduced. About once a week I find is quite enough, and sometimes not as often as that. Forgetting to water and then suddenly remembering and overdoing it makes the lower leaves drop off. This I have learned by bitter experience! Overhead spraying keeps the leaves dust-free and they seem to enjoy it. Cleaning the broad and shiny leaves with cotton wool dipped in a little milk and water gives them a nice gleam; it is amazing how much dust collects and how they benefit from a wash. A miserable-looking plant often results from over-watering and it is useless to try to feed it up. However, I find plantoids very good in the growing season, or one of the liquid house-plant fertilizers added to a little of the plant water every now and again.

Flowering plants

Flowering plants that we get in the winter, such as primulas and cyclamen, need rather special care. The colour they bring to the trough is always a delight, but I find really they enjoy more warmth and less draught than they are able to get in the sun-room in winter. Cyclamen die more quickly from over-care than from neglect. They hate both draughts and over-heating, and a constant temperature, with no watering until the leaves start to wilt, is the best. *Primula malacoides*, the small delicately-flowered tiered mauvish plants, are better if the whole pot is submerged in a bucket of warm water once a week. This is the best treatment for azaleas as well. You can quickly tell when they are very dry by tapping the pots, as they have a distinctly hollow sound. Don't forget that plants in plastic pots require less watering than those in clay pots as there is no evaporation. It is quite helpful to pack damp peat or shingle round clay pots in the trough. It retains the moisture and cuts down watering. All pot plants dislike draughts and appreciate regular watering. Green plants grow well in most conditions but

XI. A vase with an oriental flavour — one beautiful stem of Cymbidium orchids, three sprays of the winter-flowering *Garrya elliptica* and two pinky-mauve *Begonia rex* leaves seemed all that was needed to get the pleasing effect for this simple arrangement.

A *Garrya elliptica*
B *Cymbidium insigne* var.
C Leaves of *Begonia rex*

variegated ones need good light, so if you have a dark corner then put your green plant there rather than a variegated one.

A planted garden is something that I enjoy both making and, especially, having in the house during the winter and early spring. To make one, fill a shallow dish or ashet with good loam, some peat and sand; unpot the plants and press them very firmly into the dish. Firm planting is essential. Place the taller plants at the back and the shorter ones, such as peperomia, tradescantia, and small-leaved trailing ivies in front. To give the little garden a landscape effect, a path can be simulated out of gravel or finely smashed flower pots, a piece of mirror can be a pond and so on. Pieces of stone, lumps of bark or moss-covered branches all add interest and fill in the gaps, making it more economical. Cover the soil well with a layer of moss, and water as soon as it is planted; after that just test it with your finger-tips each day to make sure that it is not too dry. Spray the foliage overhead, especially if the garden stands in a hot dry room. If you have not got a syringe then place the dish on the draining board and splash the dish with cold water from a nail-brush. Allow it to dry off before putting it back on a polished surface that is liable to mark. These dishes, despite the fact they have no drainage, last extremely well and can be in the house for several months. You can replace plants and add one or two bulbs to give more colour, or even a flowering plant if you feel like it. Once the flowers in the garden become more plentiful, re-pot the plants and pop them back in the greenhouse for the summer and then you can start all over again next autumn.

Bulbs

Bulbs for indoor culture need to be planted in late September or early October. They can be planted in either fibre or small shingle. Hyacinths, crocus and daffodils are all very attractive planted in large bowls and covered in layers of shingle with just the tops of the bulbs peeping out; add water and no soil at all. Keep them in the dark until the small shoots appear. These start pale green but will soon become a brilliant green once they are in the light. They are so pretty and a constant delight to watch developing. As they get bigger they need more water, so that they end up literally standing in water. If you decide to plant bulbs in fibre, then soak it very well and squeeze out any surplus water. Put a layer in the bottom of the bowl, place the bulbs on it, giving them enough space to develop, and then fill up with fibre leaving just the tips sticking out. Keep them in the dark for several weeks, when the tips will have become pale green; then take them out and stand them in a warm room. The warmer the room the quicker they develop and it is quite a good idea to keep them all in different rooms so that you don't have them all coming out at once. Be sure to buy specially

F

prepared hyacinths if you want them to bloom by Christmas, and remember that they take fifteen weeks from planting to blooming.

TULIPS. The quality and varieties of bulbs today are good and numerous respectively. There are so many different kinds of tulips, for instance, that I find it difficult to know where to start. If you want them for bedding and colour in the garden, then beds of self-colour and strong gay colours are the most effective. If on the other hand they are for cutting, then I suggest you buy a few that really go with the furnishing and colour schemes of your rooms. There are some very attractive greenish varieties: *Tulipa viridiflora* — striped with green and soft yellow; 'Artist' — apricot-rose and green; 'Cherie' — orchid-green (but expensive); 'Greenland' — in orchid tones, green, cream and orchid-pink; *Tulipa viridiflora praecox* — rich green outside, yellow-green inside. These and the parrot-tulips are all wonderful for the flower arranger.

The parrot-tulips have a wide range of colours: 'Black Parrot' — rather expensive, but very beautiful; 'Blue-Parrot' — mauve; 'Fantasy' — good pink; 'Faraday' — a lovely ivory-white; 'Opal Queen' — with petals like ostrich feathers; and the orange and white parrots. All these are a little more expensive but so well worth growing. Moreover tulips last for quite a few years, though I regret to say that these rather more special colours and rarer varieties do not last so well.

The delicate lily-flowered type are extremely graceful and lovely as a change for arrangement. 'May Time' — purple; 'Captain Fryatt' — soft burgundy; 'Philomen' — lemon-cream; 'White Trymphator' — a beautiful white; 'Windsor Park' — a delicate soft primrose shading into cream; 'Yellow Marvel' — deep yellow; 'Red Shine' — ruby red; 'China Pink' — a soft pink. The small early double tulips are excellent for cutting and can be bought in mixed collections at a slightly cheaper price. Among my favourites are: 'Electra' — crimson; 'Aga Khan' — soft gold and copper; 'Safrano' — a delightful creamy apricot; 'Salmonetta' — apricot. The late double Peony-flowered tulips are well worth growing, such as 'Lilac Perfection' — pearly lilac; 'Mount Tacome' — pure white; 'Uncle Tom' — dark red. The Mendel, Cottage, Darwin and Striped Rembrandt tulips will make a very individual choice of colour.

DAFFODILS are best of all growing in the grass and in this way continue to bloom for many years and look delightful in the early spring. If on the other hand you want a few specials for cutting for use in the house, then some of the white and white-backed varieties are worth while. Of these, I can recommend 'Jenny' — with small turned-back petals; 'Preamble' — creamy white with a yellow trumpet; 'Cantatrice' — pure white; 'Hunter's Moon' — soft lemon-yellow; 'Louise de Coligny' — a late-flowering sweetly-scented apricot with a pink trumpet (very pretty). Again the choice is wide and varied.

CROCUSES. The early flowering 'species' varieties are lovely for the garden. They will often give you wide beds of colour in February and can be picked to put in a small moss garden, though they do not last terribly long in the house. But they are a joy for a day or so. All the wide range of crocuses striped in blue, yellow and white are good for outdoor culture and of course, as I mentioned earlier, can be grown in the house. Last year I had a large bowl of 'Snow Storm' in pebbles in the house that was a great success.

HYACINTHS grown for their scent alone are well worthwhile. Some fine ones are 'L'innocence' and 'Hoar Frost' — excellent whites; 'Myosotis' and 'Bismarck' — light blue; 'Ostara', 'King of the Blues' — deep blue; 'Flushing' — soft pink; 'Salmonetta' — salmon pink. And we must not forget the white and soft pink Roman Hyacinths that really do force in time for Christmas and are lovely either cut or growing in pots.

Other Bulbs

The new Muscari or Grape Hyacinths are interesting: for instance, *Muscari ambrosiacum* — cream and brown with a sweet scent; *M. latifolium* — a pale blue top shading down to deeper blue; *M. tubergenianum* — deep blue at the apex and shading to paler blue. Erythronium or dog's tooth violets are lovely for cutting and the new golden-flowered *E. tuolumnense* is well worth a mention. Crocosmia, a corm from South Africa, closely resembles Tritonia and has orange and deep yellow flowers.

Lilies of all sorts and kinds are wonderful material for the flower arranger. The hardy Guernsey lily, *Nerine bowdeni*, snowdrops, fritillaries, gladioli, galanthi, irises, freesias, crinum, alliums are bulbs and corms that all have a big part to play both in the garden and for the flower arranger. Their treatment and varieties are I think well covered in the Encyclopaedia section of the book.

Lime Greens and Yellows

As these are among the most useful colours in flower arrangement I thought it might be helpful to have a list, so that you can see at a glance which plants in these colours I find useful throughout the year. Lime green anyway is for me one of the most helpful of colours as it blends with all other shades — reds, blues, pinks and oranges. Here is a collection of plants:

Acer japonicum aureum.

Achillea 'Moonshine', herbaceous, pale-yellow flowers.

Angelica, perennial, leaves fade to good lime green.

Atriplex hortensis aurea, yellow-leaved annual.

Aucuba japonica, green spotted lime-coloured leaves, evergreen.

Amaranthus caudatus viridis, long tassels of green, grown as annual.

Cornus alba (Dogwood), striped green and white tapering leaves.

Cornus stolonifera flaviramea, yellow-barked dogwood.

Corylopsis spicata, shrub with bright yellow flowers in early spring.

Cupressus macrocarpa lutea, pyramidal yellow-green evergreen.

Cytisus praecox, early-flowering cream broom, low growing.

Decorative Kale and Cabbage, green and white, red grown as annual.

Daphne pontica, early-flowering daphne, yellow-green flowers in April.

Eleagnus pungens aureo-variegata, lime, green and yellow foliage in winter.

Euonymus europaeus fructu-albo, yellowish-white, form of spindle berry.

Euphorbia (spurge) all varieties, particularly *E. wulfenii*, *E. epithymoides* (or *E. polychroma*).

Fennel, bi-annual, good golden flowers.

Filipendula ulmaria variegata, yellow foliage.

Forsythia intermedia 'Beatrix Farrand', large yellow bells in spring.

Hosta fortunei albo-picta, lime-green centre, dark-green edge.

Hosta fortunei albo-picta aurea, golden small leaf.

Hosta fortunei 'Yellow Edge', a rare form with brilliant gold edge surrounding grey-green centre.

Hydrangea paniculata, pointed creamy-green heads.

Hydrangea quercifolia, white fading to green, foliage a lovely autumn colour.

Ligustrum ovalifolium aureum (Golden Privet), golden-foliaged shrub, one of the most useful.

Mahonia japonica, racemes of lime sweetly-scented flowers in winter, good foliage.

Malus 'Golden Hornet', attractive yellow berries in autumn.

Mentha gentilis aurea, lovely golden ground cover (good to pick if well conditioned).

Nicotiana alata 'Limelight', lime-green annual.

Parrotia persica, shrub, with yellow and red autumn colour.

Philadelphus coronarius aureus, golden-foliaged shrub.

Pieris, shrub with greenish-white lily-of-the-valley-like flowers.

Scrophularia nodosa variegata, lovely green and white blotched leaves.

Sedum rosea (*rhodiola*), lime-green flowers in spring.

Skimmia, shrub, if grown in full sun, leaves are lime green.

Spiraea opulifolia lutea, golden-foliaged plant.
Stachyurus praecox, 10 feet, yellow flowers in February.
Syringa vulgaris 'Primrose', primrose-yellow lilac.
Ulmus glabra aurea, the Golden Elm.
Zea mays japonica, annual with green and white striped foliage.

Grey Foliages

After green and yellows, grey foliage plants, which seem to be mostly herbaceous, are a tremendous asset for the flower arranger. You will see in the 'drying' chapter that many of them preserve extremely well which is always rather surprising. Two good suppliers of these are Mrs Underwood of Colchester and Margery Fish of South Petherton.

Artemisia, all varieties.
Cardoon (or Artichoke).
Chrysanthemum haradjenii.
Cineraria maritima (Senecio maritima).
Eryngium planum, grey-blue.
Onopordon acanthium, perennial 'Scots Thistle'.
Ruta graveolens 'Jackman's Blue', vivid blue-grey mass of tiny leaves.
Santolina neapolitana.
Senecio laxifolius, the only shrub.
Stachys lanata, 'Lamb's Ears'.
Verbascum broussa, good grey leaves and seed heads.

XII. The highlight of copper greatly enhances the subtle and subdued tones of a dried group. Copper adds so much warmth **and co**lour as a flower container. The various materials are all listed here and the methods of preserving are to be found in the chapter on drying. I really prefer dried flowers in these muted shades in winter: though I enjoy the achievement of drying for colour, and being able to keep the blue of a delphinium and red of a rose, they somehow seem oddly out of place on a cold winter's day. Yet a group of this sort brings warmth and welcome to a room in winter.

A   The common alder, *Alnus glutinosa*
B   Fuller's Teasel, *Dipsacus fullonum*
C   *Eucalyptus populifolius*
D   *Lilium martagon* seed head
E   Pressed bracken, *Pteridium aquilinum*
F   *Achillea filipendula* 'Coronation Gold'
G   Cardoon
H   Aspidistra leaves preserved in glycerine
I   Lime flower buds, preserved in glycerine
J   *Hosta fortunei* seed head
K   Cone of the Cedar of Lebanon

CHAPTER EIGHT

Ikebana

by NORMAN SPARNON

Ikebana — the Art of Japanese Flower Arrangement — or as the term implies — living flowers (from the verb *Ikeru*, to be alive, and *Hana*, flowers) is probably more expressively defined as 'An awareness of nature spiritually expressed by arranging flowers or other forms of plant life in a manner which transcends nature'. Often interpreted in the West as a simple linear style of arrangement completely symbolic, nothing could be farther from the truth. It owes its origin to the introduction of Buddhism into Japan in the sixth century. Although Buddhism was first introduced into Japan in the year A.D. 552 it was not until the reign of the Empress Suiko (593–628) who encouraged her nephew Prince Shotoku in his efforts to establish the new faith, that it gained a firm hold. Developed from the Buddhist ritual of offering flowers to the Buddha, the earliest recorded styles of Ikebana were both simple and naturalistic and were aimed at unifying the exterior of a dwelling with its interior, a feature inherent for many centuries in all styles of Japanese architecture.

Most eminent of the many masters who have contributed to the development of the art was Ono-no-imoko, first Japanese emissary to China in the year 607. On the death of his master Crown Prince Shotoku, a noted patron of the arts, he secluded himself in a priest's lodge (*Bo*) by the side of a pond (*Ike*) in the grounds of a hexagonal temple known as the Rokkakudo which had been built by the Crown Prince in Kyoto, then the capital of Japan. Taking the name of Senmu he made floral offerings to one of the Buddhist deities for the repose of his master's soul. Thus was born the Ikenobo, the greatest of all schools of Ikebana. The present headmaster is Senei XLV the 45th in direct line of descent from the original master, Senmu. The original temple is no longer in existence. Destroyed by fire several times the present structure dates from 1877; however the Rokkakudo remains the residence of the headmaster and the headquarters of the Ikenobo School.

Ikebana as practised today owes its origin to the introduction of the Rikka style in the mid-fifteenth century. Rikka meaning 'standing flowers' developed from Tatebana also meaning 'standing flowers'. Magnificent in its concept, it depicted the mythical Mount Mehru of the Buddhist and Hindu cosmology. Seldom less than six feet in height, a Rikka arrangement depicts five features of the sacred mountain — the peak, waterfall, hill, town and the trail. The whole then being divided into two — the *Yo* (sun) and *In* (shade) or the *Yang* and *Yin*, the positive and negative aspects of oriental philosophy. The perfect balance of these two aspects providing one perfect whole — the ultimate aim of every good Ikebana arrangement. This style of arrangement uses nine primary branches — the *shin* (spiritual truth), *soe* (supporting) *uke* (receiving), *nagashi* (flowing), *hikae* (waiting), *mikoshi* (overhanging), *shoshin* (perfectly straight shin), *do* (body), and *mae-oki* (anterior), and an unlimited variety of materials. If the three dominant branches of this grouping, the shin, soe and nagashi, are joined together they form a scalene triangle and it is on this triangle that all later asymmetrical forms of Japanese flower arrangements were to develop.

By the middle of the sixteenth century the Rokkakudo had become renowned for its Rikka arrangements by masters of the Ikenobo School. The art's great popularity continued and was given further impetus by the Emperor Go-mizu-no-o who by Imperial command summoned the great master, Senko XXXII to the palace where on July 7, 1629 an exhibition of Rikka arrangements was held with the Emperor himself participating. This was the origin of the Ikenobo School's Tanabata-e, an Ikebana exhibition held on the seventeenth and eighteenth of November each year at the Ikenobo School in Kyoto and at which the leading teachers from all over Japan display their art. In modern Rikka, complete freedom is allowed in the use and combination of materials and in the choice of containers. Freedom of expression is encouraged in the interpretation of the classical themes, thus producing both new and stimulating forms which have revitalised this extremely beautiful but somewhat ancient style of Ikebana and made it completely adaptable to contemporary living. The study of Rikka is a vast, complex but fascinating study which has been treated exhaustively by few authorities. Among its numerous forms are seven arrangements each consisting of a single type of material which are renowned for their classical beauty. They are the pine, cherry blossom, Japanese iris, lotus, chrysanthemum, maple and narcissus.

During the development of the Rikka style, a simple style of arrangement known as Chabana (tea flower) usually a single flower, had evolved as a necessary adjunct of the tea ceremony (*Cha-no-yu*). The tea ceremony had been introduced into Japan by the celebrated priest Eisai (1141–1215) and in Japan the austere Zen aesthetic had developed its own austere and simple flower arrangement. Sen-no-Rikyu (1520–1591) regarded as the founder of the tea ceremony was also

22. Modern Rikka—Ikenobo School. This style permits freedom of expression in varying the classical theme. Based on the classical 'split' or 'double *shin*' the beautiful Australian native *Dryanda polycephala* (Many-headed Dryanda) is arranged in two groupings with coiled cane in a modern ceramic vase.

23. Shoka style—Ikenobo School. Classical shoka—a simplification of the Rikka—developed in the seventeenth century. This arrangement of the Japanese iris (*Iris laevigata*) is known as the 'Fish-path Arrangement' (*Gyodo ike*). The wooden base, seldom used in modern Ikebana, was traditionally used in classical arrangements primarily as a protective measure against possible water stains on the straw matting (*tatami*) base in the recessed alcove (*tokonoma*) of a Japanese room.

24. Moribana style—Sogetsu School. The Moribana style introduced early this century utilizes three primary branches arranged in a low flat open container. **In this** **arrange**ment, pine — symbol of longevity — and 'Super Star' roses — symbol of **peace** — have been arranged to be viewed from any direction.

25. Nageire style — Sogetsu School. Nageire, one of the oldest of Ikebana styles, usually expresses a casual spontaneous feeling. Sometimes referred to as the 'thrown-in style', it is an arrangement in a vase. Pine and 'Super Star' roses are combined with pussy willow in an orange and black vase.

26. Free Expression, slanting style — Sogetsu School. In this mass and line arrangement emphasis is placed on form and texture of dried sunflowers arranged in a modern brown ceramic container.

a master flower arranger and is still renowned for his Ichirin or single flower arrangements. It was from this style of arrangement often done in a porcelain, bronze or bamboo vase, that the Nageire and later the Shoka styles developed. Actually any style other than the Rikka was known as Nageire which included arrangements often made in a low bowl and similar in feeling to the Moribana style which was to develop much later. However, it was the Rikka and the tea ceremony flower arrangement which have continued to the present day.

Toward the close of the seventeenth century political power began to shift from the military rulers to the merchant class and along with this transfer there arose a demand for a simplified form of the Rikka style of arrangement. To meet this demand the Ikenobo masters developed a simple three-branch asymmetrical style known as Shoka. Often referred to as the Ten, Chi, Jin or heaven, earth, man style, it offered infinite possibilities for the placement of the three branches and many new schools of Ikebana were established some of which still flourish today, viz — Enshu-ryu, Ko-ryu and Misho-ryu.

Shoka, sometimes referred to as Seika in other schools of Ikebana, combined the dignity of the Rikka and the simplicity of the tea-flower arrangement. This new style developed its own rules which governed the types and combinations of materials which could be used and the receptacles for holding them. The material was held in place in the container by a forked twig known as Matagi with a cross-bar at the back of the material to wedge it firmly into position. Materials were arranged alone such as chrysanthemums, peonies or iris or combined with one other material such as pine and chrysanthemums and with the exception of an arrangement of pine, bamboo and plum blossom, seldom were more than two varieties of material combined into one arrangement. Only one arrangement, the arrangement of the seven grasses of Autumn, permitted the use of more than three varieties of material. Such rules developed a very beautiful but highly stylised form of arrangement which demanded great technical skill of its executors.

In both the Rikka and the Shoka styles, bases of black or red lacquer or bamboo were used to elevate the arrangement and also to protect the *tatami* or straw matting in the *tokonoma* or recessed alcove into which the arrangements were placed.

To meet contemporary living requirements modern Shoka like modern Rikka was revitalised by allowing complete freedom in the use and combination of materials and of receptacles. Free expression is also encouraged in the interpretation of classical themes. A new style of modern Shoka has also been introduced known as San-shu-ike or an arrangement of three varieties of material, which also encourages free expression based on a classical theme. A feature of all classical styles whether executed in the true classical style or in their modern counterparts, is that the arrangement rises as a single unit for a height of approximately three or four inches above the mouth of the container.

Around the year 1820 a new style of arrangement was introduced, known as Bunjin-ike. This style popularised by the artists of the day followed no established pattern. However, the trend to break away from the traditional styles was not to take firm hold until the twentieth century.

During the Meiji restoration in 1868, Western culture was introduced into Japan. This brought with it new species and varieties of flowers. The Rikka and Shoka styles were governed by rigid rules which dictated the varieties of flowers and plants to be used and made no provision for the use of the new materials from the West. To overcome this, Unshin Ohara, then a master in the Ikenobo School, devised a new style of arrangement known as Moribana (heaped-up flowers). This new style utilised a low flat bowl similar to those used for Bonsai (dwarfed trees) and Bonkei (tray landscapes). This brought about the establishment of the Ohara School of Ikebana, one of the present great schools of Ikebana in Japan. As with the introduction of the Shoka style, the Moribana style offered great possibilities both in the utilisation of materials and in the placement of the three primary branches, and many new schools developed.

Another feature of this new style of arrangement was that the material was arranged in a freer and more naturalistic style and unlike the Rikka and Shoka styles which rose as a single unit above the mouth of the container, in the Moribana style, the material was brought down to cover the mouth of the container. However, this style also followed the three branch asymmetrical pattern and generally confined the combination of materials to one, two or three varieties. Also along with the introduction of this style was developed the needle-aid which is used to anchor the material in place in the container.

Concurrently with the development of the Moribana style, greater freedom emerged in the Nageire or vase arrangement style which was to popularise this style as one of the most beautiful arrangements of Ikebana. Unlike the needle-aid used to anchor the material in place in the Moribana style, two cross-bars are placed in position about one inch down from the mouth of the container or a vertical stick is attached to the end of the branch to hold it in position.

In 1930 a group of flower masters declared a break with all traditional styles of Ikebana and lifted Ikebana out of the Tokonoma into the realm of all facets of public activity. This revolutionary approach demanded revolutionary changes and this was provided by the young master, Sofu Teshigahara who in 1926 had established the Sogetsu School. In his revolutionary approach of injecting new life into an old art he used materials such as stone, tree-stumps, wire, wrought-iron etc., and handled them in a manner previously only accorded to flowers, thereby establishing Ikebana as a formative Art and giving it unlimited scope in all venues of life. Up to this time Ikebana arrangements were generally in a naturalistic style. However this intrusion into new domains seemingly beyond the realm of flowers developed styles which utilized nature and inspired the artist to express himself creatively.

This revolutionary approach to an ancient art often proves startling to Western viewers. However, to the student of Ikebana this is not so for he is well aware of the basic motivating force — design. With nature as their inspiration, the headmasters of the numerous schools who have inherited their titles, have grown up with an art which whether classical or modern, recognised a basic design. Their development of an awareness of nature enabled them to discern and utilise design in plant life and stimulated a desire toward free expression. Just as the Rikka style of Ikebana was the choice of the nobility, the priest and the warrior class several centuries ago, so is the new style of free expression the choice of today.

Among the many misconceptions of Ikebana prevalent in the West are the fallacies that only odd numbers of flowers or branches are used, that lines should never be crossed and that all arrangements are symbolic. Only certain materials hold symbolic significance and then only when arranged on certain festive occasions such as peach blossoms on Girls' Day; the iris on Boys' Day; and pine, bamboo and plum blossom at New Year.

Today in Japan, Ikebana is a vigorous and progressive Art as any living Art should and must be. It is practised by over two thousand schools with millions of followers both in Japan and throughout the world. Practically all schools of Ikebana practise the styles of Moribana and Nageire and their own approach to free expression. In addition, classical schools such as the Ikenobo practise classical Rikka and modern Rikka; classical Shoka or Seika or modern Shoka.

Apart from the Rikka, Ikebana as practised by all schools, is an asymmetrical, three-dimensional pattern based on three primary branches. The balance, angle of the branches and method of expression differs according to the school. Based on sound art principles and infinite in expression, it demands that the basic principles of the school be mastered before free expression can be successfully achieved.

Encyclopaedia

This is a list of my very personal choice of some plants that I think are lovely to grow in the garden and greenhouse, and are good for flower arranging. Of course you cannot grow all of them, but I hope that reading this section will help you to make your own selection. Each entry starts off with a brief description of the flower and its uses to the flower arranger. I have then given detailed instructions on conditioning that is, making   it last in water once it has been picked — and preserving or drying the flower, seed head or leaf for winter arrangements. In this way I have tried to make sure that the encyclopaedia section will continue to be useful after you have chosen and successfully grown a plant, for the conditioning and preserving instructions should enable you to make the most of the flowers picked for your house.

If you do not know the correct Latin name for a plant, it is sometimes quite impossible to trace a flower you may have admired in a friend's garden and want to buy and grow for yourself. On the other hand, it is an irritating fact known to all gardeners that the same plant may appear under another name in a different nurseryman's catalogue. I have tried to overcome these difficulties by listing both Latin and English names of the flowers, shrubs and trees, with the full entries under the Latin generic name. I have given the names of the species that I particularly recommend, and I have tried to include all the variants I have come across. When I have listed a plant under its generic name only, it is usually because I have recommended hybrids or because I consider that all the obtainable species are equally good. Full entries for the few kinds of fruit and vegetables are under their English names — an exception to my rule, because this is where you will find them in most dictionaries and seedsmen's catalogues.

I have not attempted to give full cultural instructions for each plant, since obviously they would vary tremendously according to your soil and locality. You probably have your own favourite gardening books, but in the short bibliography on page 201 I have given details of some works that I have found helpful.

G

Acacia (Mimosa Wattle)

Greenhouse evergreen shrubs. Most species come from Australia and make quite tall trees in their natural surroundings, with cascades of tumbling yellow blossoms, which are a sight to behold, and a wandering perfume which prevails from the trees for a long way. Some sorts can be grown out of doors in Britain against the shelter of a wall, but in very few places; the hardiest is *A. dealbata*. Lovely arranged with daffodils or any early spring flowers. Remove a certain amount of the foliage to give accent to the colour. Unfortunately the fluffy balls of gold often turn hard and dark yellow within a few hours. Keep it excluded from the air as long as possible before arranging. It keeps extremely well in a polythene bag.

CONDITIONING After removing polythene submerge the heads under cold water, then dip the stems into an inch of boiling water for a few seconds and stand in a jug of warm water until the flower heads have dried off. This should give a little longer life to the fluffy heads. Several growers now pack the mimosa in polythene bags and attach a small packet of conditioning powder to add to the water in the vase, and I find this does help.

Acanthus (Bear's Breech)

Hardy herbaceous perennial. A plant for every garden, growing well in full sun or semi-shade. (Personally I think they flower better in full sun.) The less they are disturbed, the better they grow. In ancient times the beautiful leaves were an inspiration to architects, who reproduced them on the tops of Corinthian pillars; now the plants grow wild in large clumps among the ruins of buildings in Greece and Turkey. The tall, spiky, purplish flowers last in water very much better than the leaves, though both are better cut after being left on the plant for some time. Preferably the flowers should be picked when all the buds right up the stem are nearly fully open. The leaves only last if picked in August or September and then treated as advised below. My favourite is *A. mollis latifolius*; also good, and much smaller, is *A. spinosus*. Acanthus is excellent mixed with large group-arrangements of summer flowers and its pointed shape has great structural value when used with rounded heads such as those of sunflowers or dahlias.

CONDITIONING The leaves should have the ends of the stems dipped in boiling water; then submerge the whole leaf in a solution of weak starch water for up to twelve hours. The flower stems are improved if dipped in boiling water, followed by several hours in deep cold water.

TO PRESERVE The flower heads dry very well if picked when they are all fully open all the way up the stem, then hung upside down to dry in a warm atmosphere.

Acer (Sycamore, Maple)

Hardy shrubs. My favourite of all, for flower arrangement, is a variety of sycamore, *Acer pseudoplatanus brilliantissimum*, which has apricot buds and later good apricot foliage in early spring (Colour Plate III). A beautiful tree in the garden and the foliage is a joy to use, particularly with such flowers as black tulips, to make a contrast of black and apricot. The pendulous flowers, resembling the common sycamore's, are tinged with peach and lime green. In certain soils it quickly loses colour and I am fortunate in that mine remains interesting all the year round — possibly just the luck of planting it in a soil it likes. Generally speaking, sprays of acer are not ideal material for arranging, because they do not stand well in water. *Acer japonicum aureum* will however stand better than many. Like *A. pseudoplatanus brilliantissimum*, it is such an asset in early spring for its brilliant yellow-green leaves which keep their colour well into the summer and add, as do all these plants, a touch of sunlight to the garden even on the dreariest of days. I find it hard to bring myself to cut it as it is so very slow growing, but if you have the chance then it is an excellent background to a vase of yellows and is just the right shade for soft salmon pinks. The Norway Maple, *A. platanoides*, has the most wonderful lime-green flowers that open before the leaves break, so you get vivid green sprays on coal black branches which are superb, and add a touch of sheer delight to a vase of daffodils and tulips. Unlike other acers, the Norway Maple lasts extremely well in water provided the branches are well hammered, or the bottom two inches of bark peeled off before it has a long drink.

In addition to the ones I have mentioned, there are many varieties of acer renowned for their autumn tints, and this makes them a very valuable asset to any shrubbery or heath garden. It is often possible

to use a few sprays when in full autumn colour, although they do not last for very long, but I feel even a few hours' enjoyment is well worth while for some very special occasion, provided of course that the shape of the tree is not spoilt by picking branches at random; I cannot stress too often to pick with tremendous care. Leaves of autumn colour are fading naturally and there is nothing that I can recommend to make them last in water.
CONDITIONING   Hammer the stems very well and place in deep warm water.
TO PRESERVE   Individual leaves can be pressed and then mounted on wire stems by running a wire up the back of the leaf and covering with Sellotape to make a false stem, often essential after pressing as the stems fall off easily.

Achillea (Yarrow)
Hardy herbaceous perennial. A flat-headed flower of deep yellow, useful for an arrangement in July and August as it has the great advantage of lasting well in water. There are no petals to fall and the flat heads give an excellent focal point in any vase. Dried achillea are used in the copper jug in the coloured group of dried material on Colour Plate XII. For a softer colour in pale yellow the variety I would recommend is 'Moonshine', which has a much smaller growth altogether and is good in clumps near the front of the border; the grey foliage is a considerable asset both indoors and out. There are of course many white varieties which are useful for small flower arrangements.
TO PRESERVE   Dip the heads in powdered borax and either hang them upside down or stand them in a small jug with a small amount of water. I find this latter method preferable as it allows each flower head to retain a perfect shape. If hung in bunches, the stems tend to get imprinted on the flower head and leave a mark.

Acidanthera
Bulbous-rooted perennial. The one I like best is *Acidanthera bicolor* which has drooping flowers, white with a purple blotch in the centre, and a sweet scent. Used with a few *Begonia rex* leaves and a branch of berberis, and with a predominance of water, it can make an enchanting group in oriental style, in either a shallow lead container or a grey-green dish.

Aconite, Winter *see* ERANTHIS

Aconitum (Monkshood)
Hardy herbaceous perennial. Monkshood is usually thought of as spikes of mauvish-blue hooded flowers on tall upright stems, rather like a delphinum. However, I have recently planted *A. lycoctonum* which is more delicate in form in every way, having a more branching habit and spikes of delicious yellowy, lime-green flowers, excellent for arranging.

Aconitum

CONDITIONING   Cut and give it a good long drink up to its neck in warm water.
TO PRESERVE   The seed heads dry well if hung upside down.

Acrolinium or Helipterum
An Australian wild flower growing in droves of pink and white in Western Australia, often carpeting the road verges with colour. Excellent for drying, having a daisy-like flower with dry papery petals, and very useful for small arrangements of dried flowers to give delicate colour in the winter months. It can be grown from seed, preferably started under glass and pricked out in May.

Adam's Needle *see* YUCCA

Adiantum (Maidenhair Fern)
Greenhouse plant. Sprays of heart-shaped tiny leaves on arched stems, so delicate and a delight to use for its light feathery effect in small vases. I find

Alchemilla mollis

it particularly good for trailing out of a candle cup (*see* Plate 18), or similar type of vase, with a collection of 'mixed greens' or any delicate flower such as fritillaries.
CONDITIONING Submerge the whole stem under the hottest water in which you can hold your hand, wait until the water cools, dry off and arrange.

Agapanthus (African Lily)
Cool greenhouse evergreen. One of the oldest plants, used on roof gardens in Egypt and the Near East in the time of the Caesars. Its tall, round, ball-shaped flowers on slender stems are most commonly known in blue, though I have a white one growing well against a south wall. It is not very hardy and therefore more usually a pot plant. Now marketed quite frequently and lasts well as a cut flower. It is lovely used in large groups in high summer and the rounded blue heads are particularly good to add to a blue and white arrangement in July or August. Excellent seed heads for drying.
TO PRESERVE Dry the seed heads by hanging them upside down.

Alchemilla mollis (Lady's Mantle)
Hardy herbaceous perennial. This feathery lime green flower has a long period of bloom and is useful in high summer. Its lightness of form and delicate colour make it a most popular flower for arranging. The colour blends so well with so many others — yellows, reds, blues, almost any mixture of colours. It grows easily from seed; in fact it seeds itself freely, once established, and will flourish under most conditions although as it grows wild in the ditches in Scotland this shows that it must like moisture. The leaves are beautifully shaped and silky and their centres retain drops of rain which look like jewels. This plant can be increased by division or, as indicated above, by seed.
TO PRESERVE Remove foliage and hang flower heads upside down. It keeps quite a good green colour.

Alder *see* ALNUS

Allium
Hardy and greenhouse bulbous perennials. Members of the onion family. There are many decorative varieties. My favourite of all is *A. siculum*, which unlike many of the others has pendulous bells of greenish brown, flowering in May. *Allium oreophilum ostrowskianum* flowers in July, with compact purple ball-like heads most useful for decoration, as of course is the much more unusual *A. caeruleum* for the rock garden — a real blue. *A. giganteum* has large heads, as the name implies, and these are perfect for drying to use with seed heads for winter flower arrangements. There are many more. Their rounded heads add a good focal point in any flower group and the wide range of colour makes them a most worthwhile bulb to grow. Chives' flowers are also most decorative.
CONDITIONING Never put the stems in hot water as this increases the onion smell. A teaspoonful of Milton in the vase removes any trace of smell and I can well recommend this.
TO PRESERVE Dry all seed heads by hanging them

Allium siculum and the flowers of ornamental rhubarb

upside down. Hang large heads on individual strings to prevent them from losing their shape by pressing against one another.

Almond *see* PRUNUS AMYGDALUS

Alnus (Alder)
Hardy deciduous tree. Extremely useful, especially in winter and spring. The catkins and the small cone-clusters on bare branches make lovely background shapes to set off a few flowers. *A. incana aurea* is one of the most attractive varieties, flowering very early with pink catkins. If these branches are picked in January, it is interesting to watch the catkins develop in water, and they can also be arranged with sprays of ivy or bergenia leaves in midwinter. Once it breaks into leaf, I feel it is valueless for the flower arranger.
CONDITIONING Hammer ends of stems well and put into warm water. The hotter the atmosphere, the quicker development.

Alstroemeria (Peruvian Lily)
Hardy and half-hardy perennials. Known generally as a rampant lily-like orange herbaceous plant. The new Ligtu hybrids are difficult to cultivate, but have a magnificent blend of colours from shell pink through to salmon. They need a warm well-drained position and hate disturbance. In fact it is very much better to sow the seeds where they are going to remain. Constance Spry had great success in growing some at Winkfield in open trenches. Owing to their rather stiff form and multiple flower heads I find them a little difficult to arrange, but they can be very good in a mass arrangement (with a few dark coloured leaves), because of their lovely colouring and lasting qualities in water. If the flowers are allowed to remain on the plant they form a good seed head and it is advisable to pick these early and hang them upside down to dry. If the seed heads remain too long on the plant, the stems become so brittle that they are difficult to use.

Althaea (Hollyhock)
Hardy perennial. As they may die out quickly, they are often grown as an annual or biennial. They also seed themselves very readily. Many colours from white through yellows, apricot, pinks and reds to nearly black, in tall rosettes of flowers all up the long stem. Very good to mix in a Dutch type of group in midsummer.
CONDITIONING Put ends of stems in boiling water for several minutes and then place in deep water, in the dark if possible, for at least forty-eight hours.
TO PRESERVE Once the seed head has formed, pick the stems and hang them upside down in a warm place until dry.

Amaranth Feathers *see* HUMEA

Amaranthus caudatus (Love-lies-bleeding)
Half hardy annuals. *A. caudatus viridis*, the green variety, is the one I would recommend here. The long tails of green are very good to give a change of form in any flower arrangement. There is of course the crimson variety, grown easily from seed. (See Colour Plate VIII.) Feed the plants well for best results.
CONDITIONING Remove all the leaves as they wilt easily and spoil the effect very quickly.
TO PRESERVE Will retain only a fair colour after being hung upside down. However, their shape does help to vary the form in a dried group.

Amaryllis (Belladonna Lily)
Slightly tender bulbous plant with fragrant pink or white flowers in autumn. It needs the shelter of a wall for best results. For greenhouse culture, pot in August: one bulb in each six-inch pot. I love to use a few of these white lilies in a group of foliage in autumn; or to arrange them quite alone in a slender vase to show the delicate beauty of the pendulous heads. The flower stems are thick and need a suitable vase allowing plenty of room.

Amaryllis (greenhouse) *see* HIPPEASTRUM

Anaphalis margaritacea (Pearly Everlasting)
A. margaritacea is a hardy perennial which spreads very easily, and this may make it a problem plant in the garden, but it has attractive grey foliage and clusters of everlasting-like flowers. As can be seen on Colour Plate VII, it is useful in early summer in mixed vases.
CONDITIONING The foliage in the early stages needs to have the end of the stems plunged into boiling water for a few minutes and then allowed a long deep drink. The flowers are better for this treatment too. though it is not so essential.

St Brigid anemones in a home-made container (see page 47)

TO PRESERVE Pick the flower heads in full bloom, remove all the leaves, tie the flowers in bunches and hang upside down to dry.

Anchusa

The hardy herbaceous perennial variety *Anchusa azurea*, or *A. italica*, growing three to five feet is the one I like best. The annual *A. capensis* is also good. Anchusas are not really recommended for flower arrangement as, try as one may, it is hard to make them last well in water. However, because of the superb blue I feel I must mention them. I do occasionally put in a piece on a short stem to add blue to a mixed vase and find this the best way of using it.

CONDITIONING Shorten stems, dip the ends in boiling water for thirty seconds, and then allow a long drink in cold water for several hours.

Anemone (Windflower)

Hardy herbaceous perennials, some tuberous-rooted. At the name, I always picture the brilliant colours of St. Brigid and Caen in all the flower shops just after Christmas — what a delight! Arrange in a bright red dish or glass for maximum colour effect. Also I think of the wild anemones I picked as a child and the bitter disappointment that they were dead even before I reached home. For the garden, *Anemone blanda* gives a lovely patch of pink and mauve in early spring and lasts in a vase much better than expected. *A. fulgens*, a brilliant scarlet variety with a very black centre, quite beautiful, is now marketed as a cut flower in great quantity. I cannot leave this section without a word about *Anemone japonica*, the autumn-flowering herbaceous anemone, lovely arranged with a few autumn leaves; it flowers in pink and white — I think I prefer more often to use the white, but I can never really decide.

CONDITIONING Dip the ends of the stems in boiling water for a few seconds and then allow a long cool drink. I find it better not to arrange them in Oasis as it tends to soften the ends in some way.

Angel's Tears *see* NARCISSUS TRIANDRUS ALBUS

Angelica

Hardy perennial, grown easily from seed. Confectioners use the candied stem for cake decoration, flower arrangers the foliage and flower head alike. The foliage turns a lovely golden colour as it fades and though at this stage it does not last long it is well worth including for a few days in a foliage group, or with pale yellows and creams, in August. The flat greenish-yellow heads are better if picked when mature, and I find they really last best when the seed head is formed, though still green.

CONDITIONING Place ends of stems in boiling water and then in cold water for several hours.

TO PRESERVE It is important to hang seed heads upside down so that the sap can run down to the head. Keep each head well separated from the others so that each retains its good rounded shape.

Anthemis

Hardy perennial. *A. cupaniana* is a good grey foliage plant useful in a grey border as it is dwarf and spreading, and for pieces of foliage for a small group in greys and pinks or shades of lilac. No special treatment required.

Anthurium

Stovehouse. Spade-shaped flowers with a shiny texture rather like American cloth. These last well and look beautiful arranged with their own striking foliage or with various hard green foliages. Colours now range from reds to every shade of pink and apricot. From Honolulu, where they abound, the flowers are sent all over the world.

PACKING If a small water-filled balloon is attached to the end of each stem by tying tightly with elastic bands, the flowers (packed in stiff boxes) can travel for thousands of miles.

Antirrhinum (Snapdragon)

Grown from seed and treated as an annual. The new double varieties are well worth growing; they have a good range of colours and last better as a cut flower than most people imagine. Attractive arranged in a basket with mixed annuals or alone. Often forced through the early spring and then widely sold as a cut flower; the stems tend to be brittle as they have grown to great lengths under glass and need careful handling.

CONDITIONING If cut straight from the garden, a good drink for an hour or so, up to their necks in water, is all that is necessary. If forced, dip ends into boiling water before giving a long drink.

Aquilegia (Columbine)

Hardy perennial. One of the earliest plants, often seen in old paintings. The original flower is double-petalled. The long-spurred hybrid varieties are more delicate, single and in a much wider range of colours; they look delightful arranged alone in silver or glass, or picking up a colour combination in a mixed vase, as on Colour Plate VI. Columbines also have beautifully-coloured foliage in late summer.

CONDITIONING Place in warm water for an hour before arranging. They will last very well if faded blooms are removed to allow new buds to open.

TO PRESERVE Let seed heads form, cut and hang in bunches upside down.

Aralia

Hardy shrub. *Aralia elata* (or *A. chinensis*) can be planted out of doors in a sheltered place, and grows to twenty feet in Cornwall, with heads of ivy-type flowers two feet across, and handsome large spreading leaves. *A. elata aureo-marginata* is the one I love; the green and yellow leaves are superb for a large group, and I like to use them whenever I have the chance.

CONDITIONING Dip the ends of the stems into boiling water, and then allow a long drink in deep water for several hours.

Arbutus unedo (Strawberry Tree)

Half-hardy evergreen tree with white flowers and strawberry-like fruits which keep the tree colourful most of the winter. These fruits are highly decorative and mix well with red flowers or with arrangements of fruit and flowers.

CONDITIONING Hammer stems well and keep for several hours in deep water.

Arctotis grandis
Half-hardy South African annual. The daisy-like flowers with glistening petals are white and backed with pale blue (see Colour Plate VII).

Arctotis grandis

CONDITIONING Dip ends of stems in boiling water after cutting. If possible cut in full sun, as the flowers tend to close up very quickly especially in the evening and will not reopen easily.

Artemisia
Hardy perennials. Very pretty silvery foliage and useful in all kinds of groups, especially with mixtures of greys or with pink and white. *Artemisia lactiflora* has white plumes on tall stems, excellent for large groups for church decoration during July and August.
CONDITIONING Hammer the woody stems and it will last very well indeed.
TO PRESERVE *Artemisia ludoviciana*: once the flower is over, the grey seed plumes if hung upside down dry extremely well.

Artichoke, Globe (*Cynara scolymus*)
One of the best of all plants for the flower arranger, as the leaves are very useful all the year round and the flowers in every stage, from bud to full flower to seed head. It is grown easily from seed and is edible, of course, and delicious. I am always torn between eating and decoration!
CONDITIONING The leaves last much better if they have been on the plant for several weeks before being cut. Hold ends of stems in boiling water for thirty seconds and then submerge completely in a bath of cold water for several hours. The flower heads last very well.
TO PRESERVE Hang heads upside down in a warm atmosphere, at any stage from green through purple to brown.

Arum
A. maculatum, Cuckoo-pint or Lords-and-Ladies, is more often used for its foliage. The greenish almost transparent flowers with purple stamens are beautiful, but die off very quickly. For better value, allow the berries to form and you will have a beautiful head of orange berries that mix well with flowers or foliage. The leaves last very well; their shape is so good I find I use them continually in early spring. *Arum italicum pictum* is an improved form and produces well-marked leaves in January or even earlier — this in itself is a joy — and I find it useful right through to May. It grows best in damp and partial shade, though it can be grown in open ground. A well-recommended plant. I have used the leaves in several of the arrangements illustrated in this book, including the frontispiece and Colour Plate IV.
CONDITIONING Submerge wild arum leaves in starch water for a few hours, before arranging. The flower heads last a little better if the ends of the stems are dipped in boiling water for thirty seconds.

Arum Lily *see* ZANTEDESCHIA AETHIOPICA

Aruncus sylvester (Goat's Beard)
Hardy perennial, growing four to five feet, with large plumes of creamy-white flowers in June. Formerly known as Spiraea, as so I still think of it. It very quickly loses its fluff and so can be disappointing when cut, but I do use it occasionally as the leaves are very decorative.

CONDITIONING   Boil the ends of the stems and then put into deep water.

TO PRESERVE   When the flowers fade, hang the creamy-brown heads upside down.

Arundinaria (Bamboo)

A hardy Japanese shrubby plant with slender stems furnished with grassy foliage. Generally considered difficult when cut as the leaves tend to curl; however, see the method below which is used in America to help solve this problem.

CONDITIONING   Place the ends of the stems in boiling vinegar for two minutes and then allow a long drink in deep warm water.

Arundo donax variegata (Reed)

A good striped reed in cream and green or white and green. Not very satisfactory or long-lasting when cut, as it tends to curl, but I do use it in early spring for a graceful effect in a group of foliage, and replace when necessary.

CONDITIONING   Dip ends of stems in boiling water and afterwards give a long cold drink.

Asparagus

A. sprengeri or *A. plumosus* was once almost obligatory — as the so-called fern used for all types of floristry in the early part of this century, often overwhelming the flowers themselves in, for instance, a hand-bouquet. Largely owing to Constance Spry's influence this conventional use has almost disappeared. However, I often use the autumnal sprays of foliage and berries from the asparagus bed; these delicate plumes add a transparent effect to large groups which include colouring beech leaves or other autumn tints.

Aspidistra lurida (Parlour Palm)

Certainly a plant that changed ideas on flower decoration have brought back into favour. Only a few years ago it could hardly be given away and now they are fetching fantastic prices and the demand is still rising. The variegated kind is the most popular. Used stylishly in a shallow container, it takes on excellent shapes. It preserves very well — an added delight — and needs the minimum of attention. Percy Thrower considers it stands neglect better than any other plant.

TO PRESERVE   Put the stems of the leaves in a solution of one part of glycerine to two of water and leave undisturbed. This means waiting in patience as the leaves take anything from six to nine months to dry. However, they will reward you by turning a lovely creamy-biscuit colour and with careful handling will last for years.

Aster (Michaelmas Daisy)

True asters are hardy perennials and best grown and arranged grouped alone. There is nothing more effective than a mass of their purples and pinks in the autumn sunshine, or indoors in large bowls or copper pans, rather than when mixed with other flowers. The annual china aster *Callistephus*, grown from seed, has a wide range of excellent colours, from white and pinks to all shades of mauve, and lasts in water extremely well.

CONDITIONING   Michaelmas daisies last better if the ends of the stems are well hammered and placed in boiling water; then allowed twelve hours in deep water. Pick off the faded blooms as often as possible as they can make the stem look dead long before this is actually so.

Astilbe (Spiraea)

Hardy herbaceous perennials. The hybrid varieties have a wide range of colour in delicate pointed plumes of pink to deep red. Often disappointing when used as a cut flower, but delightful as a rich brown seed head.

TO PRESERVE   Cut when the flowers have lost their colour and are a pale green or brown. Hang them upside down or stand in shallow water to dry off. *For other herbaceous 'spiraeas', see Aruncus and Filipendula.*

Astrantia major (Masterwort)

Hardy perennial. *A. major* loves shade and seeds easily. It has good foliage and pleasing star-shaped flowers with an odd crisp look — though in fact they do not dry well; these are useful with foliages or with summer flowers, having a nondescript colour they blend well in any company.

Athyrium felix-femina (Lady Fern)

Possibly the fern that I find most useful of all — you can see it in several of the illustrations.

CONDITIONING   Submerge young growths in warm water for a few hours.

TO PRESERVE   Place stems between sheets of newspaper and press under a heavy weight.

Atriplex hortensis rubra

Hardy annual with red foliage and spikes of red seed in late summer that make it a very useful plant for flower arranging. The red seed heads mix well in a vase of dahlias, and with a few bronze leaves make a good background for any brightly-coloured flowers. There is also a yellow-leaved atriplex, *A. hortensis aurea*. The spikes dry naturally in water but gradually lose their colour, so I prefer to remove them and store them away for winter use, when they add colour to a vase of dried flowers.

CONDITIONING   When the plant first comes into leaf it needs special care. The ends of the stems must be put into boiling water, and then allowed a long drink in the usual way. As the seed head forms and the plant matures, a long drink is all that is required, and it is at this stage that I find it most useful.

TO PRESERVE   The seed spikes can be dried off in water, or tied in bunches and hung upside down to dry, in a warm atmosphere.

Astrantia major (see facing page)

Aucuba japonica (Spotted Laurel)

Hardy evergreen. A shrub I never thought much of until I decided to plant one; since then I have used it often. It lightens a group of mixed ever-greens in any month of the year, though I use it most in early spring. The female bushes have clusters of brilliant red berries. It is used in pot culture, often grown on terraces in Southern Italy.

Auricula (Primula)

My grandmother called these delightful primrose-like flowers 'dusty millers' which well describes their dusty white leaves. They have a delicious smell and last much better in water than the polyanthus. A range of beautiful colours — even down to a green-and-black, though this one is not really hardy, but a plant for the cool greenhouse.

CONDITIONING   Place in deep warm water for several hours.

TO DRY   The little seed heads are charming if left till well formed on the plant, and then stood in the barest amount of water until they have really dried off.

Australian Gum *see* EUCALYPTUS

Autumn Crocus *see* COLCHICUM

Avens *see* GEUM

Azalea

Used as house plants at Christmas-time, *A. indica* (*Rhododendron simsii*) or small varieties in shades of white and pale to deep pinks are generally very popular. Bury the pot in soil and keep in the shade of a tree from May to September, repot and bring in again, and your plant can last many years. The outdoor varieties including mollis (tall), Kurume (dwarf), Ghent, and others are some of the loveliest of all shrubs. For sprays of flowers or autumn-tinted foliage they are superbly decorative. Their delicate branching habit makes them a wonderful flower to arrange — especially if you can lay your hands on enough to have a vase full of them. However, they are somewhat slow-growing and if the plants are new and small, then you must pick with care and just use a few sprays to add back-ground to a vase in shades of apricot or flame, as I have done in the arrangement shown on Colour Plate V.

CONDITIONING   As they have woody stems either remove a layer of the outer skin by paring off two or three inches, or hammer well, before allowing a long drink.

Ballota pseudo-dictamnus
Hardy perennial. The contorted, curved and almost arching sprays make it most useful for arranging, giving a lovely natural outline in any vase. The flowers are insignificant, borne as tiny grey-green funnels that ring the main stem, but they become visible as soon as the leaves are removed.
CONDITIONING Put the ends of the stems into boiling water and then stand in deep water, but do not submerge for, as with so many grey-green plants, the tiny hairs on the stems are flattened by the water and lose all their silvery-grey colouring.

Bamboo *see* ARUNDINARIA

Baptisia (False Indigo)
Hardy perennial. A pea-shaped dark-blue flower rather like a small lupin. Useful in a small mixed summer vase as blue is such an asset to a mixed group.

Barbados Lily *see* HIPPEASTRUM

Barbeton Daisy *see* GERBERA

Bay Tree *see* LAURUS NOBILIS

Beetroot (*Beta*)
Leaves and seed heads are good in a flower group. Some of the ornamental beets are most handsome with well-shaped, reddish-green leaves; *Beta vulgaris cicla* or silver beet has large green leaves with prominent midribs in green and scarlet. Even the edible beets provide some excellent leaves to use as a foil for red roses or dahlias.
CONDITIONING The leaves flag easily. Their stalks should be dipped in boiling water and then they should be completely submerged in a bath of cold water overnight. Or experiment with the starch method, by immersing the leaves overnight in a weak starch solution.
TO PRESERVE Allow seed to form, cut and hang stems upside down to dry.

Begonia
B. rex is really a greenhouse plant, but I always have it on my kitchen window-sill, and cut off leaves all the year round for use in all kinds of ways: with fruits, with tulips in spring, and with

summer flowers to add a touch of the exotic. You can see the leaves in colour on Plates V and XI and

Leaves of *Begonia rex*

I have also used it in many of the arrangements illustrated in black and white. The flowering Begonias are of little value for cutting — the heads drop off their stems so quickly; but odd blooms may be used for floating in bowls as they have a wonderful colour range.
CONDITIONING *Begonia rex* leaves should have the ends of the stems dipped in boiling water for thirty seconds. Then submerge in cold water, dry off and arrange keeping the stems as much below the water as possible.

Belladonna Lily *see* AMARYLLIS

Beloperone guttata (Shrimp Plant)
This has salmon-red bracts in drooping spikes surrounding small white flowers. A plant for the greenhouse and well worth while for small sprays picked to put in a vase, where they will add a spontaneous cascading effect. In Australia I noticed they grew in small hedges dividing gardens, with also a lime-green and yellow variety that I had never seen before.
CONDITIONING Boiling water treatment is essential.

Berberis (Barberry)

Hardy evergreen and deciduous shrubs with ornamental leaves and colourful berries — red, purple, or blue-black. My favourite evergreen kinds are *B. darwinii* and *B. stenophylla*, each with yellow-orange flowers in spring, and *B. wilsoniae* and *B. rubrostilla*, each with arching sprays of iridescent coral berries in autumn. *Berberis thunbergii* turns a beautiful autumn colour, and *B. thunbergii atropurpurea* has excellent purple foliage all summer, good as a colour contrast in any shrub border.

CONDITIONING   Hammer ends of stems or peel off some bark to make absorption of water easier.

Bergenia

Hardy perennials. The large-leaved fleshy megaseas are now better known as the the bergenias; there are many varieties and some dispute arises in the horticultural world as to the naming of them.

Bergenia cordifolia

Bergenia crassifolia has spoon-shaped leaves and very early-flowering paler pink flowers. *B. cordifolia* is one that I use all the year round; the large heart-shaped leaves are superb. Mr Foss of Constance Spry often says that if you grow only one plant in your garden, then it must be this. A plant misused in Victorian days and dumped on the flint rockery, often in the shade, because of being so good-natured, seeming to thrive in any conditions. Some of the leaves may turn a lovely colour in late summer and look beautiful with a few Peace roses. The green leaves I use in the winter with a vase of 'mixed greens'. The flowers are also effective, and are nice to cut in May, though to me they are of secondary importance. 'Ballawley Hybrid', with large handsome leaves that turn mahogany colour in the winter, is a new one that I have just acquired and am thrilled to have. I was interested to see that Bergenias have been planted in the gardens in Pompeii.

CONDITIONING   Soak the leaves completely in a bath of cold water for a few hours, dry off and arrange.

Beta *see* BEETROOT

Betula pendula (Silver Birch)

Silver birch is one of the most graceful of all trees, and I love to use sprays from the bare branches in winter, or later the young green foliage and small catkins to provide a delicate background for daffodils.

CONDITIONING   Hammer ends of stems well and stand in deep water for several hours.

Billbergia nutans

Greenhouse evergreen. Its unusual pendulous flower has the strange but attractive contrast of lime-green petals and bright-pink bracts. A greenhouse plant much recommended.

Bird of Paradise Flower *see* STRELITSIA

Blandfordia (Christmas Bells)

The Christmas plant in Australia, low-growing in fiery red, and sold as we sell holly for Christmas decoration. A fleshy-rooted greenhouse plant here.

Bleeding Heart *see* DICENTRA SPECTABILIS

Blessed Thistle *see* CNICUS BENEDICTUS

Blue Cedar *see* CEDRUS ATLANTICA GLAUCA

Bluebell (Scilla)

Wild bluebells are often thought poor flowers for bringing indoors. But this is only when they are picked on too long a stem. Cut not more than four inches long and massed tightly in a basket or tin, they will last very well and their scent is delicious. They can last as long as ten days while gradually their bright blue fades almost to white before they die off completely. When picking, never pull but cut; the white end, which must be removed in any case before arranging, provides the substance the bulb needs for flowering next year. Wrap in polythene or paper as soon as cut, as they droop very quickly if exposed to the air, and take a long time to recover.

CONDITIONING Cut stems fairly short and place in deep warm water for several hours.

Bocconia *see* MACLEAYA CORDATA

Boronia megastigma

Beautiful scented plume of magenta-maroon and yellow, growing wild in Australia and sold in small bunches by flower sellers there in September. I used it a lot in decorations there, but unfortunately never have enough to cut here. Constance Spry loved its fragrance and often had a pot of it in her room. In this country it is grown as a greenhouse shrub or house plant.

Bougainvillea

Famed for its curving sprays of rich colour on walls and arches in warm climates. A hothouse plant here and magnificent to use if there is an opportunity.

CONDITIONING I found it lasts fairly well if first the stems are dipped in boiling water and then the whole spray is completely submerged in cold water for twelve hours — not longer, or the bracts become transparent.

Bouvardia

An enchanting star-like small flower growing in trusses — white, pink and scarlet. A greenhouse plant, but sold quite frequently and used chiefly for florists' sprays or bouquets. No perfume, although I always expect one.

Box Tree *see* BUXUS SEMPERVIRENS

Bracken *see* PTERIDIUM

Briza media (Quaking Grass)

Hardy ornamental flowering grass. Graceful to use with cut flowers and, when dried, to arrange with the more solid seed heads of poppies, cardoon, and others, to add a light touch to a winter vase.

TO PRESERVE Leave on the plant until the flowers are really open; then cut and bunch, and hang upside down to dry.

Brussels Sprouts (*Brassica gemmifera*)

The red variety, besides being edible, is interesting for decoration. The purplish-red rounded leaves are most attractive. Try them in winter as a foil for a few expensive red roses.

CONDITIONING Never use hot water for any brassica. Soak well in cold water for a few hours.

Buddleia davidii

An excellent summer-flowering shrub, attractive to butterflies and often known as the 'Butterfly Bush'. Adds colour to the shrub border at rather a dull time of year. Sprays combine well in vases of mixed summer flowers; the white variety can be added to green and white groups, the mauve and the purple to pinks and blues. Does not last well despite all treatment, but can be replaced without much trouble after two days if necessary.

CONDITIONING Dip ends of stems in boiling water and then give a long deep drink.

TO PRESERVE Before picking, allow flower heads to lose colour and become a brownish spike, then store till required.

Bulrush *see* TYPHA

Burning Bush *see* DICTAMNUS

Buttercup *see* RANUNCULUS

Button Snake Root *see* LIATRIS

Buxus sempervirens (Box)

Evergreen shrub, excellently dense and slow-growing for topiary, but useful for arrangement in arching sprays, if unclipped. The variegated box, *B. sempervirens aureo-maculata* and *B. sempervirens argentea*, are especially useful and I use them a great deal in winter.

Caladium

Stove deciduous perennial. A plant with beautifully ornamental foliage: large leaves of greenish white veined in darker green, or pale-pink leaves veined with crimson. When cut from the plant, the leaves do not last very well; the best effect is gained by washing the roots and inserting the whole plant into a vase   this can add charm and lightness to a vase of foliage in greens and white.

CONDITIONING   If cut leaves are to be used, dip the stalk in boiling water, before submerging the whole leaf in cold water for several hours.

Calathea zebrina (Zebra Plant)

A good ornamental house plant which I find useful in miniature indoor gardens, in winter and early spring.

Calceolaria (Slipper Flower)

Half hardy or greenhouse plants. A wide range of orange-red slipper-like flowers. Generally used for bedding-out schemes and used little in flower arrangement, but a piece in a coppery or more subtle shade can look attractive in the centre of a small summer vase.

Calendula (Pot Marigold)

Hardy annual. A mass of marigolds in a wooden

Calendula

bowl or a basket brightens any dark corner and gives a glorious feeling of sunlight. These flowers are long-lasting in water. I am fond of the ball varieties, especially a pale lemon yellow which looks cool and fresh in high summer, arranged with grasses and green Love-lies-bleeding.

CONDITIONING   Give a large drink, up to their necks, in deep water.

Californian Tree Poppy see ROMNEYA

Callistemon (Bottle-brush Tree)

A native of Australia. The flowers are excellent for a modern style of arrangement and last extremely well. I use them as often as I can get them, liking them best when dried.

TO PRESERVE   Hang them upside down and they dry very well.

Callistephus see ASTER

Calluna see under ERICA

Camassia quamash (Bear Grass, Wild Hyacinth)

A hardy bulbous plant with spikes of blue flowers in July. A good pointed outline for a mixed group of summer flowers and excellent for a vase of blues, July being the only month for a good vase of tall blue flowers.

Camellia japonica (Tea Plant)

Hardy evergreen shrub. Now more widely grown than ever before. Though tender, they do well outside in a sheltered north or west aspect — this prevents the early morning sun from reaching the blooms while they are still in the grip of frost, when they would become scorched and unsightly. They like the dappled shade of a small deciduous tree, and acid soil. Although expensive initially, they will well reward you with an abundance of white, pink or red blooms in early spring, to say nothing of magnificent dark glossy foliage. This I enjoy in winter more than I can ever express: by itself in a white slender jug or mixed with evergreens of any kind. If you prefer not to pick the flower sprays, then use the heads alone and have them floating in a bowl.

CONDITIONING   Hammer the hard woody stems of the foliage and give a long drink.

Campanula (Canterbury Bell, Bell Flower)
Hardy annuals, biennial and perennials. In July, when many summer flowers droop readily and shed petals, these are one of the best-lasting subjects for cutting. They look cool and pretty and have become very popular over the years. Of the hardy perennial varieties, *C. latifolia*, *C. persicifolia*, *C. latiloba* and *C. pyramidalis* are some of my favourites. *C. lactiflora* 'Loddon Anna' is a delightful soft pink. The biennial Canterbury bells I well recommend both for the border and to cut. For the rock garden, there is a wide range of alpine campanula well worth growing.
CONDITIONING Place in deep water for several hours. Remove all faded flowers, and each bud should open out.

Canary Creeper *see* TROPAEOLUM

Candytuft *see* IBERIS

Canna indica (Indian Shot Plant)
Greenhouse perennial. Used for bedding and cutting, but it will not stand our winters. Handsome foliage in red and green, and yellow and flame-coloured flowers on strong, thick stems. It is marketed here occasionally and looks well with mixed foliages.
CONDITIONING For the leaves, dip the stalks in boiling water and then submerge in cold water for several hours. The flower stems need boiling and then should stand in cold water.

Cantaloup Melon (*Cucumis melo cantalupensis*)
This may seem odd to include, but its grooved shape is so decorative and gives an air of festivity, as when placed in a vase of mixed fruit and flowers for a buffet table.

Canterbury Bell *see* CAMPANULA

Cape Gooseberry *see* PHYSALIS

Cape Jasmine *see* GARDENIA

Cape Lily *see* CRINUM

Capsicum
Greenhouse. The fruits are better known as sweet peppers or chillies. I use both the red and the green fruits in vases of foliages, or with fruit and

flowers. Their shiny skins have a lovely texture and give highlights to any arrangement.

Cardoon (*Cynara cardunculus*)
Hardy herbaceous perennial. Of the artichoke family, a little hardier than the globe artichoke and therefore used for decorative purposes more widely. Good leaves and excellent seed heads. A plant I would never be without. See also Artichoke (*Cynara scolymus*).

Carnation *see* DIANTHUS

Carpinus betulus (Hornbeam)
A large tree bearing sprays of green catkins in early spring before the leaves appear; extremely pretty as background material in a vase. In the summer, they form showers of tiny keys, which turn from green to brown, delightful at all stages.
CONDITIONING Hammer the woody stems and give a long drink.
TO PRESERVE Place stems of the green keys in glycerine, remove before they turn brown, and occasionally they stay green or golden; or the keys can simply be hung upside down and when dried they are very effective.

Carrot (*Daucus carota*)
I use carrots occasionally with fruit, flowers and vegetables, but I also like to use the lacy flower (it is rather like cow parsley) after it has gone to seed, both fresh and dried. In addition carrots have good coloured foliage.
TO PRESERVE Allow the seed head to form, then hang it upside down.

Castanea sativa (Sweet Chestnut)
This is lovely to use in its flower stage, removing the foliage until you are left with the fluffy yellow spikes of the flowers, which are especially good when arranged with lilies.
TO PRESERVE THE LEAVES Put the stems in glycerine and use as a change from beech leaves.

Catmint *see* NEPETA

Cattleya (Orchid)
Stoveplant. The opulent varieties with purple colourings are usually worn as a spray or carried in a bouquet. Not really recommended for use in a

group; as well as being expensive, they are difficult to arrange as the stems are short and the petals so delicate.

Ceanothus
Hardy and half hardy shrubs, both evergreen and deciduous. 'Gloire de Versailles' and 'Lucie Moser' are two of my favourite deciduous varieties. I love a tuft of this fluffy blue flower in a vase, but I have never found any way of making it last in water, and so it does mean replacing the stem each day.

Cedrus atlantica glauca (Blue Cedar)
This magnificent tree has beautiful spraying branches and lovely cones. Its deep blue-grey goes so well with a mixture of greys and for winter decoration it can be put with eucalyptus foliage and a few pink chrysanthemums.
TO DRY A really good branch is well worth saving after use in a vase. Hang it upside down to allow the needles to fall, and it is excellent then as a background or gummed and glittered for Christmas.

Centaurea (Cornflower; Sweet Sultan)
Hardy annuals. Grown from seed, cornflowers (C. cyanus) make a good splash of colour and look their best, I think, arranged in baskets with grasses. Sweet sultan (C. moschata) in white and a soft pink-lilac is a better lasting flower for the house; it stands well and makes a good focal point in any vase.

Ceratostigma see PLUMBAGO

Cercis siliquastrum (Judas Tree)
This has showers of purple racemes and is so beautiful that I wish it were not so rarely available. A tree that is not often grown, sad to say, chiefly because it is not very hardy and is slow to flower.

Cheiranthus (Wallflower)
Hardy annual. Wallflowers as we know them come in a lovely range of warm colours — browny-golds and rich reds, through to cream and pale yellow. Because of their very woody stems they do not last very well in water unless they are picked fairly short. They seem to arrange best in a mass, either in a wooden box or basket or a copper bowl (see Colour Plate II); in this way even if the petals

do fall, they fall on each other, and the flowers do not look so sad when they gradually begin to die. 'Ruby Glow' is the most beautiful colour, almost purple, and this I think is quite one of the most unusual to grow. They are one of the few flowers that seem to last very much better if they are arranged on their own and not mixed with other flowers.
CONDITIONING Cut with stems not longer than four inches and give them a long drink in warm water before arranging.

Cherry Pie see HELIOTROPIUM

Chimonanthus (Winter Sweet)
Hardy deciduous shrub, C. praecox (C. fragrans) has pale-golden flowers deepening to red at the centre and of all winter shrubs is quite the most delightful for scent. It has, however, a rather straggly form.

Chionodoxa (Glory of the Snow)
A little bulb which produces star-shaped flowers of excellent blue colour, with white throats. Increases every year to give a cloud of blue in early spring, and is lovely when used for a touch of colour at this time in a 'moss garden', with crocus or other suitable companions.

Chlorophytum capense variegatum
Greenhouse and house plant. It ought to be called C. comosum variegatum, but I have kept to C. capense as it is invariably sold under that name. Long pointed leaves, with a cream stripe up the centre, arching over like the spray of a fountain. Useful with ornamental foliage.

Choisya ternata (Mexican Orange)
Hardy evergreen shrub. Useful both for its good green hard foliage and for its clusters of lovely white flowers in late spring.
CONDITIONING Hammer the stems well, before giving a long drink.

Christmas Rose see HELLEBORUS

Chrysanthemum (Chrysanthemum, Ox-eye Daisy, Marguerite)
Greenhouse half hardy and hardy perennials. The name covers a wide range of plants from the Ox-eye Daisy to the ones we think of as chrysanthe-

H

Yellow chrysanthemums with dried stems of the Monkey Puzzle tree and *Molucella laevis*

mums proper, the greatest standby for winter flower arrangement. There are many varieties in each class, such as incurved, anemone centred and American spray, in all colours and grown all the year round. Koreans are one of my favourites, partly because they are single; all singles are so easy to arrange and most effective for the focal point in a vase. Annual chrysanthemums with daisy-like faces are especially useful to place centrally in a mixed group.

CONDITIONING Place the ends of the stems in boiling water, then leave in deep water up to their necks.

Chamaecyparis (Cypress)
Hardy evergreen coniferous trees. These evergreens are used mainly for winter decoration, and especially for Christmas. I like to gum and glitter short pieces to arrange with fir cones and perhaps fruit and candles for a Christmas table. In the garden they have great architectural value as single trees or to contribute height and shape to a shrub border. Many different varieties in a wide range of greens and yellows.

Cimicifuga cordifolia (Bugbane)
Hardy herbaceous perennial. A plant that has become increasingly popular. Plumes of creamy flowers on coal-black stems. *C. racemosa* is taller and particularly attractive for growing in woodland.

CONDITIONING Scald the stems in boiling water and let them stand in deep water for several hours.

Cineraria *see* SENECIO

Clarkia
Hardy annual. Flowers in July and comes in a wide range of colours — purples, through pinks of all shades, to white. A very good annual to grow for flower vases as it lasts in water so well. Remember to pick when it is almost in full flower right up to the top of the stem, otherwise the budded tip of the stem tends to droop easily. It is attractive either arranged in bowls by itself or added to mixed groups of blending colour.

CONDITIONING Dip the stem in boiling water for a few seconds and allow a long drink.

TO PRESERVE Remove any foliage and arrange in full flower in shallow water. It dries off very well

and the less it is disturbed the better as this prevents the petals from falling.

Clary *see* SALVIA

Clematis (Virgin's Bower)
Hardy climbers and herbaceous perennials. The climbing varieties, both evergreen and deciduous, are very rewarding, giving a wealth of bloom if they really like their position; they like their heads

Cimifuga racemosa

in the sun and feet in the shade and prefer lime soil. As a rule they do not stand well as a cut flower, though they are ideal for the centre of a vase and I use them as often as I can. The little herbaceous one (*C. fremontii*) I have used in Colour Plate VII is one my grandmother loved, and the plant I took from her garden some years ago gives me a great deal of pleasure; unlike the climbing varieties these last very well in flower arrangement

An arrangement of purples, using lilac stripped of its leaves, *Clematis lanuginosa* 'Nellie Moser', and the small grey-purple *Iris regelio-cyclus*

without any special conditioning. The seed heads of *C. davidiana* are fluffy and very effective, as are the long sprays of Old Man's Beard, *Clematis vitalba*, the wild clematis, which I use continually in all its seed head stages.

Clematis fremontii

CONDITIONING The large-flowered and climbing varieties should have the ends of their stems placed in boiling water for a few seconds and then be given a long drink for two to three hours. The stems are sometimes short, so be sure to place in a shallow bowl and prevent the petals from getting wet, as they quickly become transparent. Although I have never tried this, the Japanese often use their alcohol treatment for clematis, placing the stems in a small bottle of pure alcohol for several minutes, before standing them in water for a long drink.

TO PRESERVE The stems of Old Man's Beard may be hung upside down to dry the seed head, though I find that if you pick before the seed is too fluffy they last extremely well in a solution of glycerine and water; I can thoroughly recommend this.

Cleome spinosa (Spider Flower)
Half hardy annual. I have used them a great deal in Australia but rarely here, where being grown under glass they are never produced in great quantities. However, if you can find them, they are certainly very attractive, with their rounded spined heads of pink or white florets.

Clerodendron bungei
Hardy shrub. *C. Bungei* with rose-purple flowers is charming and the flower sprays with leaves removed are very decorative.

Clianthus puniceus (Parrot's Bill)
Greenhouse climbing shrub. Parrot's Bill describes it very well and there is little to add. I seldom have the opportunity of using it as a cut flower, but it is most unusual and has pleasing feathery foliage which is suitable for a mixed group.

Clivia (Kaffir Lily)
Greenhouse perennial. A handsome head of upright trumpet-like flowers in shades of orange, very useful pointed leaves and lasts in water extremely well. Being spring-flowering it is an asset for a large group for a church or some special occasion — at a time when most flowers are so delicate and therefore have little substance for the centre of a vase. For a good colour combination mix it with forsythia and daffodils.

Cnicus benedictus (Blessed Thistle)
Annual. Extremely decorative green leaves with white blotches, but very prickly and difficult to handle. The flower is of little interest.
CONDITIONING Stems should have the ends well boiled; then give a soaking in cold water.

Cobaea scandens (Cups and Saucers)
A half hardy perennial, usually grown as an annual, Cups and Saucers (*C. scandens*) has trumpet or bell-shaped flowers of delicate lilac or pale green. A really enchanting climbing plant, quick growing and well worth while as an annual. Sometimes it can be persuaded to survive a winter if given a sheltered position and if the weather is not too severe. The seed heads are pretty: not very good for drying, but they last well in water.

Codiaeum (Croton)
Tender evergreen shrubs with beautiful ornamental foliage, sold here in bunches of individual leaves and extremely useful, especially in winter. I have

had the fun of picking long stems and using them in large foliage groups in Bermuda. I have found them most decorative arranged with fruit and flowers — you can see one on Colour Plate VIII

CONDITIONING The leaves last very well if the ends of the long stems are plunged into boiling water, and the whole leaf is then completely submerged in water for several hours.

Colchicum (Autumn Crocus, Meadow Saffron)
A delightful autumn bulb, very rewarding though it does need careful planting. The lovely mauve and white 'crocuses' appear straight out of the ground with no foliage at all, making a wonderful splash of colour just as it seems everything else is dying off. In spring, however, when they might well be forgotten, the plants throw up a multitude of green leaves, which are not very attractive; because of this it is advisable to plant round trees. One of the best ways of growing them I ever saw was as underplanting in a bed of azaleas, the turning foliage of the azaleas and the mass of purple colchicum made a beautiful display in autumn and the leaves were not too conspicuous in the spring. When cut the flowers last well, and one or two stems of the very large white varieties arranged on a pin-holder in a shallow silver bowl are hard to surpass.

Coleus (Flame Nettle)
Greenhouse perennial. Beautiful ornamental foliage in a wide range of colour — flames and reds, but my favourite is the lime green. It is coming into wider use as a cut plant, though usually thought of as a greenhouse or bedding-out plant for parks or gardens.

CONDITIONING The stems must be dipped in boiling water, then given a long cold drink, but do not submerge in case of transparency.

Columbine see AQUILEGIA

Convallaria majalis (Lily of the Valley)
Hardy herbaceous perennial. Sweetly-scented sprays of little bells, in pink as well as white, about six inches high. Lovers of shade, they grow well in any surroundings, doing well in small town gardens which makes them a general favourite. They are easy to force, so are in great demand for bouquets at all times of year. Almost the nicest

Convallaria majalis — Lily of the Valley

way to arrange them is to make a posy of the flowers in your hand and surround them with a frill of their leaves, tie with string to keep them in place, and put them in a small bowl or vase.

CONDITIONING If they are picked straight from the garden, little care is needed; just cut the ends of the stems and place in deep water for an hour or so. The forced blooms are rather fragile and are better if the bunch is wrapped in tissue paper and stood in a little warm water; then fill the jar right to the top and let them stay overnight in deep water.

Convolvulus see IPOMOEA

Coreopsis
Hardy annuals and perennials. Brownish-yellow daisy-like flowers with a good 'face' which makes them a useful central point in a vase. The annuals, being on rather slender stems, are more difficult to arrange than the firmer perennial varieties. Late summer plants, well recommended.

Cornus (Dogwood)

The red and yellow shoots of dogwood, indigenous to North America, are beautiful in winter, giving welcome colour to a shrub border. I recommend several species: *C. alba sibirica* 'Westonbirt' has leaves with excellent autumn colour and when these fall you are left with brilliant scarlet stems all winter. *C. stolonifera flaviramea* has bright yellow-green bark and both of these give a graceful outline shape for a winter arrangement, with perhaps a bunch of single chrysanthemums or the first daffodils of early spring. *Cornus mas* is a delightful species, flowering very early in the spring; it has clusters of tiny yellow flowers which show up well on the bare brown branches before the leaves appear. It is also excellent arranged with a few daffodils. One of my favourites is *C. kousa* with open large white bracts appearing in May or June, strawberry-like fruits in the autumn and gorgeous autumn-tinted foliage. This is a lovely flower for arrangement, for it has an oriental delicacy and one or two sprays make a decoration in themselves, arranged alone in a shallow dish or bowl. *C. nuttallii*, the famous dogwood so often seen in western North America, preserves most beautifully, though alas not so well with us, probably because of our damp climate.

CONDITIONING   Strip off up to two inches of bark from the end of the stem and give a long drink in warm water.

TO PRESERVE   The branches of fully open American dogwood can be preserved excellently by the sand method as described on p. 62.

Cortaderia (Pampas Grass)

Hardy herbaceous perennial grass with handsome white plumes growing out of tall clumps of fine grassy foliage. It was used a great deal by the Victorians as an ornamental plant in shrubberies or planted on sweeping lawns to give a feeling of height and grandeur. We use it for background for large groups in midsummer, and it has proved invaluable for flowers arranged in the Albert Hall and really large buildings. Because of its size it is of little use in the average house or for small vases, and there seems no way in which it can be cut down to look in proportion; though I think I have seen small pieces taken from the sides and used in some Australian examples. I have seen

a pink one, but it is rather unusual.

TO PRESERVE   When the grass is dry, about the end of September, pick and bunch the heads and hang them upside down to dry completely, for use in winter groups.

Corylopsis

Hardy deciduous flowering shrubs. *C. spicata*, which needs a sheltered position, flowers as early as February, with pale-yellow drooping spikes adorning bare branches. *C. veitchiana* flowers in April, and the lovely variety *C. willmottiae* flowers in March and April. I grow the first and last mentioned and although they don't really flourish in my cold garden, they always give me a few precious sprays of flowers at a very sparse time of year. (See the illustration on page 116.)

CONDITIONING   Hammer stems well and peel off up to two inches of bark from the end of the stem, before placing in warm water.

Corylus (Hazel)

Hazel catkins are amongst the first spring flowers; to get the maximum enjoyment from them be sure to bring them into the house in their early stage just after Christmas. Hammer the stems well and keep them in a warm room in deep water and you'll be surprised how quickly they come out. *Corylus avellana contorta*, with its spiral twisting and arching stems, is almost a 'must' for any flower arranger. One stem of a lovely shape is an exciting background for a few well chosen flowers at any time of year. For decoration indoors and out I love the deep purple foliage of *C. maxima atropurpurea* (the Purple-leaf Filbert). In vases it makes a good background for merging with red flowers or for contrasting with browns and yellows.

CONDITIONING   Hammer ends of stems well and peel off bark up to two or three inches. Place in warm water for several hours.

Cotoneaster

Hardy evergreen and deciduous shrubs, bearing scarlet or black berries in autumn and winter, when berries of all kinds add a brilliance of colour and form to any group of flowers. Pick with care always, so as not to deform the tree. Possibly one of the best known varieties is *C. frigida*, though *C.* 'St. Monica' and *C. watereri* are considered better,

Corylopsis willmottiae (see text on p. 115)

almost evergreen and the berries a better red. *C. wardii* is excellent, with orange-red berries and slender arching sprays with silver-backed leaves. Coming mostly from Central China they stand most conditions very well. I always feel tempted to pick the arching sprays of white blossom in April or May, but I try to wait for the berries as they are of much greater value.

CONDITIONING Sprays when flowering are better after being dipped in boiling water for one or two minutes and then given a long drink in cold water. For berries, hammer the woody stems well, before giving a long drink.

TO PRESERVE The berries can be placed in a solution of glycerine, though I have never been very successful with this method. Lately I have tried spraying the branches with hair-lacquer and found this more satisfactory (they kept their colour and it seemed to prevent them from shrinking too badly) but I still hope for the perfect answer.

Crataegus monogyna (Hawthorn)

Hardy tree that is often found in our hedges, with a wealth of pink or white blossom in May (it is often known just as 'May'), making our lanes look and smell delightful. It holds for many people a superstition that it might have been from this tree that they made our Lord's crown of thorns. From this comes the notion that it is unlucky to bring it into the house. However, having used it often in its berrying stage, I have become used to the idea of bringing it in, and love to pick its arching sprays when in flower. I remove all the leaves and use it in an oriental type of arrangement in a Chinese vase or ginger jar.

CONDITIONING Hammer ends of stems and put in warm water.

TO PRESERVE The sprays of berries remain quite a good colour for keeping to use in the winter, and if you can paint them over with a coat of clear varnish this preserves them extremely well.

Crinum longifolium (Cape Lily)
Hardy deciduous bulb. *C. longifolium* flowers well in late summer. It has trumpets of pink or white (*C. l. album*) massed at the top of thick succulent stems, and looks lovely when used with branches of lime flowers from which all the leaves have been removed. Excellent for large groups for weddings or other special occasions. *C. powellii* and its white variety is a lovely hybrid, but rather less hardy.

Crocosmia crocosmiiflora (Montbretia)
Still often listed as *Tritonia crocosmaeflora*, this is a hardy perennial with sword-like leaves and orange flowers that have a delicate habit of growing on arching sprays. Flowering late into the autumn, it is extremely useful and makes a good foil for the more solid flowers of dahlias. The leaves also are useful, and press well as they change colour and are nice to use in the winter.
TO PRESERVE Cut the leaves as they turn and press them between sheets of blotting paper to keep their colour.

Crocus
Hardy bulb. One of the greatest delights in early spring is to see a carpet of crocus growing in the grass under the trees. They cut better than is generally expected and can be used in clumps to give a splash of colour in an indoor moss garden. The species varieties, blooming so early and a joy to behold, are for me the best of all.

Crown Imperial *see* FRITILLARIA

Cryptomeria japonica (Japanese Cedar)
Hardy evergreen. An ornamental conifer with bright green foliage in early spring, turning to shades of bronze and crimson in winter. I use it at all times of the year, but mostly in autumn, as it is such a good foil for all the varying shades of chrysanthemums.
CONDITIONING Hammer the ends of the stems and place in warm water.

Cuckoo Pint *see* ARUM

Cucurbita (Gourd)
Half hardy annuals. Decorative small marrows for which seed is now easily obtainable from any reliable merchant. The gourds have all kinds of variations and combinations of colour, such as green and orange or yellow, or striped green and white. Some have smooth skins and others are very lumpy. When picked, they are very ornamental placed in a bowl or dish with a few fresh or preserved leaves, or mounted on wires and used to hang among fresh or dried material in a vase.
TO PRESERVE Never pick your gourds until they are really ripe. They are best left until the first frost. Then give a coat of clear varnish; this excludes the air and prevents them from going soft and mouldy. In this way they keep for months.

Currant *see* RIBES

Cut-leaved Elder *see* SAMBUCUS

Cycas (Sago Palm)
Stove plant. Handsome dark-green leaves with well-shaped, feathery fronds, which I rarely have the opportunity of using while they are fresh. However, they are preserved commercially and used then by many florists in wreath work. I sometimes use them at Christmas-time either glittered, or painted white or gold and then glittered. If mounted on long canes as false stems to give extra height, they are most useful in big group-arrangements for special occasions.

Cyclamen (Sowbread)
Hardy and greenhouse plants. The greenhouse cyclamen, *C. persicum*, sold in pots in autumn and winter are decorative just as they are, or when taken out of their pots and used in a planted garden with a collection of other plants; they last surprisingly well like this. Less well known, but still more attractive are the alpine varieties for the rock garden or wall. These delicate little flowers look charming in a china hand or similar small vase. It is often possible to buy them in bunches from a florist's in both spring and autumn. *C. coum* flowers in the spring; it has the most lovely cerise colouring and is delightful arranged in a bed of moss with a collection of little bulbs and spring bits and pieces.
CARE OF PLANTS The potted plants are killed more often by over-watering than by anything else. Even neglect is far better for their chance of survival. Water only when really necessary; it is often preferable to wait until the leaves start to

wilt. One old lady I know, who has a superb plant, uses cold tea every few days and it certainly looks wonderful on this diet!

Cydonia oblonga (Quince)

Hardy deciduous tree. Quinces are used more often for jelly than for flower arrangement, but a few sprays of the fruit in a vase of mixed flowers or in a combination of fruit and flowers look delicious. I only wish they were less hard to come by. I once did a vase of clusters of quince and green grapes with a collection of mixed yellow flowers and hope to try this out again one day.

Cymbidium (Orchid)

Orchids have a strong fascination for many people, and are now more widely grown than ever before; even the small-greenhouse owner is launching forth. One of their greatest merits to me is that they outlive almost any other flower in a vase. Cybidiums are one of the most beautiful of all. After being able to use them in Sydney almost whenever I liked, I felt I would never enjoy doing another fruit and flower group without putting in a spray of this orchid, which has beautiful arching sprays blooming right down the stems and a delightful colour range: soft pinks to rose red and green to cream. The bought flowers are an excellent investment in early spring; expensive as they are, they will outlive a bunch of daffodils four times over. Arrange them with a bare branch of exquisite shape, preferably in a vase of oriental design. You can see how I have used it on Colour Plate XI.

CONDITIONING   Cut the ends of the stems on the slant and stand in deep water. Every few days remove from the vase and cut a small piece off the stem. This ensures that the plant can drink properly.

Cynara cardunculus see CARDOON

Cynara scolymus see ARTICHOKE

Cynoglossum amabile

Hardy perennial. Easily grown from seed, this plant makes a lovely patch of blue in any flower border. It is better to treat it as a biennial and raise fresh stock each year. A small piece of the brilliant blue is an asset to any vase of mixed flowers. It resembles a large forget-me-not, and deserves to be better known.

CONDITIONING   Cut the stems and place in warm water until this cools; then arrange.

Cypripedium (Lady's Slipper Orchid)

Stove plant. A type of orchid that may be a little less expensive than most others. They are generally greeny-brown and yellowish in colour, though they come in a range of unusual colours in the hybrid varieties. Some time ago their prime use was to be worn as a spray or 'corsage', but they are good in vases for home decoration. They last extremely well as a cut flower. I have used them with mimosa with all the foliage removed, and placed the whole group on a convex mirror to add a reflection.

CONDITIONING   Cut the stems on the slant and cut off a small length every few days.

Cytisus (Broom)

Hardy deciduous and evergreen shrubs. Well known for their sprays of cascading bloom in spring, in all shades of yellows and reds to browns. *Cytisus praecox* is one of my favourites and one of the best varieties for flower arrangement. None last really well in water, alas, once in bloom, but the sprays add a beautiful curve to any vase or bowl. The foliage, however, is in constant demand among those who like the rather stylized effect it can produce. It has one enormous advantage, that once 'put into shape' it will remain so for a long time. The sprays can be shaped at will if the whole spray is submerged under water. First bend the branch and tie with string in the shape desired, then submerge under cold water for several hours — up to twenty-four hours at least.

CONDITIONING   Flowering broom lasts better if given a few minutes with the ends of the stems in boiling water, and then a long drink.

Daffodil see NARCISSUS

Dahlia

Half hardy tuberous-rooted perennial in many varieties: cactus, quilled, large, fancy, pompom, peony-flowered, semi-double, decorative, and so on. One of the most useful flowers of all for arrangement, having such a good 'face' for giving a central point of interest in any vase, and such a clear rounded outline for showing up from a distance; also a wide and helpful range of colour.

See especially Plates 9 and 12. With careful storing in winter, the tubers go on for many years and provide quantities of blooms.

CONDITIONING   I think a little boiling water for a few minutes for the ends of the stems, and then a long drink, is as good a method as any. Dahlias react well to sugar; if you add a teaspoonful of sugar and an aspirin to the water in your flower vase, they really should last very well.

TO PRESERVE   I have seen some extraordinarily well preserved dahlias; these were dried in a shallow box by the hot sand method.

Daphne

Greenhouse and hardy deciduous and evergreen shrubs. Daphnes of all kinds are very useful for vases and bowls and the many sweet-scented ones will fill a warm room with their fragrance in early spring. *D. mezereum*, the most common, with purple or white flowers followed by shiny red berries, often flowers in January if grown in a sheltered spot. Spurge laurel, *Daphne laureola*, the evergreen variety growing wild in woodlands, lasts for weeks in water, which adds greatly to its popularity. For its heavenly perfume *D. odora variegata* (or *D. odora aureo-marginata*) is one of my favourites — fresh and lovely with tufts of verbena-scented pinkish-white flowers and evergreen foliage — but it does need some protection. *D. pontica* is a hardy evergreen shrub that will succeed even in heavy soil or under overhanging trees, and produces its fragrant yellowish-green flowers amid bright green foliage in April.

CONDITIONING   Hammer stems well or place the ends in boiling water for a few minutes, and allow a few hours in cold water.

Daphne mezereum

Datura (Trumpet Flower)
Half hardy and greenhouse annuals. Many species I do not know at all, but the thorn apple or *Datura stramonium* is extremely useful. It has rather insignificant flowers, but lovely thorny-looking seed heads on angular branches, that dry well and are very pretty indeed, sprayed and glittered for Christmas decoration. A much-debated plant because it is poisonous to cattle; as with all such plants, great discretion should be used as to where and how it is grown. *Datura cornigera*, the greenhouse species in Britain (growing in magnificent trees in the tropics) has superb trumpet flowers; the long heads on slender stems make them difficult to arrange and they are best cut short, almost to their necks, and massed together in a shallow bowl. In this way they will last quite well. They are rare in any case and not very generally used.

TO PRESERVE Pick *Datura stramonium* when the seed heads form and start turning from green to creamy brown; remove all the leaves and hang the branches upside down.

Day Lily *see* HEMEROCALLIS

Dead Nettle *see* LAMIUM

Delphinium (Larkspur)
Hardy annual. The name larkspur is usually restricted to the annual delphiniums. A most useful annual with tall spikes of mauve, pink and white flowers, which give good outline to a group of summer flowers — lilies or roses and so on.

CONDITIONING Remove all the green foliage that goes below the water-line, as it will very quickly turn the water green; then hammer the stems and put them in warm water.

TO PRESERVE The flowers dry well if left standing undisturbed in shallow water.

Delphinium
Hardy herbaceous perennials. Showy plants for the border and one of the most popular and best of the blue plants. Their tall spikes are most suitable for large vases of any kind (see Plate 16). Beautiful for church decoration, but especially if you add some of the white species as blue is a difficult colour for artificial light — so often looking black and not blue at all. The white varieties and the pink have begun to appeal to me more and more.

The American Pacific hybrids are well worth growing from seed.

CONDITIONING If you are using the spikes for a special occasion, I think it is well worth while to fill the hollow stems with water and plug the ends with cotton wool. For general use, give a good long drink in deep water before arranging.

TO PRESERVE The seed heads can be used for winter decoration if the stems are cut when the heads are well formed, and then hung upside down to dry. To preserve the spikes for colour, hang each stem upside down when in really full bloom and dry off in a warm room. The individual florets can be dried by the warm sand method for using in jars for pot-pourri, or in miniature dried groups.

Deutzia gracilis (Japanese Snow Flower)
Hardy deciduous shrub. A lovely shrub with delicate pink or white clusters of flowers on dark stems, and flowering before the foliage — which adds to its charm. Much appreciated for cutting as it comes a little later than the spring azaleas and lilacs, and so is very useful indeed. It makes a good background for any mixed flower vase.

Garden pink (see facing page)

CONDITIONING   Hammer ends of stems well and soak well in cold water.

Dianthus caryophyllus (Carnation)

There are two distinct kinds of carnation. The border carnations grown out of doors and flowering in the garden in June and July, are smaller than the carnations that are grown so widely under glass. I love the sweet-smelling small carnations that one can grow easily from seed and propagate by layering. They have a wide range of colours — reds to deep purple, soft pinks and white. They grow on fairly long stems about a foot to eighteen inches, and for the best blooms really require staking and the flower buds reduced to one per stem. Still, I am quite happy to have them on their clustered stems and never mind if the stems have a curve or twist due to being allowed to grow freely without staking; it is often so much easier to arrange flowers that have curving rather than upright stems. These flowers scent the summer night air, and are lovely cut short and used with lavender for a guest's bedroom, or on a small table in the living-room. The larger and not so hardy carnation grown under glass is, I suppose, sold more frequently than almost any other flower, and is used a great deal in flower arrangement both in mixed groups and arranged alone. It is the one flower that really does last better if it is put into a vase and arranged alone, with no other flowers or unrelated foliage. I find them rather dull like this and much prefer, if I can, to mix them with other flowers in a combination of colours to suit the tones and hues of the vase concerned. They look particularly good with grey foliage, artemisia or eucalyptus.

TO PRESERVE   Use the hot sand treatment to keep their colour.

Dianthus (Pink, Sweet William)

Of the many hardy varieties of dianthus the best are the garden pinks — sweet-smelling, delicate and attractive arranged in bowls either alone or with little pieces of grey foliage, or mixed with summer flowers. Grow from seed or cuttings. A delightful variety of single annual pink, ranging in colour from pure white to crimson, is the 'Brilliant Fringed Mixed'.

Sweet Williams always seem oddly named *Dianthus barbatus*, but here is where they should

Dianthus barbatus — Sweet William

come. They are not only good for cutting, as they last so well in water, but they are most effective in the border, making a splash of colour for several weeks. I love to see a bowl of Sweet William just on their own, or they can be arranged in a basket. They mix well with many summer flowers, and their wide range of reds makes them extremely useful to put into a vase of 'clashing reds'. The smaller and dwarf varieties are effective in the front of the border.

CONDITIONING   Cut the ends of the stems and give a long drink.

Dicentra spectabilis (Bleeding Heart)

Hardy perennial. This very old-fashioned little flower has acquired a new popularity, thanks to the 'flower movement' of modern times. I have become extremely fond of it. There is a choice of old-fashioned names for it: Dutchman's Breeches, Lady in the Bath and many more. It has arching sprays of small flowers, rather like little lockets, hanging from delicate stems, and its strong pink with a touch of white makes it a good mixer though I really prefer to arrange it by itself, so as not to detract from the lovely form which I feel is its greatest charm. A plant that forces well and is sometimes to be found as a pot plant.

Dictamnus albus (Burning Bush)
Another old-fashioned plant that has come back into favour. I use it whenever I can. Flower-spikes in pink and white — rather like a lupin at first glance. When the flower fades, it leaves a nice-looking green seed head.
CONDITIONING   Place stems in warm water.
TO PRESERVE   Hang the seed heads upside down.

Dieffenbachia picta (Dumb Cane)
Stove plant, with lovely green and white spotted leaves. They are most decorative, and for some very special occasion it is worth while to buy a whole pot and use the leaves individually as you need them. They are such good lasters in water, that this is not as extravagant as it may sound. A few of these handsome leaves placed low in a vase just make a big group stand out.
CONDITIONING   Having cut the stem from the plant, place the ends in boiling water for a few seconds, then allow a long drink.

Diervilla florida (Weigela)
Weigela is the name I have always used for this shrub. I consider it a great asset to the shrub border, as it flowers in May to July. If you remove the leaves before arranging it, you will have delightful sprays of pink or reddish flowers that look very attractive as a background in a mixed summer vase. The variegated variety (*D. florida variegata*) with green and white foliage on dark stems is worth growing.
CONDITIONING   Strip off two inches of bark from the bottom of the stem, before placing in water.

Digitalis (Foxglove)
Hardy biennial. Suttons have the seeds of the lovely hybrids 'Excelsior' which have very nice spotted bells hanging all round the stems. (They do one called 'Apricot and Lemon' and personally I love this best of all.) They are in such delicate colours and arrange so well in a vase of mixed pastel flowers that I feel every garden should have some; liking shade, they fit into any odd corner. Quite one of the best flowers for cutting as they don't drop their petals as so many summer flowers do. There are of course some perennial varieties that are well worth growing. *Digitalis mertonensis* is crushed-strawberry pink; *D. grandiflora* (*D. lutea*) and *D. ambigua* are yellow.

CONDITIONING   Place the ends of the stems in warm water and allow them time to have a long drink.
TO PRESERVE   Gather the seed heads when formed, remove leaves and hang upside down to dry.

Dimorphotheca (Star of the Veldt)
Hardy annual. This enchanting little daisy-like flower comes from South Africa where it grows wild in drifts on the mountain sides. It stands about a foot in height and comes in shades of orange, apricot, buff and salmon. Grown here as an annual, it is charming for a patch of colour in the front of a border. Unfortunately, as it closes its petals at night, it can be a bit disappointing as a cut flower and there is little I can suggest to prevent this. I use them either alone or mixed with other small summer flowers.

Dog's Tooth Violet *see* ERYTHRONIUM

Dogwood *see* CORNUS

Dondia epipactis *see* HACQUETIA EPIPACTIS

Doronicum (Leopard's Bane)
Hardy herbaceous perennials. This yellow daisy flower is, I think, well worth growing — not because it is at all spectacular, but because it comes so wonderfully early that it is more than welcome, giving a bright spot of colour which is so cheerful on a cold day. It will grow in shade, which makes it more welcome still. It mixes well with forsythia and daffodils.
CONDITIONING   Place in warm water.

Dracaena
A hothouse plant with superb foliage. *D. fragrans victoriae* is my favourite, having broad cream leaves with a prominent green stripe down the middle. The purple-leaved varieties are most useful too, to make a good contrast in a foliage group or to give a hard outline to a more confused group of flowers.
TO PRESERVE   If you put the leaves in glycerine and water they turn a lovely colour, but it requires great patience as they can take anything from two to three months to absorb the mixture.

Dracunculus vulgaris (Dragon Arum)
Hardy tuberous-rooted arum type of exotic plant in mauvish black with mottled leaves. It would be

quite superb for flower arrangement, but gives off a vile smell — in spite of which I have used it!

Dragon's Head *see* PHYSOSTEGIA

Dusty Miller *see* AURICULA

Eccremocarpus scaber (Chilean Glory Flower)
Half-hardy. Except in mild climates, this is usually grown as climber rather than a herbaceous plant as it tends to need the shelter of a wall. It flowers in midsummer — small bells of orange and yellow — and its vivid colouring mixes well with all the 'autumnal' shades.
CONDITIONING Place the ends of the stems in boiling water for two seconds before giving a long drink.

Echinops ritro (Globe Thistle)
A hardy perennial, thistle-like, as the name implies, this has nice rounded blue heads for giving a central point to a vase. They stand well in water and look as if they should dry well, but I find this is more difficult than one expects, as they so often shed their spikes or petals.

CONDITIONING Hammer their woody stems and allow a good drink.
TO PRESERVE Strip off all foliage and hang upside down to dry.

Echium (Viper's Bugloss)
Hardy annuals, biennials and perennial. The large thick spikes of mauvey-blue flowers are one of the few good blue flowers (and it is strange that there are so few) that stand well in water. I have found *E. vulgare* growing wild in Norfolk, and it has been well worth a detour to go and look for some. They seem quite easily grown, though I am always surprised that they are not grown more often, when, because of their colour, they combine with other flowers so attractively.
CONDITIONING Place ends of stems in boiling water for a minute, before giving a long drink.

Edelweiss *see* LEONTOPODIUM

Elaeagnus
Hardy evergreen shrubs that I have come to love more and more. All the varieties are a positive

Elaeagnus pungens aureo-variegata

delight especially in the winter. The one I use most of all is *E. pungens aureo-variegata* (*E. maculata*), which has green and brilliant-gold foliage; and one can cut it the whole winter through. I like to use it with any mixture of winter flowers or foliage. In the garden it looks just like a ray of sunshine. It will do well in full sun or partial shade and can be grown from a cutting or grafted. If you have a mild climate you can grow *E. angustifolia* (Oleaster). It is a delightful shrub with the stems and leaves looking as if they are covered with a layer of white cotton wool.

CONDITIONING   Hammer the stems well, before putting in water.

TO PRESERVE   Place stems in a solution of glycerine and leave for several weeks.

Elder *see* SAMBUCUS

Embothrium coccineum
One of the most breathtaking shrubs I have ever seen, but as it is very tender it is rarely seen growing in this country — and so I have scarcely ever had the fun of using it here as a cut subject, to add brilliance to a group of mixed reds, as I did in Australia. Some of the best I have seen are growing at Bodnant in North Wales. It needs acid soil.

CONDITIONING   The stems must be placed in boiling water, before being given a long drink.

Enkianthus campanulatus
Beautiful shrub with tiny bell-shaped flowers hanging in pinky-orange clusters from the branches. They are at their best in May and in autumn. Liking peaty soil, they cannot be grown everywhere; but if conditions suit them then I can thoroughly recommend them. They are at their best arranged with apricot and flame colours, and particularly with azaleas and tulips, as in the arrangement shown on Colour Plate V.

CONDITIONING   Hammer ends of stems well.

Epilobium angustifolium (Willow Herb, Rose Bay, Fire Weed)
A hardy perennial weed that gets the name of Fire Weed because it springs up everywhere after fire. This is very noticeable in the country and it was quite remarkable in London after the Blitz in the city; seeds seemed to appear from nowhere and the following year the bomb sites were a blaze of red. Its red is a vivid carmine, and is breathtaking growing in sheets of colour in midsummer. It has tall spikes of flower and lovely pink seed heads, but these want careful watching as they suddenly burst open in a warm room and shed their fluff over everything. However, although it is a vicious weed in the garden, it is very effective picked and arranged in a mass — for either a party or some special occasion, as try as one may it is difficult to make it last with certainty even with all the known treatments. The seed heads are light and pretty mixed with more solid dried flowers all through the winter.

CONDITIONING   Pick and put it into water at the earliest minute, as it quickly wilts and is very difficult to revive once it has gone down. Put the ends into boiling water, and then allow a long drink.

TO PRESERVE   As soon as the flowers have fallen, pick the seed heads and dry by hanging the heads upside down.

Epimedium
Hardy herbaceous perennials. An attractive plant and shade-loving, which makes it the more rewarding. I like to use it in flower and for its foliage. The flowers are pink or cream according to the variety, the leaves almost heart-shaped, turning a lovely bronzey colour in autumn: it is advisable to use them only when they are mature. It is only fair to mention that the flowers do not stand very well in water; in fact, try as I may I find they last only a day or so.

CONDITIONING   The stems of both flowers and leaves are improved if you place the ends in boiling water, before giving a long drink.

Eranthis (Winter Aconite)
Hardy tuberous-rooted perennial. This delightful yellow flower has the shape of a buttercup with a frill of green round the petals. A real herald of spring that flowers before any of the other bulbs; useful in a 'spring garden' in a carpet of moss with a few snowdrops or early primroses. One of the best varieties with the longer stems and more coppery-coloured foliage is *E. tubergenii*.

Eremurus (Foxtail Lily)
Hardy herbaceous perennial. *Eremurus robustus* is

an extremely handsome plant with very tall spikes of pink flowers, slightly resembling a lupin. I have never had any luck getting it to flower a second year, but I know many people who have had great success. There is a lovely orange species, *E. bungei*, which is very much smaller in size and therefore more generally useful as the flowers can be used in much smaller vases. However, *E. robustus* has been a joy to us in really big groups in Westminster Abbey on many occasions.

CONDITIONING No special treatment required.

Erica (Heather, Heath) and **Calluna** (Ling)
Better known as heather to all of us. I use small pieces in little vases in February with winter jasmine, the odd Christmas Rose and the first of the spring bulbs. I also like to have sprays when they have died off and are a nice brown colour, going in well with an arrangement of dahlias or chrysanthemums. They are being grown more and more, and wisely so, as they make for trouble-free gardening; once established, they spread rapidly and give colour all the year round. There is a variety for every month of the year. One of the most interesting in my opinion is called *Calluna vulgaris* 'H. E. Beale', it has a crop of double flowers all the way up the stems, and lasts for weeks in a little water.

TO PRESERVE The flowers of the tall Mediterranean varieties dry naturally on the plant; they have a tendency to drop, but I feel it is well worth using a few sprays for their delightful browny colour. The 'H. E. Beale' heather, on the other hand, is better dried off standing in a little water, and retains its pink colour for months.

Erigeron (Fleabane)
Hardy herbaceous perennial. Daisy-like flowers which prefer full sun and make a splash of colour for the front of the border; good to cut and useful for putting in mixed summer flower groups. The hybrids now generally grown come in a range of pinks and mauves.

CONDITIONING Place the stems in boiling water for a few minutes, before giving a long drink.

Eryngium
E. giganteum is a hardy biennial with green and white ornamental foliage and grey-blue flowers in summer, surrounded by spiny bracts; these dry

well and can be used all winter. The best variety is 'Slieve Donard'. The wild sea holly (*E. maritinum*) is also effective in a flower arrangement and excellent for drying. The perennial *E. planum* is rather more slender, and there are many richly-coloured forms of it.

Eryngium giganteum — Miss Wilmott's Ghost

TO PRESERVE Pick in full flower, remove leaves and hang upside down.

Erythronium (Dog's Tooth Violet)
Hardy bulbous perennial. These enchanting little bulbs have delicate drooping flowers with turned-back petals in pale pinks and creams, with many variations in their hybrid forms. They flourish in the protection of grass and increase rapidly. I enjoy using them in small vases and try to show the beauty of their unusual form.

CONDITIONING Give them a drink, and as they are very fragile great care must be taken not to bruise the petals.

I

Escallonia

Hardy or half hardy evergreen or deciduous flowering shrubs, growing well in sheltered gardens or by the sea. The arching sprays of blossom, rose-tinted or white, make them very good subjects for flower arranging. They come in July and August at a very welcome time of year when not many other shrubs are in flower. On Plate 3 you will see I have used it with roses. 'Apple Blossom', with pink and white flowers, and 'Pride of Donard', with vivid red flowers, are just two of the many excellent varieties.

CONDITIONING   Hammer the ends of the stems or put them in boiling water.

Eschscholtzia (Californian Poppy)

Hardy annuals. Poppy-like open flowers, in many bright hues, that thrive on poor sunbaked soil. They have finely-cut and glaucous foliage. My very first memory of them is of my delight as a child at being able to pull off their little green hats as they were bursting into bloom, and so hasten the process! Nowadays, I like to arrange them in a basket and enjoy their blaze of colour.

CONDITIONING   Dip ends of stems in boiling water for a few minutes, before giving a long drink.

Eucalyptus (Australian Gum)

Tall trees with attractive ornamental grey foliage and flowers varying from fluffy pink to shades of scarlet and cream. These trees give Australia its beautiful hazy grey look. In Britain, we are lucky in being able to import 'pads' of E. populifolius (a lovely round-leaved variety) and E. globulus (with pointed leaves) in large quantities in the winter; these leaf sprays last well and are excellent and economical to buy. There are several hardy varieties which are well worth growing here. E. gunnii grows twelve to fifteen feet with great speed and if protected for the first winter should get well established; it is ideal for cutting.

TO PRESERVE   If the ends of the stems are placed in glycerine and water, it takes on a lovely reddish look and lasts for months. E. populifolius is particularly good.

Eucharis grandiflora (Amazon Lily)

Stove bulbous evergreen plant. I have always called this bulb the 'Easter lily'. It grows on stems about two feet in height with open drooping white flowers; when I lift its head I always think I am looking at the loveliest and purest flower of all. Because so much of its beauty is lost if the head hangs, it is better arranged on short stems and is more generally used for sprays and bouquets.

Eucomis (Pineapple Flower)

Although some species are hardy in mild climates, these plants are generally grown in a greenhouse. In early July they produce stout stems carrying spikes of greenish-white flowers, and ending in a dense tuft of green leaves — hence the name. If you can grow them, they are most rewarding. I like to use them mixed in with a green and white group.

Eucryphia

Slightly tender shrub, with open single rose-like flowers; so like philadelphus that for a long time I mistook it for a late variety. E. glutinosa is perhaps the hardiest eucryphia, though I think that the hybrid E. x nymansensis is still more beautiful in flower. It lasts very much better if you remove most of the foliage as soon as you pick it.

CONDITIONING   Having stripped off the leaves, put the ends of the stems in boiling water, before giving a long drink.

Euonymus

E. europaeus is best known as our Spindle Tree bearing lovely pink berries in the autumn. It grows wild on many of our chalky hills, in Wiltshire particularly. E. europaeus fructu-albo has white berries instead of pink. As with all berried trees and shrubs, the Spindle tree can be arranged with a wide variety of materials; because of its awkward angular habit it is better as a background. The evergreen species of euonymus are invaluable, particularly the variegated E. radicans or E. fortunei 'Gracilis', which will cling to a wall rather like ivy, and the small E. radicans variegata, with green leaves margined with white, often acquiring a tinge of pink in winter. These are both helpful to put in winter vases, and like all variegated plants immediately add a light touch to a vase of evergreens. E. japonicus argenteo variegatus, the most brilliantly variegated, has rounded leaves looking as though they were splashed with cream paint. I find I often use a spray of this to cheer up a dried group.

CONDITIONING   Hammer the stems well, before putting in water.

Euphorbia (Spurge; Poinsettia)

Tender and hardy plants of many varieties, nearly all of them useful in flower arrangement. *Euphorbia fulgens*, a greenhouse species that is on sale in January, has orange flowers all along the stems, in arched sprays; an expensive luxury, but such a glorious flower to enjoy at a sparse time of year.

Euphorbia pulcherrima — Poinsettia

The poinsettia, *E. pulcherrima*, is another lovely exotic plant, which we have come to look forward to seeing in the shops at Christmas-time; generally thought of as a flower with brilliant red bracts, though thanks to Thomas Rochford we can now also avail ourselves of all the beautiful white species that he has brought from America and propagated in this country. I have used these white poinsettias for weddings in December and consider them a godsend as they give character to any vase of mixed foliage. A point I must make clear is that they last much better if you wash the roots and do not cut the stems. All euphorbias bleed when cut and great care must be taken to condition them first. So much for the hothouse varieties. The hardy herbaceous plants are a 'must' for the flower arranger's garden. *Euphorbia polychroma* has brilliant yellow bracts in early spring, giving a touch of sunlight to the border, and is good to cut. *E. robbiae* has lovely evergreen foliage and large yellow-green flowers. It makes a useful ground-cover. *E. lathyrus*, or caper spurge as I call it, has no striking colour, only green spikes and funny green seed heads, but is good to cut in winter, and has the added advantage that it is reputed to be a mole deterrent — I think this is quite true. *E. wulfenii*, with delightful tall spikes of yellowy flowers in May is something I can never get enough of; it has the most lovely shape and colour, will mix with any other flowers and lasts for weeks in water. The orange heads of *E. griffithii* are also very worth while, lasting for a long time in the border as well as in the house. *E. sikkimensis*, three to four feet, has crimson stems and red-veined leaves, with yellow flower bracts in July. The perennial *Euphorbia marginata*, perhaps better known as 'Snow-on-the-Mountain' has leaf bracts that look like flowers in green and white and is excellent for mixing in a green and white vase in midsummer. It stands very well in water once the stems have been burnt and given a long drink. There are many more but I have covered my favourites.

CONDITIONING It is most important to treat all spurges carefully. They bleed a white liquid from their stems, so never leave them out of water for any length of time. Scald the ends of the stems in boiling water before giving them a long drink.

Evening Primrose *see* OENOTHERA

Everlasting Flower *see* HELICHRYSUM

Everlasting Pea *see* LATHYRUS

Fagus sylvatica (Beech)

Deciduous tree. Beech in all its varieties — copper (*F. sylvatica purpurea*), cut-leaved (*F. sylvatica laciniata*) and others — is used a great deal for flower arrangement. It is excellent as a background in almost any vase. It is often preserved both at home and commercially and so can be used nearly all the year round; not only the foliage, but the nuts as well in all stages of development — very recently as a new experiment, I have had great success with putting them in glycerine. You can see the result on Colour Plate X.

CONDITIONING Hammer ends of stems well before putting them in water.

TO PRESERVE Beech leaves absorb glycerine almost better than any others, turning a lovely shade of copper in a matter of days. Hammer ends of stems well, allow a long drink, then place in the solution of glycerine, in July or August. If the branches are first put in a salt and water solution, this will result in variation of leaf tones in the final result.

Fatsia japonica (Fig Leaf Plant)

Hardy, or nearly hardy, evergreen shrub, with rounded deeply-cut leaves that are extremely useful in a vase of mixed foliage as on Colour Plate III. It will grow quite well in any really sheltered garden. I am always surprised to see it growing in London gardens, but these are usually well protected by buildings. The green and variegated varieties make good house plants.

TO PRESERVE The leaves may be put in glycerine and water and removed when they have turned pale brown.

Felicia bergeriana (Kingfisher Daisy)

Annual. A slightly tender little plant, but well worth growing for its long blooming period of brilliant blue daisy-like flowers. I like to use it in very small vases, remembering that because of its delicate form it can easily be overshadowed by other flowers.

Fern see ATHYRIUM, NEPHROLEPSIS, OSMUNDA, PTERIDIUM

Ficus elastica (India Rubber Plant)

A stove or house plant that is a handsome decoration in itself, but odd leaves are effective and helpful for a touch of the exotic in a mixed green group.

Filipendula

F. *hexapetala flore-pleno*, the double form of Dropwort, is a hardy herbaceous perennial with creamy-white plumey flowers in June. It is most effective for giving a light touch to a vase of delicate summer flowers. My grandmother always grew it, and used it often with cream sweet peas

for the centre of her table. It lasts surprisingly well with no special treatment. The flowers of many varieties of *Filipendula* in a wide range of reds and pinks, to white, with fluffy flat heads, are attractive in groups of mixed summer flowers, though I often feel they are better value if you leave them until their green seed head stage; they look most attractive then in a foliage arrangement, often drying off to a desirable brown shade, when they can be used all through the winter.

CONDITIONING Hammer ends of stems well and put into warm water.

TO PRESERVE When in its seed head form, cut and remove the foliage, stand the stems in an inch of water and allow them to dry off slowly in a warm atmosphere.

Flame Flower see TROPAEOLUM

Flax see LINUM

Fœniculum (Fennel)

Really a herb, but used in flower arrangement for its feathery light foliage and attractive yellow flower. Easily grown from seed, it is a good flower for anyone making a new garden and wanting

Freesias (see facing page)

quick results for picking. Giant fennel has a big seed head much used for dried arrangements.

CONDITIONING Place the ends of the stems in boiling water for two seconds, before giving a long drink.

TO PRESERVE When the seed has set, hang the stems upside down to dry.

Forsythia (Golden Bells)

Hardy deciduous shrub. With clever pruning *Forsythia intermedia spectabilis* makes a lovely shrub, a mass of golden flowers in early spring clustered on dark stems before the leaves appear; it is a good foil for daffodils. Varieties differ in shades of yellow; one of the best is 'Beatrix Farrand'. Forsythia is quite one of the best things to force, but it does take about five weeks to come into full bloom. I find it best to pick some sprays in January, and then to hammer the ends of the stems well and put them in warm water in a warm room after twenty-four hours in the cold. This gives sprays of bloom in the house several weeks before they flower in the garden.

CONDITIONING Hammer ends of stems well, before putting in warm water for several hours.

Fortunella margarita (Kumquat)

A delicate citrus, bearing small almost oblong oranges. I have only once seen them growing, in Australia, and enjoyed using small sprays in a little vase of mixed apricot colours. I have bought the fruit here and mounted some on wires and used them in the winter quite often — but this is not quite the same.

Foxglove *see* DIGITALIS

Francoa ramosa (Maiden's Wreath, Bridal Wreath)

Slightly tender perennial plant with ornamental foliage and spikes of white flowers in late summer. The sprays are delicate and pretty in vases of all kinds of flowers, particularly good mixed with whites and ideal for wedding groups.

CONDITIONING Hammer the stems well, or put them in boiling water.

Freesia

A tender cormous plant with the sweetest smelling flowers of all. The hybrids of *F. refracta*, so im-proved in recent years, now come in every shade of yellow, and white, mauves, pinks and reds. Hybridization is largely due to the Dalrymple brothers who lived in the New Forest and spent the greater part of their lives working to get the results that we see today. It is now hard to visualize the spindly little yellow flowers they once were. I like to see them arranged in a mass on their own, or in a silver sauce-boat. However, they do mix well with other flowers and can well be put in a vase of, say, mixed pinks or reds to pick up a particular colour. The really large white freesias make a lovely bride's bouquet, as do the new and exciting double blooms.

French Marigold *see* TAGETES

Fringed Pink *see* DIANTHUS

Fritillaria (Crown Imperial, Fritillary)

Bulbous. The Crown Imperial has an elegant flower with hanging bell-shaped blossoms in orange or yellow colouring, and a tuft of leaves at

Fritillaria imperialis

An arrangement in shades of orange and flame in a dark-brown wooden milk-bowl — a suitable container to balance the stately weight of the Crown Imperials, with five Barbeton daisies and a few flame-coloured tulips

the top of the spire, rather like the top of a pine-apple. The bulbs need good drainage and as they are loved by slugs it is very necessary to have plenty of anti-slug mixture available. Excellent subjects for arranging in really large groups (they look their best in copper or wooden containers as on page 130) and one of the first of the really long-stemmed flowers to come into flower; so that they are welcomed by all who have to cope with big vases each week.

CONDITIONING They stand extremely well in water and so require no special treatment, apart from the usual long drink.

The best known of the smaller species is *F. meleagris*, or Snake's Head Fritillary, standing not more than a foot high, with delicate nodding heads chequered in pale and deep purple. They flourish in turf, growing naturally in water meadows, and seemingly enjoying the moisture and protection that grass can give them. I really feel when arranging them that one must keep the fragile effect of their delicate stems and drooping heads; so as not to detract from this, they are best silhouetted against a plain background (see colour frontispiece).

Fuchsia

Tender and hardy deciduous flowering shrubs, often growing as hedges in southern Ireland and many other places with a mild climate. They have made a big comeback in recent years, after a spell of neglect following their popularity in Victorian days. Dazzling mixtures of pinks and petunias, scarlets and purples — that sometimes seem wildly improbable. I love to use their clusters of bell-shaped flowers as a cut flower, but there are few opportunities as the hothouse varieties are seldom cut; also I think few people realise that they last so well in water. However, a chance to use them is always rewarding for the cascading bells which hang over the edge of vase or container (see Plate 9).

CONDITIONING Put the ends of the stems in boiling water for a few minutes, before standing in water for a long drink.

Funkia *see* HOSTA

Gaillardia (Blanket Flower)

Hardy annuals and perennials. Has good showy daisy-like flowers in summer, often in contrasting shades of red and yellow. They give a good centre to any vase, and mixed with any turning foliage look extremely well. The hybrid varieties last very well in water.

Galanthus (Snowdrop)

Hardy bulb, blooming in winter and spring, and not everyone realizes that there is such a large number of varieties. In fact they bloom in one species or another for about four months, the earliest coming like a breath of spring in December. *Galanthus caucasicus* is one of the earliest to flower and *G. elwesii* is one of the finest, with broad glaucous leaves. They all have drooping white bell-like heads, with a variety of markings in the form of different bands of green from the tip of the petals to the edge of the calyx. Lovely to pick for the house and to put in tiny vases or to use in a bowl in a bed of moss. Beverly Nicholls suggested uprooting a few clumps and replanting them in bowls in the house — they do look very attractive; when these are finished, the bulbs should be separated for planting again the the garden. This splitting up is a very good thing in any case from time to time and should be done immediately after flowering while still green.

Galtonia candicans (Giant Summer Hyacinth)

Hardy bulbous plant. The white bells of *G. candicans* flower in August. Its nice long stems make it a most useful cut flower to mix with shorter subjects for a late-summer wedding. There is a green variety *G. princeps* that is beautiful but very rare. See illustration on page 132.

Gardenia (Cape Jasmine)

A tender evergreen shrub with sweetly-scented white flowers; the double-flowered form *Gardenia jasminoides* is generally grown. It is used chiefly as a spray to be worn or for a bride's bouquet. However, I love to have gardenias in the house, if I can, in a small bowl or done as a pyramid as in the photograph of roses on Plate 20.

CONDITIONING Every care is required to prevent the flowers from being bruised as they get dis-coloured at the least touch. For special care over-night, stretch a piece of tissue paper over a bowl of water, secure with an elastic band, make small holes in the paper and push the stems through. This keeps the petals out of the water.

Galtonia candicans
(see text on page 131)

Garrya elliptica
Hardy evergreen shrub that grows well on a north wall, though it makes a beautiful tree of good shape if allowed to grow in the open. The male plant bears grey-green catkins in winter and is one of my favourite shrubs. You will see I have used it in many of the arrangements photographed, and I think it looks particularly effective with orchids, as on Colour Plate XI.

CONDITIONING If you want to force it, it is important to hammer the ends of the stems, before putting in warm water.

Genista (Broom)
Hardy deciduous flowering shrubs of the pea family. The Plantagenets took their badge from *G. anglica*. The spreading *G. lydia* is a delightful low arching shrub covered in spikes of clear yellow flowers in June. Small pieces used in the house add .the much needed touch of yellow to a mixed summer group. All genistas need plenty of sun, so they make good subjects for the heath garden.
CONDITIONING I find that, like gorse, the stems last best in water if they are first well scraped with a sharp knife an inch or so up from the base. Be careful that the exposed white part of the stem is well under water in your arrangement.

Gentiana
Hardy perennials. There are many varieties of this adorable little trumpet-shaped blue flower: *G. acaulis*, a lime-lover and spring-flowering; *G. verna*, small but brilliantly blue, also in spring; *G. septemfida*, with flowers right down the stem in summer; *G. sino-ornata*, the one I find I can grow most easily and I use continually in the autumn. A few of these little bright blue flowers make a charming table decoration — just on their own in a small shell or bowl.
CONDITIONING Always pick when fully open and put them in warm water immediately.

Geranium (Cranesbill)
The bedding plants generally referred to as 'geraniums' are really pelargoniums. Cranesbill are hardy perennials, ranging from dwarf kinds grown on the rockery to those for the herbaceous border. The best kinds to grow are *G. pratense* and *G. grandiflorum*, both bluish purple. *G. sanguineum*, a brilliant magenta, is one I am particularly fond of; it grows a little taller and flowers for a long period, at least three months, which is a great advantage. *G. pratense* has the added attraction of lovely coloured leaves in the autumn; although these do not last very long, they are well worth picking to use just for a day or so.
CONDITIONING Always place the ends of the stems in boiling water for a few seconds, before giving a long drink.

Garrya elliptica

Gerbera jamesonii (Barberton Daisy, Transvaal Daisy)

In a very warm part of the country *G. jamesonii* and the hybrids derived from it can be grown out of doors, but elsewhere they are really only suitable as greenhouse plants. Native to South Africa, they naturally thrive in sunshine, but are being grown in Britain, under glass, more and more, selling in great quantities as cut flowers and used for bouquets and sprays. I find they last well and I like them in vases; as they are grown nearly all the year round under glass, they are particularly useful when other flowers are scarce. I use them with dried material as all their golden and apricot shades go so well with it.

CONDITIONING Place ends of stems in boiling water, before giving a long drink.

TO PRESERVE Although I have not tried this, I feel that they are the kind of subject that should react well to the American hot sand treatment. I understand that daisy-like and open-type flowers do well in this way.

Geum (Avens)

Hardy perennial. A showy red, yellow, or orange flower only suitable for small containers as a cut flower, because it will only hold up its head if cut on short stems. I use the red ones most of all as they have such a brilliant colour, with black fluffy centres.

CONDITIONING Cut with short stems and dip in boiling water for a few seconds, before giving a long drink.

Ginkgo biloba (Maidenhair Tree)

Deciduous tree with attractive foliage rather like enlarged sprays of maidenhair fern, hence its common name. I pick the leaves in autumn, when they turn to gold.

CONDITIONING Hammer ends of stems well, before giving a long drink.

Gladiolus (Sword Lily)

Half hardy corm. Vigorous spikes of flowers in a wide variety of colours. The corms are rewarding to grow as they produce good blooms easily, though better results are obtained with additional feeding and plenty of moisture. The smaller blooms, such as the dainty *G. primulinus* and 'Butterfly', are more useful for the flower arranger; they are much easier to arrange and have a lovely range of soft colours. On the other hand, the really large stems can be a joy for a big group and give so much scope for a wide choice of reds, pinks and petunia to mix together in a big 'clashing red' vase. (See Colour Plate VIII.) By planting in batches each week, one has a long picking period. Lift and store the corms every autumn.

CONDITIONING Cut the ends of the stems under water and remove a small piece every four or five days. Always remove the dead flowers; with the stems in water, all the buds will open eventually. If by chance you have too many gladioli coming into flower at the same time, it is better to pick them when the buds are just showing colour and leave them out of water, preferably on a cold stone floor or in a cardboard box with the lid on; cut the ends of the stems and put them in warm water when you want them. They can be left like that for a week or more.

TO PRESERVE If you ever let the flowers go to seed, they are very nice in a dried group after being hung head down to dry off.

Gloriosa (Glory Lily)

Greenhouse tuberous-rooted climbers. Tender red and yellow gaily-marked lily with turned-back petals. Rare, as they are natives of tropical Africa, but they do come into Covent Garden every now and again. I have had fun using them with mixed reds or fruit and flower groups, to which they add a delightfully exotic effect.

Glory of the Snow *see* CHIONODOXA

Gloxinia

Tender tuberous-rooted plants with trumpet-like flowers, their texture more like velvet than anything else, in the richest red and purple colours. As they are greenhouse plants, they are not generally considered a cut flower. It often must seem such a waste to cut them, but for some special occasion I cannot begin to tell you how lovely they can look, their rich colouring enhancing a vase of cut flowers quite superbly. If you are tempted to cut a stem or two, I can assure you that they will last extremely well.

Godetia

A good hardy annual in long-stemmed and dwarf

varieties, with an excellent colour-range. I like the shell-pink, salmon and mauve, as they blend so well with various colours, and there are many good crimsons and reds, which go well in vases of 'clashing reds', a lovely white one and a startling shade of orange. If you don't grow them yourself, bunches are often on sale in the summer-time. They are a good standby as they last so well, and can be put in a mass in a silver bowl or used as odd stems as part of a colour scheme.

CONDITIONING   The stems are tough, so it is as well to hammer them before giving them a long drink.

Golden Bells *see* FORSYTHIA

Golden Chain *see* LABURNUM

Golden Privet *see* LIGUSTRUM

Grevillea
Greenhouse and tender shrubs. *G. rosmarinifolia*, though half-hardy, can be grown in a shrub border in the southern counties, but requires the shelter of a wall. The greenhouse shrub *G. robusta* (Silk Bark Oak) has delicate fern-like leaves, standing well when cut, which gives it an advantage over many other fern-like subjects. It is also a good subject for preserving in glycerine.

CONDITIONING   Put ends of stems in boiling water for a few seconds, before it has a long drink.

Guelder Rose *see* VIBURNUM

Guernsey Lily *see* NERINE

Gunnera manicata
Hardy herbaceous perennial. A very handsome water-loving plant with the most enormous leaves,

Gunnera manicata

rather like a rhubarb. Best used in early spring
before the leaves have fully grown. The flowers
and seed heads of *G. manicata* are superb, but so
large that they are of little value except for really
huge groups.

CONDITIONING The leaves should have their
stalks dipped in boiling water and then be
completely submerged in a bath of cold water
overnight.

Gypsophila (Chalk Plant)

Hardy annuals and perennials. This flower used to
be looked on as a foil for carnations and sweet
peas; however, I feel those days have gone, and
we now prefer these other flowers unobscured and
unfussed. By the same token we like the charming
cloudy hazy feeling achieved by having gypsophila
quite alone, arranged in a glass goblet or urn to
make the most of its ethereal lightness. There are
many kinds, both double and single, in pinks and
white.

Hacquetia epipactis (Dondia)

A delightful spring-flowering plant that is worth
its weight in gold. The small daisy-like flowers
have green petals and a yellow centre. It has short
little stems and is only useful for very small vases.
However, it gives a good centre to any really small
vase in February (*see* frontispiece), or can be added
to a 'moss garden' of early primroses and early
little bulbs. It grows well in the rock garden and
flowers freely in partial shade, but is better if left
undisturbed and if you want to split up the plant
this must be done after flowering. It lasts surprisingly well in water and needs no special
attention.

Haemanthus (Blood Flower, Red Cap Lily)

A bulbous plant for the greenhouse. *H. multiflorus*
is the one I know and like best: it has erect lily-like
scarlet flowers on stems about a foot high. The cut
flowers can be bought in the autumn, and they
make a change from chrysanthemums.

CONDITIONING Place the stems in warm water,
cut the ends of the stems under water, fill up the
vase with cold water and leave for several hours.

Halesia carolina (Snowdrop Tree, Silver-bell Tree)

Hardy flowering tree, with small white bells, as

the name implies. Very nice with the foliage
removed, used as a background to any white
flower.

Hamamelis (Witch-Hazel)

Hardy deciduous shrub flowering on bare branches
in January, with clusters of yellow that are a joy to
behold. I love to pick a small spray or two to put in
a vase of little spring bits in the very early spring.
I have seen it in bloom with the snow still on the
ground. *H. mollis* is scented, *H. japonica* is not.

CONDITIONING Hammer ends of stems well,
before giving a long drink.

Hare's Tail Grass *see* LAGURUS

Hawthorn *see* CRATAEGUS

Heather *see* ERICA

Hedera (Ivy)

Hedera, with ornamental leaves green and variegated, and much better known as ivy, is one of the
commonest of the hardy evergreen climbing plants.
Often used these days as a house plant and in pots
and troughs for house or shop-window displays of
all kinds. I grow many varieties to cut all the year
round for their foliage. The giant ivy *Hedera
colchica dentata* and its variegated form, *H. colchica
dentata variegata*, *H. canariensis*, *H. helix sagittaefolia*
and *H. helix conglomerata* are to name but a few;
there are so many kinds. Lasting extremely well in
water they are much sought after as cut sprays,
giving any vase in which they are used a flowing
line by their natural down-sweeping form; this is
an excellent help when arranging the narrow-
necked vases that are so often used in churches.

TO PRESERVE The stems of ivy berries last very
well if put in a solution of glycerine. I had great
success as soon as I tried this. They are shown on
Colour Plate X.

Hedychium gardnerianum (Ginger Lily)

Greenhouse perennial. Spikes of very fragrant
white and yellow flowers with handsome broad
green leaves, growing wild in the Pacific Islands,
where their heady scent hangs in the air. I would
use them at every opportunity, though many
people find the scent overpowering. Having nice
long stems, they are ideal for large groups.

The slice of Japanese walnut as a base, used with a "well" pin-holder makes for easy arranging of an interesting collection of material which does not require much material. Here, *Hedera helix*, Lady fern and *Molucella laevis* are used with a few tulips

CONDITIONING Put the ends of the stems in boiling water for several minutes, before giving a long drink.

Helenium (Sneezewort)

Hardy herbaceous perennials. A good plant for the back of the border, with yellow or brown daisy-like flowers that cut well and help the autumn vases. There are also dwarf summer-flowering varieties.

CONDITIONING Hammer ends of stems well, before putting in warm water.

Helianthemum (Rock Rose)

Hardy dwarf evergreen with open rose-like red and yellow flowers. Not really suitable to cut as they do not last very long in a vase, but I some-times slip one in to add a bit of colour just for an evening.

CONDITIONING The ends of the stems need putting into boiling water for a few seconds, before they are given a drink.

Helianthus (Sunflower)

Hardy annual. The single annual sunflower is popular as a cut flower and lasts well in water. The bright-yellow or more unusual browny varieties are the ones I like best and they add a focal or central point to a late summer vase. They mix well with berries and autumn foliages.

CONDITIONING Put the ends of the stems into boiling water, and then give them a long drink.

Helichrysum (Everlasting Flower)

The half-hardy annuals are grown for picking and preserving for use in winter. Their daisy-like flower heads are surrounded by papery bracts in bright orange, red and yellow. The perennials usually have grey foliage and papery-looking white or silvery flowers, which also dry very well.

TO PRESERVE The perennials are best dried by having all the foliage removed and being hung upside down. The round flowers of the annuals, however, need to have thickish florist's wire pushed right down the centre of the flower into the stalk, before being bunched and hung upside down to dry. It is always better if you can do this, as the stems tend to be brittle and so often the head falls off. Remove all the leaves before hanging up.

Heliotropium peruvianum (Heliotrope, Cherry Pie)

Half hardy perennial, but usually grown as an annual, with deep-purple flowers and a delicious scent. Lovely to use tucked into any little summer vase, but is better if picked with short stems.

CONDITIONING Pick with short stems and put the ends in boiling water for a few minutes, before giving a long drink.

Helipterum *see* ACROLINIUM

Helleborus (Hellebore; Christmas Rose; Lenten Rose)

Hardy evergreen perennials. For the flower arranger, quite one of the most useful of all the plants I can name. Starting with the Christmas Rose (*H. niger*): this is a lovely flower to have; it grows well under the shade of an apple tree, or against a wall as it likes lime, and it will give you pure white open flowers in midwinter — not always at Christmas time, alas, but if it is sheltered with a pane of glass this will often bring it into flower more quickly. The green helleborus are 'musts' for any flower arranger's garden. *H. viridis* (Green Hellebore), *H. fœtidus* (Stinking Hellebore) and *H. corsicus* all flower in the very early spring, which makes them specially useful; they cheer up the remains of a dried group, and mix well with all the early spring flowers. The Lenten Rose *H. orientalis* hybrids, with open flowers in muted shades of whites and mauves, usually have brown spotted markings; they need careful conditioning, but for me they are a joy to have, even if they do not last very long.

CONDITIONING For the Christmas Roses, it is best to take a needle and prick here and there across the stems from the flower head and especially under the water-line. For the green types, put the ends of the stems in boiling water for a few seconds and then put them in a can up to their heads in water overnight; pricking the stem is also good. Another good method is to press the point of a sharp pin against the stalk just below the flower head, and draw it down to the bottom of the stem making a fine groove along it; this should be followed by a long drink. All hellebores are much better for being in really deep water, especially the Christmas Roses. If you want to arrange them for effect in a shallow container, then it is advisable to

Flowers of the Christmas rose, *Helleborus niger*, with holly leaves

remove them at night and stand them in deep water until the next day.

Hemerocallis (Day Lily)
Hardy herbaceous perennial with yellow, orange, apricot or bronze-red flowers in summer; the flowers last for only one day, but the plants go on blooming for several weeks. Some of the hybrids have lovely colours, and larger flowers, and are well worth growing.
CONDITIONING   Cut the ends of the stems on the slant, before giving them a long drink.

Hepatica triloba (Anemone)
This is the plant still often listed by nurserymen as *Anemone hepatica*, though it is now properly called *Hepatica triloba* or *H. transsilvanica*. A hardy perennial, it is a lime-loving anemone with bright-

blue, cerise or white flowers, opening in February, at just the right time to put in a vase of little early spring flowers.

Heracleum mantegazzianum (Cow Parsnip)
Hardy perennial. Giant flat fluffy heads, like a big cow parsley, and very serrated leaves that turn a lovely lime-green-yellow as they fade; this makes them a useful addition to any flower arrangement. However, the plant grows to an enormous size, usually reaching ten feet each year, so it should only be grown if you have plenty of space.
CONDITIONING   Dip stems of leaves and flowers in boiling water for a few minutes, before giving a long drink.

Hesperis matronalis (Sweet Rocket)
This delightful perennial is a very old-fashioned little flower — with white, pale-pink or mauve

small flowers clustered on tall stems. It has a delicate appearance, that makes one imagine it would not last well, but in fact it stands extremely well in water, and adds a lovely light touch to a vase of early summer flowers. It is a plant well worth growing for a little early colour in the border and has an attractive feathery green seed head.

CONDITIONING   Lasting so well in water, it needs little special attention; but as with all flowers, it is the better for a few hours in deep water after picking.

TO PRESERVE   When the seed has formed, pick the stems and hang them upside down to dry. They add a light feathery touch to any dried group.

Heuchera

Hardy perennial. Many varieties derived from *H. sanguinea*, with attractive ornamental foliage and red and pink flowers. The delicate flower-sprays are good in mixed vases, and I like to use the small leaves for putting at the base of a little group.

CONDITIONING   I find the flowers require no special care, but the leaves are better for their stems being burnt in a little boiling water.

Hibiscus

The half-hardy tropical species are quite beautiful and have trumpet-shaped flowers in glowing rich reds and pinks, also yellow and orange, lasting only one day. They are the only flower I know that lasts as well out of water as it does in; because of this they make a lovely table decoration laid on the table-cloth, with no vase needed at all.

Himalayan Poppy *see* MECONOPSIS

Hippeastrum (Amaryllis)

A greenhouse bulbous plant with enormous red, pink or white lily flower heads and very good pointed green leaves. *H. aulicum* is the one I get in Covent Garden and use in big groups for weddings and special functions. The Barbados Lily, *H. puniceum*, makes a beautiful centre for an exotic group like that shown on Colour Plate III. It gives a vase of fruit a really luxurious look, as you can see from Colour Plate VIII.

CONDITIONING   Cut the stem, put a cane up the centre and tie firmly; this supports the head which is sometimes too heavy for the hollow stem.

Hippophae rhamnoides (Sea Buckthorn)

Hardy deciduous flowering shrub yielding a rich crop of orange berries which remain on angular brown stems long after the leaves have gone. For the berries both the male and the female kind have to be grown near together.

TO PRESERVE   Use the berries in the normal way, and they gradually dry off while the stems are in water; they may shrivel a little, but is is hardly noticeable in a winter group, and they are well worth while for the colour they give.

Hoheria lyalii

Half-hardy flowering shrub with single white flowers rather like philadelphus, but much later — the flowers appear in July and August.

CONDITIONING   Strip off all the foliage, hammer the stems and put them in hot water.

Hollyhock *see* ALTHAEA

Holy Thistle *see* SILYBUM

Honesty *see* LUNARIA

Honeysuckle *see* LONICERA

Hosta (Plantain Lily, Corfu Lily, Funkia)

Hardy perennials. I cannot praise them too highly. They are superb plants to grow, liking shade and moisture, but surprisingly easy. If they are grown in full sun you tend to get a better crop of their delicate lilac lily-like flowers; if they have more shade, the foliage is generally better and their striking spade-shaped leaves are very much larger. They are one of those dual-purpose plants that are a 'must' for the flower arranger. I can never have too many. I think I started growing them first of all for their leaves. These have such a wide colour range from lime yellow to deep green; they make excellent ground cover, in which no weeds can survive, and give good contrast in the front of any shrub border or by the water-side, their broad shape a good foil to the grassy rush and iris type of bog plants. My favourite must be *H. fortunei albopicta*, which by the middle of May has unfurled a mass of bright butter-yellow spade-shaped leaves, edged with pale green; these are ideal for the centre of any foliage group (Colour Plate IV), and add a touch of sunlight to a vase in shades of lilac

An arrangement using the young leaves of *Hosta fortunei albo-picta*.

K

or pinks; they fade to an all-over green as the summer goes on. *H. albo-marginata*, on the other hand, has reverse markings, green centre with white edge; it is a wonderful stand-by as it retains a good colour all summer. *H. fortunei albo-picta aurea* has leaves that are entirely yellow, and this makes it a valuable contribution to any small arrangement. The Sunningdale Nurseries have a new variety, *H. fortunei* 'Yellow Edge'; it is the reverse of *H. fortunei albo-picta*, with green centre and yellow edge to the leaf. *H. undulata* is a smaller plant with twisted green leaves with a band of creamy white in the middle (you can see it on Colour Plate VI). The handsome large and bold

Leaves and flowers of *Hosta sieboldiana*

leaves of *H. sieboldiana* are a real blue-grey, crinkled and deeply veined, ideal used at the base of any large group. *H. crispula*, *H. fortunei*, *H. tardiflora* and *H. plantaginea*, with its unusual white bell flowers, are all worth growing.

CONDITIONING Soak the leaves well, either by putting them in very deep water or by submerging them completely under water for several hours.

TO PRESERVE The leaves as they fade and turn colour from green to pale yellow, are well worth pressing in sheets of newspaper placed under the carpet for several days. Always be careful to see that you pick a leaf that is perfect and also that no part of the leaf is turned under before pressing. The seed heads, once formed, are also worth picking, as soon as they are set; I try to gather them before they open. If you dry them in the house, you have a better chance of the seeds staying in the turned-back petals. I stand mine in a small amount of water and keep them in a very warm place, then store them standing in a pot out of the way until I want to use them. They are worth a great deal of care as they are so beautiful. You can see a dried head of *H. fortunei* on Colour Plate XII.

Humea elegans (Amaranth Feathers)
Half-hardy biennial. Plumes of feathery red flower heads, smelling sweetly of incense. Because of this it is known to me as the Incense Plant. In the past I have used it on many occasions, arranged with lilies and heads of hydrangea. Constance Spry loved it, and for many years had it specially grown. Regrettably, one rarely sees it today, except sometimes as a bedding-out plant in parks in midsummer.
TO PRESERVE Remove the leaves and dry off for use in pot-pourri, then hang up the heads to dry for using in dried groups in winter.

Hyacinthus (Hyacinth)
Hardy bulbous-rooted perennials, with fragrant spikes of pink, blue and white flowers in spring. Generally used for pot culture and forced for the house in pans and bowls. They look so nice as a cut flower, and I find that once they become straggly in their bowls it is much better to pick them and enjoy them in their last stages in a vase. Quite one of the best flowers for indoors, as their scent prevails throughout any warm room, and I also think they are well worth growing in the garden.
CONDITIONING Cut the stems from the bulbs, leaving a piece of stem and some leaves behind for nourishment for the bulb for next year. Carefully wrap a sheet of newspaper around the bunch of flowers and put them in a jug of deep water for a few hours.

Hydrangea

Hardy or slightly tender shrubby plants. The variety that is generally grown in the garden and greenhouse is *H. macrophylla hortensis*, though *H. paniculata*, with beautifully pointed cream heads, is not one to overlook, and neither are the Lace-cap varieties. They are all very showy garden plants and excellent for cutting, lasting better if picked when they have been out on the plant for some time. They add the solidity so important to any large group of flowers if a few heads are placed centrally. With a good colour range of white, pinks and blues, they are a wonderful dual-purpose plant, used either fresh or preserved. *H. arborescens grandiflora* has slightly drooping cream heads which turn a lovely shade of green, and it is at this later stage that I love them most. The oak-leaved *Hydrangea quercifolia* is well worth growing for its superb foliage that turns a brilliant autumn colour.
CONDITIONING Place the ends of the stems in boiling water for several minutes, then submerge the whole head and stem under water for a few hours; they can be left overnight, but no longer than that in case the heads become transparent under water. They seem to drink through their heads, so it is quite a good idea to leave these covered with damp paper to be quite certain they do not flag, if you are using them in a big group for some important occasion. I find this a helpful tip for the quick recovery of a flagging pot plant.
TO PRESERVE Leave the flower heads of *H. macrophylla hortensis* on the plant as long as possible, usually until the middle of September, or until the heads are fading and turning from pink to red, or blue to green. Then cut the stems, remove the leaves, stand the stems in a little water and put the vase in a very warm place — for instance high up in the kitchen so that they get as much warm air as possible, or in a linen cupboard or boiler room. The quicker they dry, the better colour they seem to keep. Having dried them, store carefully in a box or in a dry place as they quickly lose their colour. By this method you should be at least seventy-five per cent successful, but you will find that a few curl up. Do not hang them upside down; they dry much better with their 'feet' in water and their heads in the warm.

Hypericum (Rose of Sharon, St John's Wort)

Evergreen and deciduous shrubs, mostly hardy, with many pet names. The Rose of Sharon (*Hypericum calycinum*) is a good evergreen ground-cover plant, with single yellow flowers and, later, good sprays of small fruits; these I find most useful. The new Hidcote variety is a great improvement on the older kinds. The fruits mix well in small vases of flowers and foliage in autumn.

Iberis (Candytuft)

Hardy annual and perennial. The gay little annual *Iberis umbellata* with close flat heads of pastel pink, mauve and white, is good grown in the garden as a border plant or for edging. I like to use it in the house in a mass in a small low bowl or basket. Small pieces mix well in groups of summer flowers, picking up the soft colours. The evergreen perennial, *I. saxatilis*, which has white flowers, is a very good rockery plant as it blooms for such a long time. Suttons have the seed of both white and pink perennials (the pink *I. gibraltarica*, best-treated as a biennial, and only six inches high, is new to me but sounds most attractive); they also have a dwarf mixed annual hybrid which should be very useful.
TO PRESERVE If the flowers are allowed to seed, they form effective open green seed heads. Wait until these are well formed before picking, and hang them upside down to dry. As the stems are quite short, they are only suitable for small groups.

Iceland Poppy *see* PAPAVER

Ice Plant *see* MESEMBRYANTHEMUM

Ilex aquifolium (Holly)

Hardy evergreen trees and shrubs with deep green or variegated foliage. It is only in very recent years that I have become acquainted with the fantastic numbers of varieties of holly that there are; I would guess at least a hundred. Welcome for its bright red berries for Christmas decoration — in fact the house never seems decorated until the holly is up. Used then for decorating our churches, and hung in bunches or made into garlands for our front doors. It is so much a part of Christmas. The yellow-edged holly, *I. aquifolium aurea* was the very first tree that I planted when we came to our cottage; this because it is slow growing, and variegated holly is a lovely tree to have in a garden.

A Christmas table decoration using fruit and dried seed heads with holly leaves

CONDITIONING Holly is really better if it is kept out of water; if it is standing in water, the leaves tend to fall off very quickly. It is a good idea to spray the leaves with Polycel; it certainly seems to keep them on rather longer.

Impatiens (Busy Lizzie)
Stove perennial. Busy Lizzie, a plant so well-known to everyone, is an *I. sultani* hybrid, a fleshy-leaved and brittle-stemmed plant that flowers continually all the summer with a mass of pink or white flowers. It is of no value as a cut flower, but I mention it all the same, as it is so very much a house plant, flourishing on many window sills.

Incarvillea delavayi
Hardy perennial, with pink or rose-coloured flowers and attractive deeply-cut leaves. Not a well-known cut flower, but the few times I have had the chance to use it I was agreeably surprised how well it lasted.

Incense Plant *see* HUMEA

India-Rubber Plant *see* Ficus

Ipomoea (Morning Glory, American Bell-bind, Convolvulus)
Tender perennials and half-hardy annuals. *I. rubro-coerulea* (or *Pharbitis tricolor*), the blue Morning Glory, is the best known. Growing at random in parts of Australia, it makes a glorious mass of brilliant blue, quite breathtakingly lovely. Grown here in pots as an annual, it gives very good results; the flowers start bright blue in the morning, fading to purple as the day wears on. Try as one may, they will only last an hour or so in water; I have used them only once for a lunch table, and they just survived and no more. Of the same family, the common white convolvulus, a rampant weed, can also be used as a table decoration, and looks pretty, but again, it will only last for an hour or two. The wood rose of Hawaii is the seed head of Ipomoea. It dries naturally on the plant before it is picked, and in the last few years has been sold in large quantities all over the world. I like to use them in dried groups. They need careful handling as they are very brittle.

Iris (Flag, Orris Root, Fleur de Luce)
Hardy perennials, some are bulbous-rooted and some rhizomatous. The most popular are the June-flowering Bearded iris, useful plants for the flower arranger's garden as the foliage is most decorative, as well as the flower. They have the most unusual dusky colours, which lend themselves to some lovely flower groups, and large heads on long stems, in soft mauve, purple, yellow, brownish and orange, shades, also grey and pure white. Useful for any large flower vase. The Dutch, Spanish and English irises are a little shorter, growing just a foot in height. These come in stronger, harder colours, blues and yellows, flowering in June and July (though they are forced under glass so that we are able to buy them in the early spring; they are more popular then, as of course there is not such a wide choice of flowers in general, and they are a good buy as they last well in water).

Iris histrioides

The genus is large and varied, with a long period of bloom, starting in January with *I. stylosa* (*I. unguicularis*); its delightful mauve blooms are greeted with open arms, being one of the very first flowers to cut. They last only a day or so and are better picked in bud. It is fun to see them actually burst open in a warm room, and as flowering continues it is possible to replace them daily. These are followed by *I. histroides*, which is my favourite, china blue and enchanting. *Iris reticulata*, in all its blue and purple shades, is another charmer. *Iris tuberosa*, the snakeshead or widow iris, is one that is worth a mention as it has such enchanting little green heads with black velvety petals; it is a bit difficult to grow, but comes into Covent Garden in the spring, and is lovely with a few foliages or arranged with the striped *clusiana* tulips. Altogether, there is something from the iris world for the first six or seven months of the year.

Three irises that are worth growing just for their foliage alone: *I. foetidissima variegata* has cream striped leaves, evergreen and quite easy to manage. *I. pseudacorus*, the common yellow-flowered pond iris, has excellent tapering green leaves which last well in water and are a good background for a summer vase; like all irises they stand well in shallow water and are nice in an oriental group, with a predominance of water. The yellow-striped leaves of this form, *I. pseudacorus variegata*, are most useful, especially in early spring when the foliage is buttercup yellow before fading to plain green in late summer. *I. pallida dalmatica*, a very old plant with deliciously fragrant lavender flowers, is really most helpful as it retains its exceptionally grey foliage through the summer.

Finally, three irises that have good seed heads. *I. foetidissima* is quite one of the best: not only has it good dark-green foliage, but beautiful seed heads that burst open to display bright orange seeds. *I. ochroleuca* and *I. pseudacorus* both have excellent green seed pods that dry well.

CONDITIONING Cut the ends of the stems on the slant, before giving a long drink. Carefully remove each flower as it fades, so that the next one can open.

TO PRESERVE When the seed pods form, pick and hang them upside down to dry. With *I. foetidissima*, I find that is is better to stand the stems in a little water and dry them off in the warm, as sometimes the seeds fall out if they are hung upside down.

Ixia (African Corn Lily)
Half-hardy bulbous plant, with clusters of star-like

Ixias

flowers of many different colours on very slender stems. They last well in water and are useful when you need a slender flower in a particular vase.

Jasminum (Jasmine, Jessamine)
Tender and hardy climbing plants. The best-known to everyone is *Jasminum nudiflorum*, which has sprays of yellow flowers in winter — a most popular visitor, bringing the spring feeling in January! Nice to use with the odd Christmas rose, or later with a few snowdrops or early iris. The white variety, *J. officinale*, has slender sprays of sweetly-scented white flowers in midsummer; although this one does not last so well in water, it is worth picking for the fragrance it gives to any room. *J. polyanthum* is a cool-greenhouse plant with a heady scent; it is easily grown and can be treated as a house plant. The yellow *Jasminum primulinum*, scentless, is not well-known, but is another cool-house plant, well worth trying for its enormous star-like yellow flowers.

CONDITIONING The winter yellow jasmine needs little extra care, but the summer white one is better for having the ends of the stems in boiling water, before being given a long drink.

Jerusalem Sage *see* PHLOMIS

Jonquil *see* NARCISSUS

Judas Tree *see* CERCIS

Juglans (Walnut)
This is not commonly used as a cut flower, but the catkins that precede the nuts are the most wonder-

A well-shaped branch of walnut with two peonies

ful purple-pink colour, growing on such artistic-ally-shaped branches that if you ever get the opportunity of using them, never miss it. I would sacrifice the few nuts any day for the chance of using a spray, with two or three tree peonies — an outstanding combination.

Kaffir Lily *see* CLIVIA

Variegated curled kale

Kale (*Brassica fimbriata*)
Decorative Kale and Cabbage I like to grow as I find them extremely useful in the winter and early spring. They have the most glorious leaves, finely cut, and good colour — green and white, and purple-red; quite beautiful as a foil for the last of the red roses (see Colour Plate VIII), or in winter with a group of fruit and flowers. In spring-time it is possible to use the whole head, and this not only fills the centre of a really large arrangement, but looks so exotic that it can fool the experts and set everyone guessing. The cabbage is more compact in growth, as one would expect, and the solid

heads are often quite pink and even more effective as a single stem than the kale (see Plate 12), but I can thoroughly recommend sowing a little of both; although they are edible vegetables, they will be really much too precious to eat!
CONDITIONING Never use boiling water on the stems or you will never get rid of the 'cooking cabbage' smell. Pare the end of the stem to a tapering point and make cross-cuts up the stem, one way then the other; then push the whole point as deeply as possible into the water.

Kalmia latifolia (Calico Bush, American Laurel)
Hardy evergreen shrub with good glossy foliage and delicate clusters of frilly-edged pale-pink flowers, rather like the bunches we wore on our Sunday straw hats as children. They are a showy compact shrub and once blooming well give a lot of colour to the shrub border when the rhododendrons have finished. To keep the shrub small and a good shape, it is as well to cut short flower stems. Tuck them in low at the centre of a vase.
CONDITIONING Well scrape the ends of the stems up to about an inch and give a long drink, over-night if possible.

Kerria japonica pleniflora (Jew's Mallow)
Hardy deciduous shrub which produces a mass of double flowers in the very early spring. It does better in the shelter of a wall facing south or west. I like to use the sprays by removing all the leaves and so getting the full value of the yellow blossoms to mix with daffodils and other early spring flowers.

Kniphofia uvaria (Red-hot Poker, Torch Lily)
Hardy perennial. A very handsome plant in any border. Tall stems that stand very erect with a mop of tiny bell-like flowers that hang in a cluster from the top of stem, starting greenish and changing to yellow and red. They are useful in late summer and autumn as they add a change of shape to a group of late flowers. Having very thick stems, they require a large vase, or of course can be arranged in a shallow dish with their stems on a pin-holder. There are many varieties in shades of coral, red and orange. Lately the hybrid yellows have become most popular, my favourite being *K. uvaria* 'Maid of Orleans'; this one is pale straw-colour, gradually fading to ivory white and lovely to arrange with creams and browns.

CONDITIONING Cut the stems on the slant and give a long drink of water.

Kumquat *see* FORTUNELLA MARGARITA

Laburnum (Golden Chain)
Hardy deciduous flowering tree with racemes of yellow flowers which are such a delight in spring. *L. alpinum* (the Scotch Laburnum) is better than common Laburnum; but the hybrid *L. vossii* is perhaps best of all. I like to use it with the foliage removed so as to get the full benefit of the long, yellow chains of flowers shown off against the almost-black branches. In a Chinese vase it seems completely right. Also it lasts very much better without the foliage.
CONDITIONING Scrape the bark off the ends of the stems up to about two inches, then place the stems in warm water and leave as long as possible.
TO PRESERVE When the seed head has formed, remove all the foliage and hang upside down to dry.

Lachenalia (Cape Cowslip)
Greenhouse bulbous flowers with bell-shaped heads on very fleshy stems. *L. bulbifera* has coral-coloured bells tipped with green, and *L. nelsonii* is a clear yellow; I think these are the two most popular and I am very happy to use either. They are charming as a pot plant and so good to cut as they last well in water; also pretty arranged with little spring flowers in a 'moss garden', or in a candle cup with a mixture of small pieces of greenhouse foliage.

Lagurus ovatus (Hare's Tail Grass)
An attractive annual grass that seeds easily and is most useful in a summer vase, as a background for a few cornflowers or poppies. It dries so well that it becomes even more useful in the winter, as a feathery foil for more solid and heavy dried leaves.
TO PRESERVE Leave on the plant until midsummer so that the seed is well set, and then pick, remove all the green leaves, bunch and hang upside down to dry.

Lamb's Ear *see* STACHYS

Lamium (Dead Nettle)
Hardy perennial. *L. maculatum* has good orna-mental foliage; it acts as an excellent ground-cover spreading rapidly and allowing little else to take over. *L. maculatum aureum* has good golden foliage and gives a glow of sunlight to any dull corner. They do need careful conditioning to be of use as a cut flower, but if great care is taken it is really worth while as they last extremely well and provide nice trailing sprays that give a flowing line to a vase.
CONDITIONING Put the ends of the stems in boiling water for a few seconds, and leave submerged under water for twelve hours or more.

Lapageria rosea (Chilean Bellflower)
Greenhouse plant. I understand that it can be grown out of doors, against a sheltered west wall in the south, but I have never seen it so. The transparent waxy-looking bell-shaped flowers come in red and pure white and soft rose-pink. They are superb for a bride's bouquet, as you can imagine. I think I could count on one hand the number of times I have ever had the opportunity of using them as a cut flower: then just as a very special table decoration, with a few stephanotis and one or two leaves of delicate tradescantia and maidenhair fern.

Larix decidua (Larch)
A deciduous conifer with the most graceful habit: the sweeping branches tip upwards at the ends. The trees can reach a great height and are usually grown for timber, but I love to pick branches in the spring when the new brilliant green growth is forming and you can see the young, reddish-pink cones lying along the top of the branches. Later, when the cones have formed fully, they can be picked in sprays and used as an arching background for late dahlias and then chrysanthemums; they of course dry naturally on the trees and are useful all winter, in sprays or as separate cones for Christmas and other decorations.
CONDITIONING Hammer the ends of stems well, before giving a long drink.
TO PRESERVE Pick the cones from the trees as soon as they are dry, and pack away in a safe place; or pick when green and hang upside down to dry off.

Larkspur *see* DELPHINIUM

Lathyrus (Everlasting pea; Sweet pea)
Hardy annuals and herbaceous perennials. *Lathyrus* is the generic name for our favourite Sweet Pea, *Lathyrus odoratus*, an annual grown by expert and amateur alike. Although I love to arrange large bowls of beautifully grown long stems, with the much-coveted four, five or even six blooms per stem, I am quite happy to have a handful of shorter stemmed and not so well grown blooms, as to me the scent is of paramount importance. For this reason I think they are best put into large bowls in self-coloured bunches which as soon as you see you just long to lean over to drink in their scent. They do of course, mix well with flowers of matching colouring.

The small everlasting peas, the perennials, *Lathyrus grandiflorus*, have no smell at all, but last very well when cut and are nice used in small mixed vases in late summer. They have a good colour range in shades of pink, puce and apricot, softening to white.
CONDITIONING The annual sweet pea is better handled as little as possible; give a drink in deep water for several hours before arranging. The everlasting needs no special care, as it stands very well.

Laurel *see* PRUNUS

Laurus nobilis (Bay Tree)
Sweet bay is used as a flavouring, but sprays of the pointed green leaves look nice in the house and give off a spicy aroma.

Laurustinus *see* VIBURNUM TINUS

Lavandula (Lavender)
Hardy evergreen shrub with aromatic grey foliage and spikes of purple flowers which we all know so well, if only from the old-fashioned lavender bag — a nice idea that seems to be dying out. The little dark-purple French lavender is the one I like to grow, and I use some of the flowers in small vases in summer.
TO PRESERVE Gather the heads as soon as they are starting to fade, spread them out well to dry and then shake off the seeds; these retain their scent for a long time and can be a nice addition to pot-pourri.

Lavender *see* LAVENDULA

Leek (*Allium porrum*)
Annual vegetable, but the seed heads can be of great value to use, either fresh or dried, in a vase. They add a good solid centre to a vase of foliage, as they do equally well to a dried group.
TO PRESERVE When the seed heads are well set, pick and hang them upside down to dry. They are better tied up individually as they tend to lose their neat round shape if they press together.

Lenten Rose *see* HELLEBORUS

Leontopodium alpinum (Edelweiss)
This attractive small pearly-white flower growing wild in the mountains of Switzerland is the Swiss national emblem. Although it has the appearance of being dried, it needs to stay on the plant at least a month before it is actually dry, and it is most useful at this stage. I used to grow it for many years, but it was never really happy and survived rather than thrived; but it will grow quite well in many English gardens if it has the warmth and protection of the rock garden and, as it dries so well, it can be used in winter vases of other dried flowers to great effect.
CONDITIONING Put the ends of the stems in warm water and allow them to have a long drink, being careful that none of the heads get below the water, as they soak it up quickly through their hairy heads and it spoils the colour of the flowers.
TO PRESERVE Cut the heads when they have been on the plant at least a month, and bunch and hang up to dry.

Leptospermum scoparium (South Sea Myrtle)
Half-hardy evergreen shrub with white flowers in June. (*L. scoparium nicollsii* has bright red flowers, but is not quite so well known.) Not very often available as it is not very hardy, but attractive with mixed green and white groups in midsummer.
CONDITIONING Hammer ends of stems well, before giving a long drink.

Leucojum (Snowflake)
Bulbous perennial. The spring-flowering variety, *L. vernum*, is the one I grow and find so useful, coming just after the snowdrops — although they are rather alike, the snowflake has a larger head, with green tips at the ends of the petals, and very much longer and stiffer stems which make it more

useful in slightly larger vases. Later still is the Summer Snowflake, *L. aestivum*, with larger, pure white flowers in April and May.

Leycesteria formosa (Elisha's Tears, Flowering Nutmeg)

Hardy deciduous flowering shrub which has clusters of pendulous dark-purple flowers with a touch of white; these are often rather obscured by their leaves, so that it is important to remove quite a lot of the foliage before putting them in a flower vase. The purple berries that follow are, if anything, even more attractive, and as they last a little better it is sometimes better to wait for them. This shrub is a rapid grower; once established, it gives plenty to pick from. I love it and used it most successfully recently with heads of mauvish hydrangeas and some bunches of hothouse purple grapes, in an elegant Japanese vase.

Leycesteria formosa

CONDITIONING Remove as many leaves as seems best, then pare the outside skin off the bottom of the stems and put them in very hot water for several minutes.

Liatris (Button Snake Root)

Hardy perennial *L. spicata* has purple flower spikes that are almost unique in that they start flowering at the very tip of their spikes and work down, unlike lupins and delphiniums that start opening at the base of the spike and work up! A nice flower to have in August when colours tend to be mostly yellows. Adds good spikes to vases of sweet peas and mauve roses, godetia and so on.

Ligustrum ovalifolium (Privet)

Hardy evergreen shrub with green or golden foliage; the latter (*L. ovalifolium aureum*) is one that I use continually, but was the first tree I took out of my cottage garden as soon as we moved in — and how I have lived to regret it! It is one of the best standbys possible as background material for large groups (see Colour Plate VIII) as it holds its leaves for weeks, even in winter, and adds a lightness to any flower arrangement. If grown as a tree and not clipped, it produces delicate branches of very good foliage and fine crops of black berries in the autumn.

CONDITIONING Hammer ends of stems well, before giving a long drink.

Lilac *see* SYRINGA

Lilium (Lily)

Hardy and half-hardy bulbous plants. A wide and wonderful range of distinguished and elegantly beautiful flowers in all colours save blue. *Lilium candidum* (Madonna Lily) is one of the first to flower at the end of June. *L. testaceum* has heads like clotted cream, *L. henryi*, *L. davidii*, *L. tigrinum* and *L. hollandicum* (*umbellatum*) all come in varying shades of orange. *L. brownii* is one of the loveliest of all the trumpet lilies, cream with a brown back; *L. regale* is pink-backed and *L. longiflorum harrisii* pure white; the latter is forced and we can buy it for many months of the year, as we can the arum (see *Zantedeschia aethiopica*). *L. martagon* (the Turk's Cap Lilies) grow on tall stems and have small turned-back heads — and are now to be found in a wide range of colours, white (as seen on plate 2), mauve, bronze and almost black. They are all lovely to use and have very good seed heads. *L. speciosum album* is fragrant and white, with such slender stems that they arch and hang most gracefully over the edge of a vase. *L. speciosum rubrum*,

Lilium martagon

the pink variety, is rose-coloured with purple spots and has the same form; this lily is generally forced, but will grow out of doors and I have seen it thriving in Cornwall. *L. giganteum*, as the name implies, is the tallest, and most handsome of all, growing as tall as six feet on thick fleshy stems, with an abundance of creamy white trumpet heads hanging well down the stem; this is a difficult lily to grow, but most rewarding once it is established; it has beautiful seed heads. *L. auratum* is probably my favourite — if it is possible to have a favourite in such a field; known as the sun lily of Japan, it has heavily-scented open flowers, cream with distinct dark reddish-brown markings; in recent years it has been more widely grown out of doors, and does very well, and I would thoroughly recommend it. The new American De Graaff lilies are superb; 'Limelight', one of the most beautiful, is a clear-yellow trumpet lily and I cannot begin to describe how good it can look in a vase of green and golds. Here are but a few of this very wide

range. They are a great stand-by as a cut flower and anyone who has to do many flower groups welcomes them with open arms as they have a quality and shape that makes them invaluable, they show up well from a long distance — an important asset — and also they last longer in water than almost any other flower.

CONDITIONING Cut the ends of the stems on the slant and give a long drink in deep cold water.

TO PRESERVE The seed heads of *L. martagon* and *L. giganteum* both dry very well. Pick when the seed head has formed, and either hang them upside down to dry or place the stems in a very small amount of water in an open-necked vase, so that the air can circulate round them; then leave them in a warm temperature.

Lily of the Valley *see* CONVALLARIA

Lime Tree *see* TILIA

Linaria (Toadflax)
Hardy annuals and perennials. The annuals, in various shades, make a good splash of colour especially the small rock varieties. The perennials are spiky and not outstanding, though they look well in a bowl of mixed sweet peas.

Linum (Flax)
Hardy annuals and perennials. I advise either *L. perenne* or *L. narbonnense* (both perennials), both of which are the most lovely blue and open in a mass of colour as soon as the sun appears. Better as a garden plant, since they do not really last well in water.

Liquidambar styraciflua (Sweet Gum)
Deciduous tree with the most lovely autumn colouring. Like all falling leaves, these will not last for long when standing in water, but a few branches even for a day or two give real pleasure and add colour to any autumn group.

CONDITIONING Hammer the stems before giving a long drink.

Liriodendron tulipifera (Tulip Tree)
Hardy deciduous tree with green and yellow cup-shaped flowers on upturned branches — consequently they are best cut on fairly short stems so as to get the curved stems under water. The most suitable way of arranging them is to float them in

a shallow bowl. They are lovely used in floristry; I have seen a bride's bouquet made of them and it was most unusual.

Lobelia (Cardinal Flower)
Hardy perennials and half-hardy annuals. Perhaps best known to most of us as a little blue or white edging plant, *L. erinus*, though the scarlet-flowered and crimson-foliaged perennial called *L. cardinalis* or *fulgens*, which is unfortunately only half-hardy, is good as a cut flower and can look very effective if used with mixed reds or in a group of autumn colours.
CONDITIONING Put the ends of the stems in boiling water for a few minutes, before giving a long drink.

London Pride *see* SAXIFRAGA

Lonicera (Honeysuckle)
Hardy and half-hardy deciduous and evergreen shrubs. Honeysuckle means to me a wonderful sweet scent which fills the air as soon as we open

Lonicera etrusca superba

the door on a summer's night. I have four varieties on my cottage so that I can have them blooming as long as possible all through the summer. The best known are the Dutch Honeysuckles, *L. periclymenum belgica* and *L. periclymenum serotina*; these have well-scented flowers in spring and summer. The evergreen *L. japonica halliana*, with pairs of small blooms on arching sprays, is enchanting used for its scent in a vase in mid-summer, and its variety *L. japonica aureo-reticulata*, has good sprays of delicate golden foliage which gives excellent shape to any vase, though it rarely flowers. *L. etrusca* is exceptionally fragrant but unfortunately not hardy in colder districts. All these flowers mentioned here are well worth putting into vases, even if they do not last so very well, as the scent of even a small spray will fill a room. If you grow plenty, then the nicest way of arrangement is to put a tin or bowl into an old wooden tea-caddy, or box with an open lid, and pack it tightly with stems of honeysuckle.

Lonicera nitida
A small compact-leaved evergreen shrub that is used for making a good hedge. If the bushes are left unclipped, the foliage is useful in winter.

Lords and Ladies *see* ARUM

Love-in-a-Mist *see* NIGELLA

Love-Lies-Bleeding *see* AMARANTHUS

Lunaria (Common Honesty; Money Flower)
Lunaria biennis (or *L. annua*) is the best-known variety, generally used as a winter decoration; the seed heads contain a satiny 'partition' that is very attractive for using with dried flowers in a winter group, or painted with gum and then sprinkled with glitter and used with red holly berries for a Christmas decoration. Its purple flower in early spring is nice to have for the colour it gives to the garden and to mix in with a bowl of spring flowers.
CONDITIONING Put the stems of the flowers in very hot water as soon as they are picked, then give a long drink in cool water.
TO PRESERVE As soon as the seed has formed, hang them upside down to dry, then take each dried head between finger and thumb and slip off the outside case to reveal the satiny part. The seed

heads can be left on the plant until this takes place naturally, but they so often get badly damaged in wet weather that I would really recommend doing as I suggested at first.

Lungwort *see* PULMONARIA

Lupin *see* LUPINUS

Lupinus (Lupin)
Hardy perennials and annual. The familiar herbaceous lupins stand about two to four feet in height, coming out in June as one of the earliest and showiest of the herbaceous plants. Thanks to Mr George Russell, who spent the greater part of his life hybridizing these plants, we have today a vastly improved strain, with multi-coloured blooms and a very wide range of colours — bluish-mauve, reds, pinks, yellow, orange and pure white. I like to use, say, a few stems of apricot colours, to add to a vase of apricot foxgloves and some early roses in this colouring, or to add lupins to any vase of really mixed summer flowers (see Colour Plate VI). The tree lupin, *L. arboreus*, which is a perennial, has a mass of yellow or white flowers and the most delicious scent in late June. The annuals come from *L. hartwegii*. Although all the lupins tend to shed their flowers fairly quickly, I still feel they are well worth using in the house.
CONDITIONING There are many different ideas about what is the best way to make these flowers last. One method is to put the ends of the stems into boiling water for a few seconds, before giving a long drink. Another is to fill the hollow stem with water and then plug the end with cotton wool; this is a lot of trouble, but worth it for some special occasion. The really old-fashioned idea of putting the stems into a weak solution of starch water has the advantage of keeping the flowers from dropping and so is quite a help. They tend to go on growing in water and so to twist their heads round when first picked, but a night in water as soon as they have been picked prevents this from taking place in an arranged vase.
TO PRESERVE Pick when the seed head has formed, remove all the foliage and hang in bunches upside down to dry. I should mention here that the Russell and good hybrid varieties should not be allowed to seed, so of course use your discretion.

Lychnis (Campion, German Catchfly, Scarlet Lychnis, Jerusalem Cross)
Hardy perennials. A widely diverse race, varying from tiny *L. alpina* for the rock garden to *L. chalcedonica*, scarlet, and *L. coronaria*, magenta or white, both of which are tall herbaceous plants. Both the white and magenta campions are useful for small groups and have attractive grey foliage. *L. chalcedonica*, the Scarlet Lychnis, with flat heads of really scarlet flowers in July, is a joy to use in a mixed red group. *L. fulgens*, with a mass of vermilion double flowers, is nice to cut and a very useful edging to the border; it has the added advantage of a long flowering period.

Macleaya cordata (see facing page)

Lysichitum (Skunk Cabbage)
Hardy perennial. Water-loving plant with spathes of yellow or white in April and May, followed by a handsome crop of shiny leaves. *L. americanum* has the yellow arum-like spathes and is spectacular rather than beautiful, but is very effective if used in a flat ovenware type of bowl, by impaling the

stems on a pin-holder and covering this with some suitable leaves. I also find the bold green centres useful for putting into a green foliage group, long after the outside of the flower has faded.

Lythrum (Purple Loosestrife)
Hardy perennial. Tall stems of magenta flowers in late summer, useful to add a touch of the unusual to a vase of other shades of red. It also adds good colour to the flower border.
CONDITIONING Put the ends of the stems into a little boiling water, before giving a long drink.

Macleaya cordata (Plume Poppy)
Hardy perennial. Useful for the back of the border and as a background for large groups of flowers. The fine sprays of buff flowers fade as the summer goes, forming elegant tracery for use in winter.
CONDITIONING Never pick until the flowers are fully open up to the tip of the stem. The stems must be boiled for a few minutes and then left to stand in deep water for twelve hours.
TO PRESERVE Cut sprays from the plant when already dry and store till required.

Madonna Lily *see* LILIUM CANDIDUM

Magnolia (Cucumber Tree, Yulan)
Hardy deciduous and evergreen shrubs and trees. Of the deciduous ones a favourite is *M. stellata*, flowering early in spring; its white star-like flowers burst out of grey-green fur coats, on beautifully shaped branches that need little or no arranging as they look quite their best alone, in a bowl of celadon green or a glass bowl. *M. soulangeana* has large chalice-shaped white flowers flushed with purple outside, flowering on bare branches in April, but it has one of the longest flowering periods and often the flowers are still visible in June when the leaves have opened out. Again it is quite lovely alone in a vase, or it can be arranged with any other flower that picks up the colouring. *M. watsonii* has a more open flower and a very sweet scent. Of course there are many more of these deciduous varieties. Among the evergreens, *M. grandiflora* (or laurel Magnolia) is usually treated as a wall plant as it needs this protection in a cold climate; its beautiful large glossy leaves are from my point of view even more valuable than the flowers, very handsome as these

are — and sweetly scented; these flowers are only suitable to use in really large groups, or perhaps floating in a bowl.
CONDITIONING Hammer the ends of the stems very well, before putting into really hot water, and allow this to cool off before taking out the stems to arrange.
TO PRESERVE The leaves of *M. grandiflora* take up a solution of glycerine with very worth while results. It is also possible to skeletonize the leaves in a strong solution of soda and water. As this is a very slow and rather difficult process, many people prefer to buy them ready treated — they are preserved in this form in the East and sold here in large quantities. The method is a well-kept secret and I would just love to know how they do it!

Mahonia
Mahonia japonica, *M. bealei*, the hybrid Mahonia 'Charity' and *Mahonia aquifolium*, related to the berberis, are winter-flowering with beautiful foliage and sprays of pale-yellow, sweet-scented

Mahonia 'Charity'

flowers from January onwards; after the flowers have fallen the berries are bluish-green, turning purple on arching delicate sprays which look well in a small vase.

CONDITIONING Hammer the ends of the stems, or peel off some bark — up to about two inches — to make absorption of water easier.

Maidenhair Fern *see* ADIANTUM

Malcomia maritima (Virginia Stock)
Hardy annual. Star-like flowers in various colours on seven-inch stems; useful for small mixed vases or to add a spiky background to self-coloured arrangements.

Malus (Crab Apple)
Ornamental trees, spring-flowering in shades of pink, red and white. Many produce decorative fruits in autumn. One of the most popular is *M. baccata*, the red Siberian crab, with richly-coloured autumn fruits, and white flowers in April. *M. eleyi* is perhaps my favourite as it has coppery-coloured foliage, rosy when young, with red flowers and purple-red fruit, so that it is decorative all the year round; I like to use it in all its stages. It is lovely in the spring with pink tulips, and the fruits are attractive in autumn groups. It lasts better than any other blossom. *M. floribunda* has dark-green leaves and red flower buds opening to pale pink. The fruiting crabs are also well worth a mention as they are excellent for using in the autumn, 'Dartmouth', 'Golden Hornet' and others, all making trees about twenty feet high.

CONDITIONING Hammer or scrape the stems, before giving a long drink in water.

Maranta
M. leuconeura kerchoveana is a good ornamental house plant which I find useful planted in miniature indoor gardens, in winter and early spring. The leaves have dark spotted markings, but although extremely decorative, they do not last well in water.

Marguerite *see* CHRYSANTHEMUM

Marigold *see* CALENDULA

Masterwort *see* ASTRANTIA

Matthiola (Ten-week, Brompton and Night-scented Stocks)
Hardy and half-hardy annuals and biennials. With the exception of the sweetly scented *M. bicornis*, or Night-scented Stock, which is lovely in the garden but of little value as a cut flower, the stock family provides some of the best flowers for arrangement. They are widely grown and also cultivated under glass, so that they are available for many months of the year. The Ten-week Stock, so named because it flowers about ten weeks after the seed has been sown in March, has a very good range of delicate off-beat colours, in pale yellow, soft pink, deep crimson, pale and deep mauve, and a new one called 'Antique Copper' which is just as its name suggests. These mix well in all types of arrangements, they add a useful splash of colour, and tuck well into the centre of any vase. East Lothian stocks, if sown in February, usually come into flower in July. The Bromptons, on the other hand, are hardy biennials and the seed should be sown in June to produce flowers the following summer.

CONDITIONING Stocks have a very woody stem that needs to be treated rather like a branch and should be hammered well; or the ends should be put into boiling water for a few minutes, before having a long drink. It is also very important to remove any leaves that go under the water-level, as they quickly make the water smelly and unpleasant.

Meadow Saffron *see* COLCHICUM

Meconopsis (Himalayan Poppy, Welsh Poppy)
M. betonicifolia baileyi, the glorious blue biennial poppy, I have only now and again had the chance of putting into a flower arrangement, but on those few occasions they were really delightful. However, as they do not last very well in water, it is perhaps better to enjoy them out of doors. The yellow varieties (*M. cambrica* and *M. integrifolia*) are also attractive and have such beautiful hairy foliage that this is an added inducement for cutting. When using the flowers, it is better to cut the stems fairly short so as to see into the face of the flower, as they tend to hang their heads.

CONDITIONING Put the ends of the stems in boiling water, before giving a drink.

Megasea *see* BERGENIA

Melissa officinalis (Common Balm)
Hardy herbaceous perennials which I like to grow
for the fun of pinching the leaves as I pass to keep
the delicious scent of the aromatic foliage on my
hands. The yellow variegated balm (*M. officinalis
variegata*) is the nicest one for effect. You can see it
in Colour Plate V.
CONDITIONING The foliage does not last well,
but I love it so much that I use a branch for a day
or so and then replace it. It helps to put the ends of
the stems into boiling water for a few seconds and
then give a long drink; or better still submerge the
whole stem under water overnight.

Melon *see* CANTALOUP MELON

Mentha (Mint, Pennyroyal)
Hardy perennial with aromatic foliage, best known
for its culinary use. However, there are many
varieties that make it worthy of mention here: one
with attractive green and white foliage, another
the golden yellow *M. gentilis aurea variegata*. They

Meconopsis cambrica (see facing page)

make excellent ground-cover, and are nice picked
and put into small vases in late summer. It is also
nice to dry the leaves for mixing in pot-pourri.
CONDITIONING Put ends of stems in boiling
water and give a long drink before arranging.
TO PRESERVE Strip the leaves from the stems and
dry in a warm place for mixing in pot-pourri.

Mesembryanthemum
The half-hardy annual *M. criniflorum* is a brilliantly
colourful little daisy-like flower, used as a rock
plant or edging plant and at its best when enjoying
hot sunshine. Not really a very good subject from
the flower arranger's point of view; it can look
attractive at the centre of a small vase, but has the
habit of shutting up at night, which can be
disappointing.

Michaelmas Daisy *see* ASTER

Mignonette *see* RESEDA

Mimosa *see* ACACIA

Miscanthus sinensis
Hardy ornamental green and creamy-yellow striped
grass, decorative in the border and when used to
add a spiky effect to a group of rounded and more
solid leaves. More effective in its early stages in
May, when the leaves are at their best.

Mistletoe *see* VISCUM

Mock Orange *see* PHILADELPHUS

Molucella laevis (Molucca Balm, Bells of
  Ireland)
M. laevis, sometimes better known as the Shell
Flower, is grown in this country as an annual —
and what a popular plant it has become! It produces
spikes of shell-shaped flowers all up the stem,
green to start with but a soft parchment-colour
when preserved. The stems take on lovely shapes,
which for the flower arranger is an added attraction.
They are charming arranged alone on a pin-holder
in a shallow dish, or in a dried group with pressed
ferns and seed heads, to which one can add a few
fresh flowers.
CONDITIONING Remove all the leaves so that the
shell flowers are shown off to their best advantage,
cut the stems on the slant and give a long drink.

Molucella laevis

The piece of driftwood mentioned in the chapter on drying, with a brown and cream collection of dried materials, which is a standby for many months. The dried flowers are of *Molucella laevis*, *Eryngium giganteum* and a seed-head of hosta. The leaves are of aspidistra and preserved lime.

TO PRESERVE When the leaves have been removed, the flowers can be preserved for winter by putting them into glycerine or by hanging the heads upside down. The former treatment is, I think, the best, as they turn such a lovely soft cream colour. It is then advisable to spray the stems with clear lacquer or a hair-spray to prevent the flowers from falling off.

Monarda didyma (Sweet Bergamot)
Sweet Bergamot is a hardy herbaceous plant, with fragrant mint-like foliage and whorls of pink or red hooded flowers on erect stems' in August. 'Croftway Pink' and 'Magnifica' are clear rose and deep rose pink respectively. 'Cambridge Scarlet' is a good clear red.
CONDITIONING Put the ends of the stems into boiling water, before giving a long drink.

Money Flower see LUNARIA

Monkshood see ACONITUM

Monstera deliciosa (Shingle Plant)
Tender greenhouse evergreen climber with outstandingly handsome deeply-cut large leaves. The pineapple-flavoured cylindrical fruits are very good to eat, but are also excellent as the centre of a vase, especially a vase of foliage. The leaves can be used very effectively at the base of any large group. They grow to immense height in the tropics, and they make a distinctive decoration. They are in front of the town hall in Brisbane, growing to well over eight feet.
CONDITIONING The leaves need several hours in deep water once they have been cut; to maintain their glossy appearance it is a good idea to wash them in milk and water every few weeks. The fruits are best given a long drink and then placed in rather shallow water, either on a pin-holder or with the stems just under the water-level.

Montbretia see CROCOSMIA

Moraea (Butterfly Iris)
M. spathacea has clear yellow iris-like flowers that last well in water and mix well in a vase to give a good colour contrast, such as green and yellow or — better still — black and yellow with near-black tulips. They also have good seed-heads for winter.

TO PRESERVE Let the seed heads form, and then bunch and hang upside down.

Morina longifolia (Whorl Flower)
This handsome herbaceous plant is valuable for foliage, flower and seed head. As the pet name implies, the flowers, borne on stout stems, are in whorls, hooded and tubular, in white turning to pale and then deep pink. The stems dry well for winter.
TO PRESERVE Hang the heads upside down once they are well matured.

Mullein see VERBASCUM

Muscari (Grape Hyacinth)
Hardy bulbs. Six inches high, with blue heads in

A miniature vase with stems of muscari, *Anemone blanda* lilac-blue scillas and the button-daisy Sutton's Quilled Salmon Pink.

spikes of very close bells, suitable for small borders or the rock garden. Useful in spring to add to a moss garden in the house (Colour Plate II), taking the place of the earlier Glory of the Snow; or they can be used in a mixed vase of, say, fritillaries and some of the species tulips. The small white one, *Muscari botryoides album*, fairly new to me, is a pet. The blues are very varied and have quite a long flowering period.

TO PRESERVE The seed heads are very effective and although it is not advisable to let too many go to seed, the delicate stems are nice to have. I think it is best to stand them in a little water, and let them gradually dry off; if they are hung bunched upside down, they shed very quickly.

Myosotis (Forget-me-not)

Hardy perennial but usually grown as a biennial. Short-stemmed blue flowers in May and June, compact and good as an edging or in a small border. They add just the right touch of blue to a small vase and look childlike and pretty used with small pink and white daisies for a font decoration.

CONDITIONING Cut in small bunches and give a long drink before arranging. If used in small bunches for a font decoration, I would advise securing with elastic band or tying with string for easier handling.

Myrtus communis (Myrtle)

Greenhouse and half-hardy evergreen shrub with compact green leaves and small fluffy white flowers in January and February under glass, or following later outdoors in the extreme South of England. A traditional flower for a bride's bouquet. I often have the opportunity of using it in the very early spring, and it looks most attractive with white hyacinths and sprays of the indoor *Jasminum polyanthum*, arranged in a white porcelain vase or a trumpet-shaped glass vase which allows the stems to cascade.

Narcissus (Daffodil, Jonquil)

Hardy bulbs. We commonly apply the name narcissus to the small-cupped varieties, though the daffodil in all its forms comes under this heading in all the botanical journals. The genus is enormous and I cannot begin to name even half of them. I personally really prefer the short trumpet types for flower arrangement, and find the very big heads of 'King Alfred' extremely difficult to do anything with. The very first narcissi to come on the market just before Christmas are paper white, worth buying for their lovely scent alone; they arrange well in a vase of evergreen oak with some lemons, as they look so like orange or lemon blossom. The first of the trumpet type could be 'Golden Harvest', and to make the most of these I suggest arranging them in a basket, in which a baking tin or an ovenware dish is filled with wire netting and disguised by a layer of green moss; place the flowers in clumps with a branch of forsythia or catkins, and a single bunch will go a long way. A basket is always a nice container for these flowers (see Colour Plate II) and later on, if you can pick them freely from the garden, you can discard the moss and just have a mass of blooms. Having straight stems they do not lend themselves to complicated groups of mixed flowers. The dwarf varieties of narcissus such as *N. cyclamineus*, *N. bulbocodium* and *N. triandrus albus* (the Angel's Tears daffodil) are suitable for the rock garden. Two dwarf varieties that I love are 'Silver Chimes' and 'April Tears', and I use them for small vases in the spring, as you can see from the colour frontispiece. Many types force very well in bowls for the house in either fibre or shingle and water. Some of my pet varieties are 'Beersheba' (a large pure-white trumpet), or any of the white-backed types, 'Geranium', 'February Gold' (as it comes so early), 'Primrose Phoenix', 'Pheasant Eye' . . . , but there are of course so many more.

CONDITIONING Bear in mind that the flowers last better in shallow water.

Nasturtium *see* TROPAEOLUM

Nemesia

Half-hardy annuals. The new hybrid varieties have a good range of colour, in tones of pinks to a lovely blue. They are generally used as edging plants, but small pieces picked for the house and put into little mixed vases are pretty.

Nepeta (Catmint)

Hardy herbaceous perennial. *N. mussinii*, sometimes known as *N. faassenii*, is really loved by cats and this is surely how it got its pet name. It has feathery spikes of purple flowers in June and July; useful as a background in a vase of summer

Another home-made container (see page 47) used for a spring group: a lichen-covered branch, bright-coloured anemones, hellebores, a leaf of *Arum italicum*, with narcissi to give height to the arrangement.

flowers. My earliest recollection of it is seeing it arranged with pink or white garden pinks; my mother always used it in this way on our dining-room table at home. It lasts extremely well in water and needs no special treatment.

Nephrolepsis exaltata (Ladder Fern)
N. exaltata is not hardy but can be grown very easily as a house plant. The unfurling shoots of the new growth are enchanting and from the moment they appear I use it all the time. It sometimes remains green for much of the winter, but even when it goes rather brown it nevertheless looks effective to add delicate outline to a few flowers.
CONDITIONING Lasts extremely well, but the young growth is better if it is submerged in warm water for a few hours.
TO PRESERVE Place the stems between sheets of newspaper and press under the carpet or some heavy weight.

Nerine (Guernsey Lily)
Greenhouse bulbous plant. *N. sarniensis* has brilliant scarlet flowers in the autumn. They are quite one of the most lovely of all the bulbs; their petals have a sheen that makes them look as if they had been painted with a touch of gold on the brush. *N. bowdenii*, a semi-hardy bulb, is grown out of doors in a mild climate; with upright pink lily-like flowers, and flowering as it does in the autumn, it is a great attraction to any garden and a joy to pick. I love to use the scarlet variety with some autumn-tinted leaves and sprays of berries; or sometimes to stand just three in a shallow dish with a branch of lichen. The pink variety also looks well when arranged like this, or it can be put with a mixture of varying shades of pink.
CONDITIONING Cut the ends of the stems on the slant and give a long drink.

New Zealand Flax *see* PHORMIUM

Nicotiana alata (Tobacco Plant, Sweet-scented Tobacco)
Half-hardy annuals in soft mixed colours, but the green variety sometimes called 'Limelight' has become extremely popular with flower arrangers — and rightly so. Its soft lime colour blends well with almost any colour combination that you can

Nicotiana alata

think of. Its starry open flowers look nice in a mixed green group or with summer flowers as you can see on Colour Plate VII.
CONDITIONING These flowers last better, I think, if they are placed in warm water before they are arranged.

Nigella (Love-in-a-Mist)
Hardy annual with small blue flowers that are surrounded by a frill of feathery green. They produce a good seed head in autumn, useful for winter decoration. The flowers themselves are most attractive arranged with small rose-buds and garden pinks. They are so delicate that they are welcome for any posy, to put on a coffee table or in a guest's bedroom.
TO PRESERVE As soon as the seed head has set, pick carefully and remove all the foliage before hanging in bunches upside-down to dry.

Night-scented Stock *see* MATTHIOLA

Norway Maple *see* ACER PLATANOIDES

Nymphaea (Water Lily)
Tender and hardy aquatic plants that flower on our ponds in July. The flowers are so lovely to use but they have one great snag, as they close up after they have been cut; there are several ways of trying to prevent this but I have never been very fortunate with them. They are most effective used for a table arrangement, and can be persuaded to last just long enough. Arrange them with the leaves of *Bergenia cordifolia*, which are as like their own as any you can find and they last so much better. I remember once using these flowers with blocks of polished glass on a large circular glass tray, giving the effect of clear water; the effect was delightful. I have also seen a bride's bouquet made of them, which looked simply lovely. It is possible to wire them so that they will keep open.
CONDITIONING There are several methods, but the one I would suggest is to try the Japanese idea of injecting them with pure alcohol; I understand this usually keeps them open successfully. Some people hold the flowers very near to the light, which seems to encourage them to unfold. For very important occasions we can keep them open by force, by dropping melted wax between each petal; in this way they cannot possibly close.

Odontoglossum
One of the loveliest of Orchids. Very small mauve, brown and greenish flat flowers on arching sprays, unlike the lipped orchids. Some of the varieties are imported nowadays from the East, and so we have the opportunity to buy and enjoy them.
CONDITIONING Cut the ends of the stems on the slant and give a good drink. Remove and recut before replacing in fresh water.

Oenothera (Evening Primrose, Tree Primrose)
Hardy biennials and perennials. The most popular biennial is *O. biennis*, with pale yellow flowers, growing about four to five feet tall. The perennial *O. fruticosa* has golden-yellow open cup-like flowers alternately up the stem; it lasts better in water than one would think, as every flower bud will open out, but I find it almost more useful in the green seed head stage; this I use whenever possible, in cool green groups for a hot sunny day.
CONDITIONING Put the ends of the stems into boiling water for a few seconds, before giving a long drink.
TO PRESERVE When the green seed heads have formed, pick them and remove all the leaves, then bunch and hang them upside down to dry. If, however, you are using these heads in a vase, you will find that they will dry off by themselves; after that, you can store them away until you need them.

Old Man's Beard *see* CLEMATIS VITALBA

Olearia (New Zealand Daisy Bush)
Hardy evergreen bush with clusters of white daisy flowers. The one I like best is *O. haastii* because it flowers in July and August and is very useful to mix with white godetia, a white lily or two, and perhaps some sweet peas.
CONDITIONING Scrape well up the ends of the stems and place in warm water.

Oleaster *see* ELAEAGNUS ANGUSTIFOLIA

Onopordon acanthium (Cotton Thistle, Scots Thistle)
The hardy perennial 'Scots Thistle' *O. acanthium* is

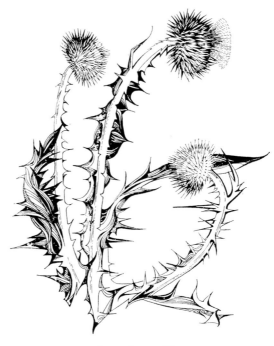

Onopordon acanthium

an outstandingly beautiful plant. As it grows to at least six feet, it naturally needs a lot of space, but is well worth growing if you have room. It has a statuesque beauty that is excellent in silhouette. Extremely prickly, the stems are flanged with grey cotton-wool-like flounces, making a candelabra effect with the grey thistle heads, at which stage they are quite lovely before the heads burst into purple. I like to use them in all stages: the grey leaves in winter, with 'mixed greens'; then the whole branch in midsummer, beautiful either alone or in a big church group, with whites and greys or blues; the flowers of course look good in a vase of purples or mauves. They dry well and add to any collection of other grey dried flowers or seed heads.

CONDITIONING   The stems are better if they are put into boiling water for a little while before they have a long drink.

TO PRESERVE   When the thistles have reached the seed head stage, pick and hang them upside down to dry.

Opium Poppy *see* PAPAVER

Orchid
I have mentioned earlier some of the best orchids for flower arrangement (see cymbidium, cypripedium, odontoglossum) but as this is such a large family, with perhaps well over five hundred, genera, you may well have the opportunity of using many more. They are quite one of the best-lasting flowers in water and personally I love to use them whenever possible.

Oriental Poppy *see* PAPAVER

Ornithogalum (Chincherinchee; Star of Bethlehem)
Hardy and greenhouse bulbous plant. The best-known to most of us is the South African Chincherinchee (*O. thyrsoides*), which gets its name from the funny squeaky sound the stems make as the wind blows them across the Veldt. They are imported here, arriving with a great welcome at Christmas time, and when the wax end is cut off and they are placed in warm water, they gradually open out and last in water for weeks. They look most attractive if arranged with berried holly, or with sprays of yellow jasmine just after Christmas.

Ornithogalum nutans

The hardy variety that I like to grow here is *O. nutans*, which has spikes of white starlike flowers with greenish-grey centres; they flower in June and are a welcome addition to a green and white vase. *O. umbellatum*, which most of us know as Star of Bethlehem, grows wild in the West of England, and spreads almost too rapidly for the average garden. It must be picked for the house in full sunlight or when the flowers are open, as they are temperamental about opening indoors. I like their starry innocent-looking flowers massed in a shallow bowl. The chincherinchee is also grown here, but flowering as it does in July is not nearly as desirable then, when we already have so much to pick.

CONDITIONING   The chincherinchees come with wax on the bottom of their stems which must be cut off. Then they need to be stood in warm water for a little while, remaining afterwards in deep water for several days to open out well, before they are arranged.

Osmanthus (Fragrant Olive, Holly-leaved Olive)
Hardy and half-hardy evergreen shrubs. The spring-flowering *O. delavayi* (now also called *Siphonosmanthus delavayi*) has small white flowers and a delicious scent. *O. ilicifolius* (*O. aquifolium*) on the other hand, flowers in July. Both are good as a background for delicate flowers.

Osmunda (Royal Fern, Flowering Fern)
Hardy deciduous ferns with tall handsome fronds.

Fronds of *Osmunda regalis* and *Osmunda regalis cristata*

They are water lovers and thrive in moist conditions. It is advisable to press them before using them, as they quickly curl if brought into a warm room. They turn very good autumn colours and make a delightful backing for autumn and winter flower arrangements. *Osmunda regalis*, the Royal Fern, is better known than *O. cinnamomea*, which has wide curling fronds at the tip of the stem.

TO PRESERVE Press the fronds at all stages, so that you get a wide colour range: some while green, and some when they have changed to their lovely golden and bronze tones. Spread them carefully between newspaper and place them under the carpet or under some suitable weight.

Ox-eye Daisy *see* CHRYSANTHEMUM

Pasque Flower *see* PULSATILLA

Paeonia (Paeony, Peony)

Hardy herbaceous and shrubby perennials. The shrubby kinds, or the 'tree peonies', are lovely to grow and much hardier than is often supposed. Native to China and the Himalayas, they can stand quite a lot of frost in winter, but the young growth objects to cold winds and needs a little protection from a wall. They are slow-growing except for *P. lutea ludlowii*, with its single sweet-scented flowers and good seed heads. *P. delavayi* has the small single maroon blooms that are particularly nice to arrange with sprays of purple plum, and yellow-green leaves of the hosta for contrast (see Colour Plate V). The Japanese, Chinese and French varieties, either double or single, but all with enormous heads that look as the stems could not hold them, are in my opinion quite wonderful. They come in shades of pink, red, orange and white. To name a few: 'Hakugan' (single white, with golden stamens and petals like silk), 'Haru-no-akebono' (white, flushed with pink), 'Elizabeth' (coral pink double, of great beauty), 'Souvenir de Ducher' (double magenta flowers), 'Horaisan' (clear pink).

Paeonia delavayi

The herbaceous peonies are some of the loveliest subjects for flower arrangement; they are so bold that they can take the centre of any group, and are wonderful to use in any large flower vase for church or a special occasion. The delicate pinks and whites are my favourites, but I have found that the magenta red does something to a vase of mixed reds that is hard to describe. The soft shell pinks seem more delicate than in any other flower; a vase of these with branches of lime flowers stripped of their foliage, and apricot foxgloves, is about as perfect as any arrangement I know. Good varieties are 'Messagera' (creamy white), 'Mai fleuri' (ivory), 'Phillippe Rivoire' (crimson), 'China Rose' (pink), 'Sarah Bernhardt' (deep pink). Two of the singles I would recommend are *P. lactiflora whitleyi major* (superb white with golden stamens, and with dark reddish foliage) and *P. emodii* (a smaller white flower, often bearing more than one head on a branch; it has clusters of yellow stamens, a delicious scent and a good seed head).

CONDITIONING   The French peonies come over in pads, never having been in water at all, and as they last so well it started us thinking at Winkfield, and we have done a little experimenting. I find that if I pick peonies fresh and leave them out of water to dehydrate, as it were, this is all to the good; they can be left on a cold stone floor for some days. Or if they are cut and placed in a polythene bag, they will keep for several weeks in a cold room. Then cut the ends of the stems and finally put them in warm water for a long drink.

Pampas Grass *see* CORTADERIA

Pansy *see* VIOLA

Papaver (Poppy)
There are both hardy annual and perennial poppies and I like them all, though my favourites are, I think, the Orientals and Sutton's art shades. These latter have a range of off-beat colours which look as if they have all been painted with a touch of grey. They have all the soft pink and mauve colours and are so muted that they blend with anything, for instance with any bluish colours, the soft pink of the Preston hybrid lilacs, muted pink and mauvey delphiniums, and of course pink roses. *P. nudicaule*, or the Iceland poppy, is a perennial, though it is often better grown as a biennial. Its flowers come in the clearest orange, apricot and yellows, and are best picked in bud and allowed to open in water. They look well when arranged in a basket or bowl with a collection of feathery grasses; or some of their subtle colours blend well with a vase in tones of cream or apricot. The Shirley poppy, *P. rhoeas*, is truly an annual and gives a lot of colour in the garden, and the pink and white are pretty for use in midsummer. The Opium poppy, *P. somniferum*, is worth growing for the seed heads alone.

CONDITIONING   It is very important to burn or boil the ends of the stems, by dipping the stems into boiling water for a few minutes, before giving a long drink. The flowers tend to fall quickly; to make the most of every minute of their short lives, pick them just as they are bursting and showing colour.

TO PRESERVE   The seed heads of *P. orientale* and *P. somniferum* dry very well. Remove all the foliage and bunch them, then hang them upside down to dry.

Parrot Tulips *see* TULIPA

Parrotia persica (Persian Ironwood)
Hardy deciduous tree. *P. persica* makes a beautiful specimen tree with ovate green leaves in summer and rich autumn colouring. Any shrub with a good tinted foliage is well worth growing, and small pieces added to a vase in September and October give a glow that is hard to describe. However, pick with great care so as not to spoil the shape of a young tree, and remember that no foliage that has gone a good colour will last very long.
CONDITIONING Hammer the ends of the hard woody stems well and give a good drink in deep water before arranging.

Parthenocissus (Virginia Creeper)
Climber with brilliant coloured leaves in the autumn. The leaves do not last at all well in water, but it is possible to use them for a day or so although you will find that they quickly curl up. They must be pressed.
TO PRESERVE To press the leaves when coloured, put them carefully between sheets of newspaper and place them under a weight. The stalks usually fall off when pressed, so that it is necessary to make a false stem; this can be done by putting florist's wire up the back and securing with Sellotape. In this way the wire can be put into the vase in place of the stem.

Pasque Flower *see* PULSATILLA

Passiflora (Passion Flower)
The flower gets its name from the idea that it represents features of the Crucifixion. *P. coerulea*, the almost-hardy blue passion flower, is well worth growing where the climate permits. It does better with the heat from a wall, so that the warmth ripens the wood and enables it to withstand the winter. The flowers are quite beautiful, and make a spectacular addition to a fruit and flower group in the summer. The orange fruits are also attractive for flower arrangement. The greenhouse species, *P. incarnata*, white and purple, is a fine specimen if you have the space for it.
CONDITIONING The flowers themselves last quite well when picked, but if you are picking a trail it is important to put the ends of the stems into boiling water, afterwards submerging everything in a bath of cold water for several hours.

Passion Flower *see* PASSIFLORA

Pearly Everlasting *see* ANAPHALIS

Pelargonium (Geranium)
Greenhouse perennials. I always find their naming confusing, *Pelargonium* being the authentic botanical name, but then so-called 'Geraniums' being so well known as such that I never think or talk of them as anything but Geraniums. I am by no means alone in this; there is even a 'Geranium Society'. The scarlet 'Geraniums' are all *Pelargoniums* of hybrid origin. These are now divided into several groups: Zonal, Variegated-leaved, Ivy-leaved, Scented-leaved, and Show or Regal Pelargoniums. I love all the unusual colours of the Ivy-leaved and Zonal varieties; the flowers range from petunia and scarlet to the softest pink and lavender. They are all fun to use, giving plenty of scope for ideas, and can often pick up unusual colourings in a flower arrangement. I have put them in a group of mauves with some 'Sterling Silver' roses, purple *Begonia rex* leaves, and side shoots from pink delphiniums. They are splendid arranged in a mass in a shallow bowl with some of their own leaves; packed tightly like this they often seem to last better, or perhaps it is just because they are packed so closely the petals do not get a chance to fall! The Regal *Pelargoniums* have a more open flower and usually a blotch on the petals; these flowers stand very much better in water, and give a different colour range. The soft pinks look well with pink roses and, to provide a contrast, a few deep scarlet roses such as 'Crimson Glory'.
CONDITIONING By spraying some florist's gum on the backs of the petals, it is possible to prevent them from falling so quickly. It could be that hair-lacquer would be as good.

Penstemon
Hardy and half-hardy shrubby perennials. One of the best kinds for a flower vase is the little blue one called *P. heterophyllus*, which stands well in water and is hardy except in the coldest gardens. This adds a lovely bit of blue to any mixed summer vase. The hybrids are in a magnificent colour range and are excellent in the border, but disappointing when cut as they do not last very well. This is always so sad as the colours are more than tempting to use.

CONDITIONING   Although they do not last well, I have had a certain amount of success by burning the ends and leaving them to have a really good soak, up to their necks in cold water for two days, before arranging.

Peony *see* PAEONIA

Peperomia
A collection of good house plants with decorative leaves, some variegated and others plain, that are most useful to put into planted indoor gardens. The small leaves are individually distinctive at the base of a small mixed green group.

Periwinkle *see* VINCA

Pernettya (Prickly Heath)
Low-growing evergreen shrub that has prettily coloured berries in the autumn — crimson, pink and white. Mixed with small button chrysanthemums or pink and red dahlias, they are most unusual and decorative. They are lovers of peat so are not always easy to grow, but they come as cut bunches into Covent Garden in the autumn and are deservedly popular.
CONDITIONING   Hammer the stems well, before giving a long drink.

Petasites (Butterbur)
A rampant weed, but it blooms in January and February, and so can be most welcome if you have somewhere for it to 'ramp'. *Petasites fragrans* is known as Winter Heliotrope because the vanilla scent of its pink-tinged white flowers is very like that of Cherry-pie. *P. japonicus giganteus* has a cone of lime-green flowers and a frill of leaves at the base of the stem. The flower grows straight out of the ground before the leaves appear. At this stage I use it in a vase of catkins with some of the green hellebore as a focal point. It is very unusual and despite its enormous leaves in summer I am extremely fond of it. The leaves are so large that in Japan the children use them as a sunshade.
CONDITIONING   As the flowers have very short stalks when they first appear, it is well to stand them in a tea-cup of water overnight, when they will grow a little and so be more easily put in a vase.

Petunia
Half hardy annual. The three best-known kinds are the large-flowered grandiflora, the bedding or multiflora and the double-flowered. The double are, I think, the best for cutting, they last remarkably well; they are most effective alone arranged in delicate porcelain or glass. The bedding varieties, in their vivid colours, make a long-lasting show in the garden and a splash of colour in any small vase.
CONDITIONING   Put the ends of the stems in boiling water for a few minutes, before giving a long drink.

Philadelphus (Mock Orange, 'Syringa')
Beautiful flowering shrubs with a heavy scent and a wealth of white blossom. With such a number of different kinds, you can have a succession blooming through June and July. *P. coronarius*, very early, flowering in June, has rather a twiggy habit, but a lovely scent; it is not grown so much these

Philadelphus 'Beauclere'

days. *P. microphyllus*, with small flowers, and *P. grandiflorus*, scentless, but with large flowers, are perhaps more popular. The hybrid *P. lemoinei* has given rise to many varieties with masses of fragrant flowers. Good single ones are 'Avalanche', 'Mont Blanc' and 'Belle Etoile'. 'Boule d'Argent' and 'Virginal' are lovely double varieties. For me they are all lovely, and I think they are perfect for weddings. By removing all the leaves you are left with a mass of white blossom on coal-black branches; add to this some tall stems of white delphiniums, a bunch or two of white peonies, a few pink or white roses, and you have the most beautiful bridal flower group imaginable (see Plate 16). June to July is the only time of year for a really large, completely white flower group. At any other time there is always an element of green. The small golden-leaved philadelphus, *P. coronarius aureus*, I find extremely useful; it is a compact shrub with delightful lime-green foliage — sweetly-scented, but blooms reluctantly.

CONDITIONING Hammer ends of stems well, or pare up the bark, and put into warm water immediately. Never leave the stems out of water for long, as if they once flag it is very hard to revive them. Remove as many leaves as possible as this shrub finds it difficult to take up enough water to supply both leaves and flowers at once.

Philodendron

P. scandens with its deep-green glossy leaves has become a very useful house plant and is used for many displays for show-rooms, restaurants, and hotels.

Phlomis fruticosa (Jerusalem Sage)

P. fruticosa is a hardy evergreen shrub with whorls of yellow flowers in June. I remove some of the leaves and use these flower spikes quite often; their soft yellow colouring mixes well with a really summery group of lupins, spurges and the lime-green hosta leaves. The green rounded seed heads are nice in late summer for arranging with mixed green foliages.

TO PRESERVE Remove all the leaves and hang the seed heads upside down to dry.

Phlox

Half-hardy annuals and hardy perennials. The perennial phlox has become a great favourite of mine over the years, as they bloom for such a long time. Although they thrive on good food and plenty of moisture, they do well in my clay soil and give a wealth of colour for weeks. They are lovely to arrange with a really lavishly mixed summer group. Their vivid colours add gaiety, and the deep reds and petunia shades are excellent for a vase of mixed reds. As soon as the petals start to drop it is important to remove each one of these, or the sprays will look faded long before they are over. The variegated 'Norah Leigh', although a slow grower, is both an asset to the border and lovely in a mixed green group. The annual *Phlox drummondii* are so pretty in the border, in a wide range of colours. Small pieces used for a vase look gay and colourful and last much better than expected.

CONDITIONING Hammer ends of stems well and give a good drink in warm water before arranging them.

Phormium tenax (New Zealand Flax)

Regrettably only half-hardy. I have used these delightful sword-shaped leaves and their strange spiky flower whenever I have had the chance. Fortunately, they are imported into Covent Garden. They are excellent used as a background for large groups in autumn and winter, and last for weeks. Besides the plain green, there is a green one with a cream stripe (*P. tenax variegatum*), and another one which has reddish leaves (*P. tenax atropurpureum*); all are most welcome.

CONDITIONING These leaves last extremely well in water. It is a good idea to trim the ends of the leaves to a point, so that you get the end easily into the vase; they are very square and difficult to handle, and can take up far too much room in the container unless they are trimmed in this way.

Phygelius (Cape Figwort)

P. capensis is a half-hardy herbaceous perennial with orange-scarlet flowers from midsummer onwards; these are nice to arrange with the orange and red dahlias and some autumn or colourful foliage.

CONDITIONING Put ends of stems into boiling water and then allow several hours in deep water.

Physalis (Cape Gooseberry, Winter Cherry)

Greenhouse and hardy perennials. *P. peruviana* is known to most of us as the Cape Gooseberry; it has orange balloon-like seed vessels, containing a bright orange berry. These can be used when fresh, but are more commonly dried off and used in the winter (see Colour Plate IX). I prefer to use them before they have turned orange: I put them into a vase when they are green and find them very effective at this stage, with a collection of other green seed heads or foliages. The hardy species usually cultivated is *P. alkekengi*, the Bladder Herb or Winter Cherry (though the latter name is more often applied to *Solanum capicastrum*). *Physalis franchettii* is a giant form that has been recommended to me by Mrs Margery Fish, from whom it is obtainable.

TO PRESERVE   Remove all the leaves when the heads have turned orange, then bunch and hang upside down.

Physocarpus *see* SPIRAEA

Physostegia virginiana (Obedient Plant, Dragon's Head)
Hardy perennial, blooming in pink and carmine, 'obedient' because the individual little flowers swing round on the stem to face any way you want.

Physostegia virginiana

These spiky flowers mix well in any group in pink and mauve colours.
CONDITIONING   Give a long drink in warm water before arranging.

Phytolacca americana (American Poke Weed, Red-Ink Plant)
Hardy perennial. This is a plant that I love — I think I have been partly responsible for its growing popularity in flower arrangement in these last years. I grew it from seed a long time ago, and use it continually. It is attractive in the green flower stage, but even more useful when the berries form; the heads then look like clusters of blackberries and go well with so many different things, but particularly with the red heads of the sedum 'Autumn Glory' and a few stems of red or pink hydrangeas.
CONDITIONING   When using the flower stems, place the ends of the stems in boiling water, before giving a long drink. When using the berries, remove all the leaves and give a long drink in tepid water, though as they last so well no extra care is really necessary. One point I must make here is the fact that they stain very badly, so be very careful when the seeds are really ripe as they fall easily and the stains are so difficult to remove.

Picea (Spruce, Christmas Tree)
A word about the decorations for the Christmas tree. If it is possible to adopt a colour scheme, it makes just all the difference. For instance, if one year you decide to have all the decorations green and gold, or red and silver, or gold and silver, red and gold, and so on, I cannot begin to tell you what a good effect that it makes. When using branches of spruce in water for a decoration, the blue-greys are the most effective. *P. pungens* is very blue and most striking for a winter group, with sprays of lichen-covered branches and some of the lovely blue-grey eucalyptus leaves.

Pieris
P. japonica is a hardy evergreen shrub with cascades of white flowers in the early spring like trusses of white lily of the valley. At Winkfield we get it up from Cornwall in March. It looks well in so many vases. Try one elegantly-shaped stem alone in a Chinese jar, or use it with a collection of foliage — eucalyptus in its various forms, forsythia branches,

green guelder rose (this is of course imported as early as March), stems of green hellebores. A stem or two will transform a vase of white tulips. *P. forrestii* has the additional distinction of producing

Phytolacca americana (see facing page)

striking new growths of leaves in early spring. They are brilliant red looking at first sight rather like poinsettia flowers. The red persists until after the flowers appear so that when it is in full bloom the shrub is a magnificent sight. All pieris are peat lovers.

CONDITIONING   Well hammer the ends of the stems, before giving a long drink.

Pineapple Flower *see* EUCOMIS

Pinks *see* DIANTHUS

Pittosporum tenuifolium
Evergreen, slightly tender shrub, growing well in Cornwall and Ireland. It has very shiny small leaves and is in great demand by the florists in winter and

early spring. It has the advantage of lasting a long time in water. I don't think I ever use it very much; I find it slightly difficult, as the stems are often clumsily laden with foliage. However, it can be a good stand-by in early spring and can be used with other foliages, but avoid crowding it into a vase so that it overshadows the blooms of tulips or daffodils; it can hide so much of their colour. On the other hand, if you can get a delicate well shaped branch, it is very effective alone as it has such beautiful dark stems — almost black. *P. tobira* has larger leaves and more conspicuous creamy-white flowers, sweetly scented.

Plantago (Plantain)
This you may think is an odd choice, but the red-leaved and the double are very decorative and I find if I do not weed them all out by mistake (as I have a habit of doing!), they are useful to pick for any small foliage group.

Plantain Lily *see* HOSTA

Platycodon grandiflorum (Balloon Flower)
Hardy herbaceous perennial. *P. grandiflorum* has blue or white flowers that are effective when cut, but it is not a plant that is very widely grown. I think it looks extremely well in a shallow bowl, with a few glass blocks to hide the wire or pin-holder; in this way you get the beauty of every flower and stem.

CONDITIONING   Put ends of stems into boiling water for a few minutes, before giving a long drink.

Plumbago capensis (Leadwort)
A charming plant, *P. capensis*, a lovely pale blue, can be trained in the cool greenhouse to cover a trellis. *Ceratostigma* is a hardy shrubby related genus that has very good blue flowers in the summer; it is nice to use in small pieces for a really mixed vase in August.

CONDITIONING   Put ends of stems into boiling water for a few minutes, then give a long drink.

Plume Poppy *see* MACLEAYA

Poinsettia *see* EUPHORBIA

Poke Weed *see* PHYTOLACCA

Polianthes (Tuberose)
Half-hardy bulbs. These arrive here in spring from France or any warm climate. The scent from their creamy-white flowers, backed with pink, is delicious. Added to a vase of white and cream flowers they not only look lovely, and rather exotic, but scent the whole room exquisitely.

Polyanthus *see* PRIMULA

Polygonatum multiflorum (Solomon's Seal)
Hardy perennial. Has arched wands of green leaves and hanging white flowers. It is often found growing wild in the woods, and is happy growing in shade. I find that I use it a lot in the early spring, to mix in with green groups (see Colour Plate IV). The leaves turn a lovely shade of yellow in autumn, and I like to use it then in vases of mixed autumn colours — the stems add such good curves, giving balance to the base of a vase. There is a new one with variegated foliage which I haven't tried yet.
TO PRESERVE After flowering, the leaves absorb glycerine well: leave them in the solution for four or five days, and then hang them upside down to dry.

Polygonum (Knotweed)
Hardy herbaceous perennials and climbers. The best known is *P. baldschuanicum*, the Russian Vine, which climbs rampageously and will cover an arch or wall more quickly than any plant I know. The herbaceous varieties with their pink and white flowers are very useful in the late summer. They stand well in water, and are good in small vases. *P. vacciniifolium* is more suitable for a rock garden, but its pink spiky flowers dry well and I use them in a small dried group in the winter. If you have an odd corner, *P. cuspidatum* has beautifully variegated leaves and is another asset for picking, adding as all variegated plants do a touch of sunlight to garden and vase alike.
TO PRESERVE Cut the flowers just as they turn colour, and hang them upside down to dry.

Poppy *see* PAPAVER

Portugal Laurel *see* PRUNUS LUSITANICA

Potentilla
Hardy herbaceous perennials and sub-shrubs. Starry-faced little flowers in bright red and yellows.

There are many kinds and I find I have grown very fond of the shrubby varieties (*P. fruticosa*) as they give almost continuous bloom for months. I use sprays of the little yellow flowers in the summer and autumn, to add the touch of yellow that is so important in any mixed vase.
CONDITIONING Put the ends of the stems in boiling water for a few minutes, before giving a long drink.

Prickly Heath *see* PERNETTYA

Primrose *see* PRIMULA

Primula malacoides

Primula (Auricula, Cowslip, Primrose, Polyanthus)
Greenhouse and hardy perennials. This family is enormous, and I hardly know where to begin. The primrose is one of the best known of our wild flowers and I use them in posies, in 'moss gardens' and in church for the Easter festival, often in a mass to decorate the window-sills of the church.

A Victorian watch-case which makes an interesting container for a few pretty bits from the spring garden, including auriculas and primulas. The flower stems are pressed into a well-soaked lump of oasis. A lump of sugar should be placed at the back of the group to absorb the moisture and prevent the glass from steaming up

M

When using primrose and polyanthus massed, you can get the best effect if you have them in bunches, surrounded by their own leaves, as you can see from Colour Plate II. Never use them on very long stems as they quickly droop. Auricula I have mentioned already (see under 'A'). *P. obconica* and *P. malacoides* we know of as pot plants that give a long flowering period and are to be seen on many a window-sill. *P. denticulata*, with its rounded heads, is used as a cut flower and can be bought in bunches in spring; they are nice to use with the purple hellebore as the colourings go so well together. There are many bog varieties but these rarely come on the market, and so they are little used as a cut flower; if however, you have them, they mix in with groups of summer flowers.

CONDITIONING Primroses need little special care; bunch and place in the vase. Polyanthus, however, are better if the ends of the stems are put into boiling water as soon as they are picked; afterwards give a long drink. Another method which gives excellent results is to prick the stem just below the flower head to release any air bubbles. The same applies to the bog varieties.

TO PRESERVE The only seed heads that dry well are those of the bog primula *P. sikkimensis*. Allow the seed heads to form on the plant, pick and bunch and hang them upside down to dry.

Privet *see* LIGUSTRUM

Protea
This is a South African flower, imported here quite often now that they can be flown over. Their flower heads are large and star-shaped, with fluffy centres surrounded by pointed petals in pinks and reds. They are used in large groups with success, and both *P. grandiflora* and *P. cordata* dry well.

CONDITIONING Put ends of stems in boiling water for a minute, then give a long drink.

TO PRESERVE Put the flowers into a warm oven (about 200° F): the centres will fall out as they open, but you are left with the lovely star-shaped outer petals.

Prunella
P. grandiflora is a deep purple hardy perennial, which makes good ground cover and is excellent for cutting.

TO PRESERVE The seed-heads dry well if hung upside down.

Prunus amygdalus (Almond)
Almond blossom forces well to give delicate sprays of pink blossom indoors as early as February. A few sprays of this add so much to a collection of very expensive spring flowers that it cannot be valued too highly. Sprays of almond fruits are beautiful in the autumn in a mixed green or foliage group.

TO FORCE If branches are picked after Christmas, remember that they will take about five weeks to open into blossom. Hammer stems well, place in warm water and keep in a cold room for the first two days, then bring into warmth.

Prunus (Plum, Cherry, Apricot, Peach)
A wide collection of trees and shrubs, including useful fruits and some decorative species. The peach, apricot, cherry and plum are of course edible species and although the blossom is lovely to use, it is often too precious for arrangement. This can only be managed by extremely careful pruning, and small pieces can be picked to use in a vase to great effect. Among the best flowering cherries are *P. serrulata* (Japanese Cherry); varieties include double and single blooms in pink and white. One of the best known is the variety 'Kanzan', which I have used in two very different arrangements shown on Colour Plates II and III. *P. subhirtella autumnalis* is one of the best for growing to pick, and flowering as it does in the winter is a joy to have. Of the doubles, the lime-green heads of *P. serrulata grandiflora* 'Ukon' are indescribably lovely. Some of the cherries have good autumn colour and although the leaves may not last very long in water, I love using a spray or two for special effect, even if only for a day or so.

Prunus (Portugal Laurel; Cherry Laurel)
These laurels are hardy evergreens with bold shiny green leaves that are a constant standby for the flower arranger. Useful as a good solid background for large church-groups as they act as an excellent shield for screening light — this is very often a problem when doing flowers on church window-sills and chancel steps. Portugal laurel, *Prunus lusitanica*, has sprays of delicate pendulous white flowers, and with the leaves removed, these branches can be most decorative, having a good Chinese effect with the white blossom on dark stems. The flowers are followed by dark purple

fruits; I find these useful as well. The variegated *P. lusitanica variegata* is a plant that lights up any dark corner and I use it more and more.

The cherry laurel, *P. laurocerasus*, is an excellent evergreen for the town, with clusters of pink flowers in very early spring; these show best if some of the leaves are removed and then it can be effectively used with tulips or daffodils.

CONDITIONING Hammer ends of stems well, before giving a long drink.

TO PRESERVE Laurel takes glycerine very well and I find this worth applying, even though the plant is an evergreen, to have a good solidly-shaped leaf to add to a dried collection.

Pteridium aquilinum (Bracken Fern)

I feel I must mention bracken as it is pressed a great deal for winter arrangements. It will not stand in a hot room without curling unless it is treated; then it is excellent used with some dried seed heads and cut chrysanthemums. A few sprays look surprisingly well with laurel leaves to help out a bunch of early daffodils; I think it is the mixture of textures that is so effective.

TO PRESERVE Cut the stems of bracken in various shades of cream, brown and green, lay them carefully between newspaper and place them under a weight. If they are to be used for Christmas decorations, it is advisable to soak them in a solution of weak starch water; this stiffens them so that they take the paint and glitter better.

Pulmonaria officinalis (Lungwort)

Low-growing hardy herbaceous plant. For me its great attraction is the fact that it is often in bloom in February. It has strange little flowers that are pink and blue on the same stem. The foliage is prettily mottled, but it is a little difficult to make it last in water. The small flowers, however, look well in a 'moss garden' and add a very helpful early touch of blue.

Pulsatilla (Pasque Flower)

This small hardy perennial has anemone-like flowers surrounded by soft grey serrated leaves. They are one of the joys of the spring rock garden and last well in water. They look pretty arranged by themselves, but as they are rather special it is difficult to pick a great number without spoiling the show in the garden, so I usually add one or two

to a small mixed vase or to a 'moss garden'. They grow wild in Switzerland in a pale lilac colour, but some of the new hybrids are in lovely colours of pale lilac to deep reds.

CONDITIONING Put the ends of the stems into warm water, not allowing the fringe of fluff to touch the water.

TO PRESERVE Cut the seed heads when they are well formed and hang them up to dry. These are fluffy balls and dry very well to mix in small dried vases.

Pyracantha (Firethorn)

A thorny, berried evergreen shrub. The variety I like most is the yellow-berried *P. rogersiana flava*, for arranging with dahlias and all the autumn shades. Large sprays of all these berries are very good as backing for large groups, lasting well and in churches for instance, giving a glow of colour against a background of stone or wood. All the colours are excellent and the brilliant orange berries of *P. coccinea lalandii* last well on the bushes and give colour to the garden for many weeks.

TO PRESERVE The berries last a long time, but to avoid shrivelling it is helpful to paint them with clear varnish.

Pyrethrum

Hardy perennials with single or double daisy like flowers in pink, white or red, properly called *Chrysanthemum coccineum*, but nearly always catalogued under Pyrethrum. They are useful for cutting as they flower at rather a sparse time of year, and as they last well in water they have become a popular cut flower. Personally I find them difficult to arrange as they have such stiff form; though they are suitable to add as a centre to a mixed garden-basket or vase in June.

Pyrus (Pear)

Branches of any fruit blossom are always a joy to pick — but of course only do so if you have old and well-established trees. Gnarled and well-shaped branches are most useful in winter as a background for a few flowers.

CONDITIONING When using the branches in flower, hammer ends of stems well, before giving a long drink in warm water.

Quaking Grass *see* BRIZA

Quercus (Oak)

Hardy deciduous and evergreen trees with many varieties. I use the evergreen oak (*Quercus ilex*) in the winter; arranged in January with some of the very early paper white narcissi and a few lemons, it can look like the leaves of an orange tree at a quick glance. The flowers of the male oak have pendulous catkins in spring and I love to use a well-shaped branch in a shallow dish with a few tulips. Branches of really good shape are useful in winter as a background, as I have mentioned before.

Quince *see* CYDONIA

Ranunculus (Crowfoot, Buttercup)

Hardy and half-hardy herbaceous and tuberous-rooted perennials. The tuberous-rooted French and Turban varieties (R. *asiaticus*) single and double, are sold in our florist's shops in bunches in early spring, and there is a lovely small button red one that arrives in time to add to a candle cup for a Christmas arrangement. Just after that, we get a small delicate pink one with a really lime-green centre; these are quite adorable in January and placed with a few sprays of forced lily of the valley make a charming group for a piece of delicate china. Any flower of subtle colouring is always of greater value for easier mixing. The later-flowering ranunculus imported from France are a great asset as they have a wide colour range and mix well with self or contrasting colours.

CONDITIONING The ends of the stems are best put into boiling water for a few seconds, before being given a long drink.

Reseda odorata (Mignonette)

Perennial, but more often grown as an annual. It requires plenty of sun and does best in sheltered beds. A strange greenish flower that is effective with leaves and seed heads in the summer, though it is chiefly grown for its lovely scent.

TO PRESERVE If the flowers are allowed to seed, they have pretty seed heads, which should be picked and bunched and then hung upside down to dry.

Rheum (Rhubarb)

The ornamental-leaved species have magnificent red and coloured leaves in the spring; it is possible to use them at this time as they have not yet grown too large, though it is advisable to condition them well before you put them in a vase. They make an excellent base for a spring group of forsythia, green hellebore and a few white-backed daffodils. The flowers are tall, handsome plumes of delicate pink or white (see page 97) but it is better to use them when they are fully mature or even in their seed head stage, as they will then last longer.

CONDITIONING Put the ends of the leaves in boiling water for a little while, and then completely submerge the whole leaf in a bath of water overnight. This may have to be done again after the first day, as so much depends on the maturity of each leaf.

TO PRESERVE When the seed heads are drying off, pick them and finish the process by hanging them upside down. It is possible to dry them on the plant but if the weather turns wet, you will find that they quickly spoil, so it is better to be on the safe side and pick them.

Rhododendron

An enormous family of shrubs, which includes the azaleas (see p. 103). They grow from the Himalayas to the tropics in various forms. This genus, given lime-free soil, has done so much to enrich our gardens, possibly more than any other. For the flower arranger they are pure joy, and I can say no more than that. Rhododendrons, which are evergreen, have rounded heads with clusters of flowers in all the pinks, purples and reds, also white. There are endless varieties, and there has been much hybridizing through the years. They are wonderful for large groups with their nice long stems. They can also be picked with short stems, or just the flower head itself can be used. These heads give a focal point to any group, and are rewarding whichever way you decide to use them. It is often better if you remove some of the leaves, so that the flower is not obscured in any way. I use either azaleas or rhododendrons, in all their forms, to mix with other flowers or to have on their own, whenever I can get them. You can see them on Colour Plate V.

CONDITIONING As they all have very woody stems, it is very important to hammer the ends of the stems well and to put them into quite hot water and leave overnight or longer if necessary. Overhead spraying helps to keep the heads of some of the rhododendrons from flagging.

Rhus cotinus

Rhus (Sumach)

R. *cotinus* (or *Cotinus coggygria*) is sometimes known as the 'Smoke Tree' because of the lovely fluffy flower and seed head that it produces. It is a deciduous tree with good autumn-coloured foliage either reddish brown or maroon in the case of R. *cotinus purpureus*. It does not stand well in water, and so needs special care, but it looks well in the autumn arranged with other leaves and autumn-coloured flowers in orange or red. The Staghorn Sumach, R. *typhina*, is not so good for cutting, though it is very tempting to use it in autumn as the leaves turn the most lovely colours, but they die almost as soon as they are picked. The seed heads, however, which stand up like candles on the branches and have a very pretty 'red velvet' look, last well in water and are effective in a mixed fruit and flower group; as the stems curl upwards, they can only be used rather short.

CONDITIONING For *Rhus cotinus*, with its lovely but delicate foliage, the ends of the stems should be well boiled and then the whole spray submerged right under water for several hours.

TO PRESERVE The seed heads of the Sumach will dry if you hang the heads upside down, but they do tend to lose their colour quickly.

Ribes sanguineum (Flowering Currant)

Hardy shrub with pink or red flowers in spring. It is useful to arrange in a vase, though it has the disadvantage of what some people consider rather an unpleasant smell when cut; however, I find that this wears off very quickly as soon as you stop handling it. It is one of the best shrubs to force, and will come out well in water, when brought into the house in early January. It forces white or very pale pink, and not the strong colour you might expect. It is then lovely to use with a few daffodils and tulips. Also attractive are the yellow-leaved *R. aureum* and *R. alpinum aureum*. As I think you must already have realized, I love plants with golden foliage!

Ribes sanguineum

CONDITIONING Hammer ends of stems well, before putting in water for a long drink. When forcing it, always stand it in the cold, indoors, for a day, before you bring it into the warm. Allow four weeks for it to come into full bloom.

Ricinus communis (Castor-oil Plant)
Half-hardy annual. This is grown here mainly for flower arrangement, as it has large palm-shaped leaves that are good to use with foliage groups. The one with red foliage (*R. communis sanguineus*) is the most popular and to my mind the most effective. The perennial castor-oil plant is *Fatsia japonica*, q.v.

Rodgersia
Hardy herbaceous perennials which seem to enjoy really wet conditions. *R. podophylla* (Rodgers'

Bronze Leaf) has handsome bronze leaves which make a decoration in themselves, just two or three in an oriental arrangement. They can also look effective with branches and flame tulips, or later in the year with a few bronze-coloured roses or dahlias.

CONDITIONING The leaves are very tender and need careful attention, especially in the early spring. Put the ends of the stems into boiling water for a few minutes, and then submerge completely in a bath overnight.

Romneya (Californian Tree Poppy)
R. coulteri has enormous single white heads with a tuft of yellow stamens in the centre of the flower. Quite beautiful, and superb in a white and green group, but it is a little tender and is not often available as a cut flower. *R. hybrida* is perhaps a little hardier.

CONDITIONING Put ends of stems into boiling water and then give at least twelve hours in a cool place in deep water.

Rosa (Rose)
What flower gives more pleasure to the grower and the arranger? Roses are more widely grown these days than ever before, partly as they make for such easy gardening. The Floribundas are becoming increasingly popular, because of their long period of flowering and being so useful to pick. Of the Floribundas, to name but a few: 'Iceberg' (white), 'Magenta' (purple), 'Elizabeth of Glamis' (apricot), 'Fashion' (salmon), 'Dearest' (soft pink), 'Rosemary Rose' (cherry red) ... though of course one could go on for ever.

The Hybrid teas are numerous; try to grow some in the newer and more unusual colours, as well as established favourites. Of all flowers I think they are the least complicated to deal with; they are excellent on their own, either just a few stems or grouped in a mass, either self-coloured or mixed. They can be arranged in almost any type of container, be it glass, china, metal, wood, or pottery. Personally, I like them best in a mass by themselves with their own foliage, but I also use them as the centre of many a large group, as you can see, for instance, from Colour Plate VI.

The old-fashioned shrub roses have a special charm and are being widely grown, for their profusion of bloom and their exquisite scent. For

Rose 'Constance Spry'

arranging in the house they are not really so reliable as they do not last very well; however, they are a pleasure to cut and enjoy just for a couple of days. As they bloom so freely, it is possible to bring in a nice lot of them for a real wealth of colour, and not detract from the show

Rose 'Constance Spry'

in the garden. The modern shrub rose 'Constance Spry', is the only name I am going to mention here, as I feel it is as yet little known and is a 'must' for the flower or rose lover. It has large delicate-pink blooms, shading to a deeper-pink centre, with the sweetest musky scent. A word of warning — it needs space, as it does grow enormous! Do not overlook the foliage of the older roses. R. *rubrifolia* has the most attractive silvery-purple leaves and good hips. When the bush is large enough for picking, the branches make wonderful backing for a mauve-pink vase, but in fact I find I can use it for almost any colour scheme. The species roses R. *virginiana* and R. *nitida* both have foliage with rich autumn colour. Lastly, the rugosa roses 'Frau Dagmar Hastrup', R. *typica* (*rubra*) and R. *scarbosa* all have excellent hips.
CONDITIONING Put ends of stems in boiling water for a minute, and then give a long drink.

Rosemary *see* ROSMARINUS

Rosmarinus officinalis (Rosemary)
Hardy evergreen shrub with fragrant foliage that is useful to pick and use all through the year. The flowers are delicate blue and these can be added to a mixed vase in July or August.

Royal Fern *see* OSMUNDA

Rubus (Blackberry, Raspberry, Wineberry)
Hardy perennial fruits and shrubs. They can all be used in sprays as available. The wineberries (R. *phoenicolasius*) with their downy red fluffy coats are most decorative; sprays of these and blackberries are all exceedingly helpful to add interest and contrast to a vase in late summer. I have used blackberries and red roses to great effect.

Rudbeckia (Coneflower, Black-eyed Susan)
Hardy annuals and herbaceous perennials. Double and single, with showy yellow, brown and orange flowers in late July and August. Their vivid colouring makes them a welcome centre for a late summer vase of browns and yellows. They last well and their daisy-like flowers with dark centres are very effective. The annuals derived from R. *hirta* are the most showy, and well worth growing.
CONDITIONING Put the ends of the stems into boiling water and leave for a few minutes, then allow a long drink.

Ruta graveolens (Rue)
A small herb with a close crop of divided leaves that are generally grey-blue in colour, though there is a variegated green and white one. As it is evergreen, I use it often in a small vase in winter to eke out a few precious flowers. R. *graveolens* 'Jackman's Blue' is particularly good.

St John's Wort *see* HYPERICUM

Saintpaulia (African Violet)
Small violet-like flowers in shades of pink and mauve; for the warm greenhouse, though they are used as house plants as well, very decorative.

Salix (Willow)
Hardy deciduous trees of many varieties. The

golden weeping willow, *S. vitellina pendula* (which you may find catalogued under a large variety of names, including *S. babylonica ramulis aureis*, *S. chrysocoma* or *S. alba tristis*) is one of the most decorative for the garden, and I enjoy using wands of its weeping branches for a large group in March. The pussy willows, as they are commonly known (*S. discolor*), are delightful in early spring as a background for daffodils and tulips. You can gather them from the hedgerows, or many people grow them in the garden, though as they grow rapidly and very large this is not advisable unless you have plenty of room for them. *S. matsudana tortuosa*, the contorted willow, I have become very fond of as it grows in superb shapes and gives a wonderful outline for an oriental type of vase; it has many uses and I should like to grow many more.

CONDITIONING The weeping willow needs to be very well looked after; hammer the ends of the stems or boil them in an inch of boiling water, and then allow twelve hours completely submerged in cold water.

Salpiglossis
Half-hardy annual. *S. sinuata* has open cup-shaped flowers not unlike alstroemeria, except for colour; the colourings are most varied and you can often get a most unusual combination of 'dirty' brownish and reddish shades. Although they are delicate to handle, they last very well in a vase. I find that I often build up a vase in July around one particular stem, and it makes for something of great interest.
CONDITIONING Place the ends of the stems in very hot water and leave them until it cools. Avoid boiling water unless you shield the blooms, as they burn so easily.

Salvia (Sage, Clary)
Hardy and half-hardy perennials with a wide range. Probably the ones I use most are *S. haematodes* (good clear blue) and *S. turkestanica* (tall stems of whitish flowers surrounded by pink-edged bracts). *S. turkestanica* tends to be rather short-lived and is often best treated as a biennial. Both of these flower in midsummer and are extremely pretty mixed with summer flowers, either to add a touch of blue or as a blue foil for a muted vase of mauves. *S. splendens* is not hardy and is quite different from the others, having glowing scarlet flowers and

bright foliage; it adds distinction and impact to a mixed red vase of dahlias and roses, phlox, and anything else that suggests itself.

Sambucus nigra (Elder)
Hardy deciduous shrub with flat round white flowers and black berries, that grows wild in the south of England. I enjoy using it both in the flower and fruit stage. The big clusters of flowers are most effective if the leaves are first removed and the sprays then put with other white flowers, such as lilies, for a large group, or the late double tulips and lilac; or just with a collection of wild cow parsley. The clusters of black fruits that follow need careful handling as they drop when ripe and stain badly, but look so good with reds, black grapes and red roses. The golden-foliaged species, *S. nigra aurea*, is very effective. *Sambucus nigra laciniata*, the cut-leaved elder, is a good hardy deciduous ornamental-leaved shrub which I like to use in a vase of foliage in late spring and early summer. It is found growing wild in parts of Scotland. The flower, in spring, is a small fluffy plume and so attractive that one is tempted to pick it, but it simply does not last.
CONDITIONING If you are picking branches of elder for their leaves alone, then you will find the following method quite effective: hammer ends of stems well and then soak for several hours in warm water. Restand in hot water and finally allow a long cold drink. For both flowers and foliage I use a slightly different treatment: put the ends of stems into boiling water for a little while, and then allow a night in deep water.

Sanguinaria canadensis (Bloodroot)
Hardy perennial flowering herb with double and single white flowers in spring. They last surprisingly well in water and are effective in small spring groups, or in a shallow dish alone, and are also very effective in silver or glass.

Sansevieria (Bowstring Hemp)
These plants are generally grown as house plants. They have sword-like fleshy leaves, usually well variegated, and are often known as Mother-in-law's Tongue. Much in demand by the flower arranger as they last for weeks in water and are so useful for a severe upright effect; they can look well in a shallow vase (as on Colour Plate IV), with

a few rather choice yellow arum lilies to complete the arrangement.

Santolina (Lavender Cotton)

S. chamaecyparissus (or *S. incana*) is a hardy evergreen shrubby plant with aromatic small feathery green or grey leaves, and button daisy-like flowers in pale and deep yellow in late summer. I like to use small pieces of the foliage in the winter or early spring; when greenery is really scarce, they are more than useful. The little daisy flowers are nice to mix in a small summer group (as on Colour Plate VII).

CONDITIONING Hammer ends of stems well, before giving a long drink.

Saxifraga (Rockfoil)

Hardy perennial rock and border plants. The rock saxifrages are not used very much in flower arrangement as they have such short stems, though I do occasionally use a whole cushion of the encrusted silver and green, or the yellow variegated, in a small group in early spring. *Saxifraga umbrosa* (London Pride) with its delicate stems of bell-like flowers mixes well with a vase of dianthus, candytuft and any small summer flowers. The large-leaved pink-flowering plant formerly known as a saxifrage or megasea, is now called Bergenia, q.v.

Scabiosa (Scabious)

Hardy perennials and annuals. The most commonly used and valued flower in this family is the perennial *S. caucasica*, 'Clive Greaves', a rich clear blue, with wonderful lasting qualities, which endear it to any flower arranger. The white one is also becoming very popular. They can be arranged either alone or with a mixture of self-coloured flowers; they are lovely in a mass in a silver bowl or in delicate china. The mauves and pinks of the annual scabious are effective in small summer groups, though the perennials last a little longer, and don't shed their petals, and are invaluable in hot summer days as a cut flower for the house.

CONDITIONING Cut the ends of the stems and give a long drink, preferably overnight.

Schizanthus (Butterfly-flower)

A pretty annual with curiously-shaped blossoms in clustered heads of many colours on the same stem: rose-pink and orange, lilac and violet with an orange blotch — all with a strange pansy-like flower. They are usually grown in a cool greenhouse, and so it is not very often that one can use them as a cut flower, though they last extremely well and are nice in a vase on their own or mixed with a collection of summer flowers.

CONDITIONING Put the ends of the stems into boiling water for a few seconds, then give a long drink before arranging.

Schizostylis coccinea (Kaffir Lily, Crimson Flag)

Hardy perennial. Pink or red flowers, rather like a miniature gladiolus, lasting well in water and flowering in the autumn so that they make a useful change for a vase. They are very attractive arranged with a few autumn leaves.

Scilla (Squill, Bluebell)

Hardy bulbous plants. The rock variety *S. sibirica* has bright blue flowers and these add just the right touch of blue to a small 'moss garden' in the early spring. The common bluebell *S. nonscripta* has a lovely scent and can be used as a cut flower (see under 'Bluebell'). The garden variety *S. hispanica* in blue, white, or a delightful lilac pink, has large flowers and stiffer stems and therefore is really better for cutting; they arrange well and look very effective by themselves, or mixed in a vase of self-coloured flowers.

CONDITIONING Cut the ends of the stems and give a long drink in cold water.

TO PRESERVE The seed head of the scilla is very graceful when allowed to form and dry. Pick in the green seed head stage and hang upside down.

Scrophularia (Figwort)

The only species which I feel is worthy of a place in the garden is *S. nodosa variegata*, a statuesque plant with strangely square stems and green leaves striped and blotched with cream. It is a delight in the border as it keeps its leaves well into the winter and is attractive in the house when cut. Unfortunately it does not last well in water, but nevertheless it is worth picking as it can easily be replaced after a day or so.

CONDITIONING Put the ends of the stems in an inch of boiling water for a few minutes and then completely submerge the whole stem in warm water for as long as possible.

Sea Buckthorn *see* HIPPOPHAE

Sea Holly *see* ERYNGIUM

Seakale (*Crambe maritima*)
This is of course a vegetable, but if you can get the chance of using it the blue-grey leaves are delightful, especially as a foil for a summer vase of blues and greys.

Sedum (Stonecrop)
Hardy perennial rock and border plants, that are excellent for cutting. *S. spectabile* is probably the best known variety, and the hybrid 'Autumn Joy', which has slightly larger heads and a deeper colour, is one that I use continually; it gives a good focal point to a large vase in the autumn (see Colour Plate VIII). The rich red colour is good to mix with the black heads of *Veratrum nigrum* and the berried spikes of *Phytolacca americana*. The dark maroon leaves and flower heads of *S. maximum atropurpureum* look well with any autumn group

and add a touch of darker colour to a vase of dahlias, roses and others, in shades of pink. The variegated green-and-white leaved *S. spectabile variegatum* I would also recommend to the flower arranger. *Sedum rosea* (or *S. rhodiola*) has peculiarly-scented greenish-yellow flowers in spring.
CONDITIONING   Cut the stems on the slant and allow a good drink in deep water.
TO PRESERVE   The flower heads of the sedums dry well and make a useful contribution to a dried group. Pick when well matured on the plant and hang them upside down to dry. Or they can be left to dry on the plant.

Sempervivum (House Leek)
Hardy perennial succulent with rosettes of leaves that are much sought after by flower arrangers, to use as the focal point of a small group.

Senecio (Ragwort; Cineraria)
Hardy and slightly-tender perennial herbs and

Silybum marianum

hardy flowering shrubs. The grey-foliaged ciner-arias are often tender, but are well worth growing for cutting almost all the year round. The delicate leaves of *S. maritima* I like to use complete on the chunky stem — or just the individual leaves, with garden pinks and small roses for posies in the summer as on Colour Plate VII. *S. laxifolius* is perhaps one of the most useful small shrubs for cutting; it has rounded grey leaves and pretty yellow daisy-like flowers in midsummer.

CONDITIONING   The soft-stemmed cinerarias need to have the ends of the stems put into boiling water for a few seconds, before they have a long drink. The hard woody varieties should also have a long drink and the ends of the stems should be hammered beforehand.

Shortia

Hardy perennials. Small plants with rounded leaves of good colour in the spring, with shading in red on green foliage. Enjoying shade and peaty soil, they have often been used to edge rhodo-dendron beds. Pretty in a small vase of spring flowers, with some fritillarias and a stem or two of auriculas; they add weight and interest to the base of the vase.

Sidalcea

Hardy perennial herb. Tall stems of single pink mallow-like flowers, in various shades. Useful to cut in midsummer and add to a really mixed summer vase. It lacks sufficient distinction of form for arrangement on its own.

CONDITIONING   Put the ends of the stems into boiling water for a few minutes, before giving a long drink. This is very important as it will not stand well unless it is treated in this way.

Silene (Catchfly)

The hardy perennial *S. schafta*, with a brilliant pink single flower, is the one that I like best of all to use in a flower arrangement. It adds excellent colour to a small vase in late summer.

Silk Bark Oak *see* GREVILLEA

Silybum marianum (Milk Thistle, Holy Thistle)

S. marianum, an annual, is good to grow for its very decorative leaves — green, spotted with white. These are so prickly that they are hard to handle, but highly effective if used in a green or green-and-white group in July. (See illustration p. 183.)

CONDITIONING   The ends of the stems must be put in boiling water for a few minutes, before being given a long drink.

Sisyrinchium (Satin Flower)

Hardy perennials. *S. striatum* has yellow flowers in June. I find that these flowers when cut tend to fade quickly in water, but I sometimes use them just for a touch of pale yellow in a mixed vase. I prefer their green seed heads and use these continually in vases of foliage and seed heads. They also dry well and, turning almost black, look very effective with berries and bright autumn colours, as you can see from Colour Plate IX.

CONDITIONING   Put the ends of the stems in the flower stage into boiling water and then allow a long drink.

TO PRESERVE   Pick the green seed heads, remove all the foliage and hang them upside down.

Skimmia japonica

Hardy evergreen shrub. Attractive, shiny foliage, pretty flowers in pointed clusters of cream, and beautiful scarlet berries, all make this a good shrub for the flower arranger. The berries form only if you grow both male and female plants. They are a good substitute for holly, so that if it is a bad holly year, they are a great help for the Christmas decorations. *S. foremanii* has pale-green leaves and the flower heads are more than useful in April and March.

Snapdragon *see* ANTIRRHINUM

Snowball Tree *see* VIBURNUM

Snowdrop *see* GALANTHUS

Snowflake *see* LEUCOJUM

Solanum capsicastrum (Winter Cherry)

Tender berry-bearing plant that we have come to associate with Christmas. Grown under glass, and used as a house decoration at Christmas-time.

Solidago (Golden Rod)

Hardy herbaceous perennials indigenous to North America, where I understand there are literally hundreds of varieties. It has bright, showy, fluffy, yellow heads of flower in the autumn and grows readily in almost any conditions, which makes it generally popular as a herbaceous plant. It is rather difficult to arrange as the heads are often rather large and bulky and it is better if some of them are removed first. I think I really like it best when it is nearly over; the creamy-brown colour as it fades

The berries used in this pyramid arrangement are from the mountain ash, *Sorbus aucuparis*

is more subtle and, to my mind anyway, prettier than the strong yellow in its full-blown stage. It goes well with the autumn tones of gladiolus and dahlias. *Solidaster luteus*, a hybrid between an unknown solidago and *Aster ptarmicoides*, has paler yellow flowers, in narrower panicles than Golden Rod, and is therefore a better plant for the flower arranger.

CONDITIONING Remove most of the leaves, before giving a long drink.

TO PRESERVE Allow the heads to dry off on the plant, and try to catch it before it reaches the fluffy stage, then pick and store.

Solidaster *see* SOLIDAGO

Solomon's Seal *see* POLYGONATUM

Sorbus (Rowan, Mountain Ash; Whitebeam)
Hardy deciduous trees with white flowers followed by berries of red, white or pink. The Rowan or Mountain Ash, *S. aucuparis*, is perhaps the best known. I love to use it in autumn in a vase of colourful foliages, with a few dahlias and late roses; the clusters of shiny red berries add much interest to a group of this kind. The Whitebeam, *Sorbus aria*, which grows so readily in the chalk hills of the Chilterns, unfurls in early spring with silver-grey tufts of leaves, which from a distance can be mistaken for flowers, on coal black stems. These grey-leaved branches make a lovely background for a vase of white or pale pink flowers.
CONDITIONING Hammer ends of stems well, before giving a long drink.

Sowbread *see* CYCLAMEN

Sparmannia africana
S. africana is an African tree or shrub, as the name implies. It has clusters of white flowers and beautiful spade-shaped green leaves. It will only grow here in a cool greenhouse, so that it is not widely used in flower arrangement; but small pieces of the white flower sprays, in June, arranged in a candle cup, give a touch of the exotic.
CONDITIONING Dip the ends of the stems into boiling water and give a long drink before arranging.

Spartium junceum (Spanish Broom)
S. junceum is a hardy deciduous shrub with sweetly-

scented yellow flowers in midsummer, giving a gay splash of colour to the shrub border. As a cut flower it is rather difficult to keep alive, so use it sparingly, but it provides the touch of strong yellow that is often so necessary to a vase of yellows and orange in July.

CONDITIONING   Put the ends of the stems into boiling water, then give a long drink.

Spathiphyllum floribundum

A cool-greenhouse plant with shiny pointed leaves and a small spiky flower enclosed by a spathe-like white leaf. It lasts well, and I like to use both leaf and flower when possible. The flowers make an excellent centre for a mixed white vase in early spring. I was once able to use some quite large ones for a wedding in a country church, grouped with anthurium leaves and flowers and a few white lilies, but this was exceptional — the flowers are small as a rule and therefore not really suitable for anything larger than a container about a foot high.

Spider Flower see CLEOME

Spindle Tree see EUONYMUS

Spiraea

Hardy deciduous shrubs. The shrubby spiraea *S. arguta*, commonly known as Foam of May, has delicate sprays of white flowers which I love to use with early tulips and daffodils. *S. vanhouttei* has plumes of white flowers and these dry well in seed head form, turning a beautiful creamy brown, and this is how I really like to use them. *S. bumalda*, 'Anthony Waterer', carmine, flowers in July and this good red colour looks excellent in a vase of mixed reds, but again the seed heads are lovely, in the form of a small flat brown head which is invaluable in winter. *S. opulifolia lutea* may be known to you as *Physocarpus opulifolius luteus*. It was recommended to me by Sybil Emberton, who describes it as having leaves rather like those of a flowering currant only smaller, and borne on immensely tall shoots and on shorter curving sprays, both making a useful contribution for arranging. However, it is for its lime-green colour that I have grown to like it, most vivid in spring, but useful in the autumn when the leaf ends become tinged with bronze.

CONDITIONING   Hammer ends of stems well and put into warm water. I find that the leaves of *S. opulifolea lutea* last better if the ends of the stems are plunged into boiling water before they are given a long drink.

TO PRESERVE   When in seed head form, cut and remove the foliage, stand the stems in an inch of water and allow them to dry off slowly in a warm atmosphere.

For the herbaceous 'spiraeas' see Aruncus, Astilbe and Filipendula.

Spotted Laurel see AUCUBA

Squill see SCILLA

Stachyrus praecox

Half-hardy deciduous shrub growing well in Cornwall. It has hanging trails of pale yellow flowers that are a great delight as they come so early in the year — often in February — like a real breath of spring.

Stachys lanata (Lamb's Ears)

Hardy herbaceous perennial, useful for borders and rough ground. Its leaves are densely covered with

Stachys lanata

silky grey hairs, and are very effective for a small group of whites and greys. The flower is pretty when picked in midsummer, but I think I prefer to save it for drying: you then get a beautiful spike of grey to add to a vase of grey dried material and pink chrysanthemums in midwinter.

CONDITIONING The leaves are better if you give them a long drink before arranging, but try not to submerge them or they will lose their silvery appearance.

TO PRESERVE As soon as the seed heads have formed, pick and bunch and hang them upside down to dry.

Star of Bethlehem *see* ORNITHOGALUM

Star of the Veldt *see* DIMORPHOTHECA

Stephanotis floribunda (Clustered Wax Flower, Madagascar Jasmine)
Winter evergreen climbing greenhouse shrub. The beautiful star-shaped waxen flowers have a delicate perfume. Generally used for brides' bouquets or wedding head-dresses, but a cluster just laid on a cream-coloured shell with a few of the waxy leaves makes a superb decoration for the centre of a dining-room table. We used these clusters of flowers with green grapes, on a large gold platter, as a table centre for the dinner in Lancaster House after the Queen's Coronation.

CONDITIONING Stretch a piece of tissue paper over a shallow bowl of water and fix with an elastic band; then make holes in the paper and insert the flower stems. This prevents the waxy flowers from touching the water, which is very important as they would quickly turn brown. Given a few hours in water like this they will stand quite well for an hour or two for bouquets or flower arrangements.

Sternbergia lutea (Winter Daffodil)
Bulbous plants with yellow crocus-like flowers, blooming surprisingly enough in the autumn. Although I have grown these for many years, mine rarely flower, alas; when they do, they provide me with a touch of real spring in November, and I put them into a little green 'moss garden', with any of the little bits that I can often find at that time of year, such as a *Primula* 'Wanda' and a spray or two of *Viburnum fragrans*.

Stinking Hellebore *see* HELLEBORUS

Stonecrop *see* SEDUM

Strelitzia reginae (Bird of Paradise Flower)
Warm-greenhouse plants that are natives of South Africa. They have angular orange flowers with a purple tuft. They are a little awkward to arrange, and, generally speaking, are most effective alone in a shallow dish with a few of their own leaves. Constance Spry had the fun of arranging quantities of them at the time of the Queen's Coronation. We grouped them massed in large boxes in Parliament Square, with other rare flowers flown in from the Commonwealth.

CONDITIONING Cut the ends of the stems on the slant and give a long drink.

Summer Snowdrop *see* LEUCOJUM

Sweet Pea *see* LATHYRUS

Sweet Rocket *see* HESPERIS

Sweet-Scented Tobacco *see* NICOTIANA

Sweet Sultan *see* CENTAUREA

Sweet William *see* DIANTHUS

Sycamore *see* ACER

Symphoricarpus (Snowberry)
Hardy deciduous shrub with clusters of white berries in autumn. I am always amazed how long these stay on the bushes, right into the winter. The best variety that I know of is obtainable from the Sunningdale Nurseries, and they call it 'Constance Spry' as she used and loved it so much. By removing all the leaves, you get lovely sprays of berries to cascade from the front of a small vase. Use them either with green-and-white groups or with a vase of autumn colourings.

Syringa (Lilac)
Hardy deciduous flowering shrub known to us all as Lilac, and known best for its trusses of purple

Stachys lanata in leaf and flower, with sedum, *Leycesteria formosa* and seed-heads of poppies

flowers with a very sweet scent. Nowadays there are many lovely hybrids as well, and the pink Preston Hybrids are well worth growing; their subtle soft colourings are lovely to use in a vase of pastel flowers, with some of the Suttons art-shade poppies, and pale pink peonies. There is also a new and beautiful yellow one *S. vulgaris* 'Primrose' that I have refrained from growing for a long time, but have recently come to enjoy. It makes a valuable and interesting contribution to a soft-yellow and cream arrangement in May and early June.

CONDITIONING It is most important to remove nearly all the foliage, as the stem does not seem able to take up enough water to supply flowers and leaves. If you want to arrange a vase of just lilac alone, then you must use separate branches of leaves. Hammer the ends of the stems very well, and then give a long drink in warm water. When using forced lilac in early spring, I find it will not last well on short stems; it needs hammering and the stems should be put into really boiling water, before they have a long drink.

Tamarix (Tamarisk)
Hardy evergreen and deciduous shrubs, growing well near the seaside. They have plumes of feathery pink flowers in summer, which make a good background for vases of flowers at this time.
CONDITIONING Hammer ends of stems well and stand them in warm water.

Tellima grandiflora
Hardy perennial. A close relative of the *Heuchera* and *Tiarella*, this plant grows easily in woodland and makes a good ground cover. I grow it primarily for its leaves, which are heart-shaped and beautifully marked, often pinkish in their early stages and turning to a lovely bronzy colour in winter. I have used them very effectively at the base of a small arrangement in a candle cup with the October flowering gentian *G. sino-ornata* and a few sprays of *Viburnum fragrans*. The flowers of *T. grandiflora* are 2 ft. spikes of small pink bells with a touch of green. They are a little insignificant but can nevertheless look well in contrast to bolder flower heads, as on Colour Plate V.
CONDITIONING The flowers and the leaves last better if their stems are plunged in a little boiling water before being given a long soaking.

N

Telopea speciosissima (Waratah)
Australian bush with superb large flowers, slightly resembling a red protea. It is the New South Wales State flower, and I enjoyed using them in large arrangements in the British Pavilion at the British Fair in Sydney.

Thalictrum (Meadow Rue)
Hardy herbaceous perennial with finely-cut green and grey-green leaves, and fluffy yellow and purple flowers in the summer. I find it most useful for the foliage as the flowers do not last very well in water. *T. glaucum* is my favourite as the foliage is blue-grey and I find it very good as a background in summer vases of greys and pinks as can be seen on Colour Plate VI. *T. dipterocarpum*, growing so well in Scotland, has the loveliest flowers and if it is ever available I am delighted to use it; it is so delicate with sprays of mauve flowers and looks charming arranged with a few sweet peas, or just alone in a glass vase.
CONDITIONING The foliage is better if given a really good soak, in deep warm water, but avoid submerging, which will diminish the grey effect of *T. glaucum*. I can recommend no special conditioning for the flowers, though a long drink is always a help.

Tiarella cordifolia (Foam Flower)
Hardy perennial herb with a spreading habit which makes it suitable for ground cover. The heart-shaped leaves with dark veining are nice to use in small arrangements (see the frontispiece). It has small, white fluffy flowers in spring, which I use in small vases, but I grow it really for the leaves.
CONDITIONING Soak the leaves completely under water for several hours.

Tilia (Lime Tree)
Hardy tree that from the flower arranger's point of view is quite wonderful. By removing the leaves when it is in blossom, you uncover the delightful small flowers and bracts of palest green which lend themselves as background to any summer flowers — to suggest but two, peonies and lilies. The stems, I discovered a few years ago, take up glycerine very well and you have delicate sprays of pale-brown bracts which add lightness to any dried group as in Colour Plate XII or make an unusual background for chrysanthemums.

CONDITIONING Peel off the bark up to about two inches, before giving a long drink.

TO PRESERVE Before the flower actually opens, pick the branches, remove the leaves and place the stems in a solution of glycerine and water.

Tobacco Plant *see* NICOTIANA

Tradescantia
Hardy herbaceous and tender perennials. The best known is *T. fluminensis*, a popular house plant with green and white leaves, pink-tinged if the plant is kept in a sunny position. It is most useful in bouquets and sprays, and I like to use small pieces in little vases, in winter especially. It has a sprawling, drooping form so that it is ideal to use falling from a candle cup. The hardy flowering form, *T. virginiana* (Moses in the Bulrushes), has showy blue, white or mauve flowers with three petals, and these can be used in mixed groups, but they need much of the foliage removed as the flowers are overshadowed by the leaves.

Transvaal Daisy *see* GERBERA

Tree Primrose *see* OENOTHERA

Trillium (Wood Lily)
Hardy tuberous-rooted perennial, not widely grown. They thrive in moist leaf-mould and have attractive lily-like leaves and white or mauve three-petalled flowers, which look well when arranged in a shallow bowl. Fix the stems on a pin-holder, so that the full beauty of the flower is displayed.
CONDITIONING Put the ends of the stems into boiling water and then allow a long drink.

Tritonia (Montbretia) *see* CROCOSMIA

Trollius (Globe Flower)
Hardy herbaceous perennial rather like a double buttercup, with round heads in orange or yellow. *T. chinensis* is my favourite and has pale-yellow heads that I like to use with small sprays of *Acer pseudo-platanus brilliantissimum* and dark heads of auricula.
CONDITIONING Dip the ends of the stems into boiling water, before putting them up to their necks in cold water for a long drink.

Tropaeolum (Nasturtiums)
Greenhouse and hardy perennials, dwarf and climbing. The hardy perennial creeper *T. speciosum* (Flame Flower) has scarlet flowers, and *T. polyphyllum* is a small yellow-flowered trailer. The yellow-flowered Canary Creeper, *T. peregrinum*, is best grown as an annual. The flowers of these climbers, and of the annual nasturtium, last exceedingly well when cut. The Shrewsbury show always has a class for nasturtiums and it produces some lovely arrangements; this is such a good idea as it gives everyone a chance to compete. I love to arrange the flowers with their own trails (all the buds open out in water), and find them most effective arranged in wood or metals, with their brilliant colours set off against a dark background.
CONDITIONING Give a good long drink before arranging.

Trumpet Flower *see* DATURA

Tuberose *see* POLIANTHES

Tulip *see* TULIPA

Tulipa

A candelabrum converted to hold tulips and azaleas

Tulipa (Tulip)

Hardy bulbs with very many varieties; it is difficult to choose which to mention. From the flower arranger's point of view, undoubtedly the delicate lily-flowered 'Moonlight' and many similar ones, are lovely to work with. So of course, are the May-flowering doubles, 'Mount Tacoma' (white), 'Eros' (pink), 'Lilac Time' (mauve), and so on, which give a good centre to any large group; grown well, they make enormous blooms that resemble a peony. The green tulips, hybrids of *Tulipa viridiflora*, are very striking. I have used 'Artist' in the arrangement shown on Colour Plate V. Parrot tulips are always decorative, with their feathery petals streaked with green on various colours, from almost black to shades of pink to pure white. The striped Rembrandt tulips are so typically Dutch that no modern Dutch group seems com-

plete without them. At tulip time one can work out some beautiful colour combinations: black and apricot, pink and black, soft yellow and creams, apricot pinks . . . tulips make all these possible. The dwarf tulip species should not be overlooked. They cut well and make a striking feature for any small spring vase, as you can see from the colour frontispiece. As the bulbs are small and need care, it is best to grow them in a rock garden or trough so that they are not likely to be dug out during the summer. *Tulipa clusiana* is one of my favourites: its alternating pink and white petals give it a striped effect. *T. hageri* is bright orange flushed with green back and the scarlet *T. linifolia* add a vivid spot of colour. As they are very delicate, they want careful arrangement so that they are not overshadowed by larger flowers.

CONDITIONING   Cut off the white end of the stem,

wrap the bunch in newspaper with all the heads together and put in deep warm water for several hours. Tulips react well to the addition of a teaspoonful of sugar to the vase water. Just recently I have found that pricking with a pin right through the stem just under the head makes the tulips last much better.

Tulip Tree *see* LIRIODENDRON

Turk's Cap Lily *see* LILIUM MARTAGON

Typha latifolia ('Bulrush'; Reed Mace, Cat's Tail) Very useful for adding pointed shapes to a large group. The small bullrushes I find the most generally useful, they last extremely well and look attractive arranged with rushes and other water plants in shallow dishes, so that the impression of water predominates.
TO PRESERVE   Try spraying the heads with hair-lacquer to prevent them from bursting, as when this happens the fluff seems to travel everywhere.

Ulex (Gorse, Whin) Hardy evergreen shrub growing mainly on common land, and giving a blaze of yellow to the countryside in spring. The double variety, *U. europaeus plenus*, makes a good garden shrub. Branches are effective for the house, but they need careful handling as the prickles are quite vicious. Pick with gloves on, and strip off the lower branches, and it is then possible to handle it. I like to use the burnt stems of dried gorse for a dramatic effect in the early spring, with scarlet tulips. Of course it is important to select well-shaped branches.
CONDITIONING   Remove the lower prickles and put into very hot water for a few hours.

Ulmus (Elm; Wych Elm) Hardy deciduous trees with green or variegated foliage. Branches of the golden elms *U. procera aurea* and *U. glabra lutesceus* are glorious in a large group in spring time. The Wych Elm, *U. glabra*, has clusters of brilliant-green flower bracts, on slightly weeping branches, and these are interesting to use with a few tree peonies or tulips, or to add to mixed green foliages. I also like to pick the pink flowers on the ordinary elm trees in February or

March and have them for a background for a vase of daffodils. The best-shaped bare branches are lovely for Christmas time; painted with gum and sprinkled with glass glitter, they look as if they were covered in frost. Branches that have become diseased and look like cork, are effective arranged with a few chrysanthemums, as a background for some dried seed heads.
CONDITIONING   For the flowering sprays and stems of the Wych Elm, it is important to hammer the ends of the stems very well, and then put them into boiling water for a minute or two before giving them a long drink.

Vallota speciosa (Scarborough Lily) Greenhouse evergreen bulbous plant. I enjoy using its brilliant scarlet lily flowers in a fruit and flower group in the early autumn. The vivid colour adds so much to a vase of late gladioli, dahlias and red roses, for a brilliant mixed red group.

Veltheimia Tender bulbous-rooted plants for a cool greenhouse. In early spring they produce orange and reddish flowers closely resembling a red-hot poker. I used these recently for the very first time in a vase with red *Begonia rex* leaves and budding pink flowering cherry.

Venetian Sumach *see* RHUS

Veratrum (False Hellebore) *Veratrum nigrum* is the plant I know best. It has beautifully pleated leaves (which the slugs adore), and long slender spikes of almost-black flowers; these are a joy to use and are particularly effective with the seed heads of *Phytolacca*, some almost-black dahlias and a bunch of white 'Iceberg' floribunda roses.
CONDITIONING   Cut the ends of the stems on the slant and give a good long drink.

Verbascum (Mullein) Hardy biennial and perennial herb with yellow or pink flowers in summer. The wild yellow mullein, though quick to shed its flowers, has a good flower head and a very nice seed head. The mauve and pink spikes of *V. chaixii* are attractive in the border, but my favourite is *V. broussa*, with its

Wild mullein with montbretia and peony foliage pick up the colours of the brown and yellow lustre jug

'cottonwool' leaves and stems; it is useful to put in a vase in its leaf stage and when in full flower.

CONDITIONING For the individual leaves, remove the fleshy part from the base of the leaf, especially the part that goes under water. If you fail to do this, you will find that the hairy leaves pick up the water and drip it off.

TO PRESERVE When the seed head has formed, remove the leaves and hang the heads upside down to dry.

Verbena

Half-hardy annual, flowering in a wide range of mauve, petunia and pinky shades. They make a good splash of colour in the garden and are effective in a small flower vase. They add gaiety to a vase of mixed annuals, and the double varieties last extremely well in water.

Verbena

CONDITIONING Put ends of stems into boiling water, and then allow a long drink.

Veronica (Speedwell)

Hardy herbaceous perennial with blue, pink or white flowers in summer. The blue varieties add a welcome touch of blue to an early summer vase of mixed flowers, and are pretty in the front of the border. The shrub varieties are helpful in late summer, and though I never want them just alone, they are useful in a mixed vase.

Viburnum (Guelder Rose; Snowball Tree;
   Wayfaring Tree)

Hardy deciduous flowering shrubs with white and pink flowers, which most of all I enjoy for their lovely scent. To pick a sprig of *V. fragrans* in the late autumn or even midwinter, and put it into a small vase either alone or added to a few freesias, or into a 'moss garden' of little flowers, is a joy. They scent the whole room. *V. carlesii* or *V. carlcephalum* in April have rounded heads of sweetly-scented pinky-white flowers; these, added to a few pale-pink tulips, a spray of azaleas, and some bronze peony foliage, make a charming arrangement. *V. opulus sterile*, better known as the Snowball Tree, hanging with little green balls that turn white as they open, is a shrub that I love, and I like best to use it in the green stage. It is forced in Holland and sold in long sprays here during the early spring; its touch of emerald green enhances any vase. *V. tomentosum mariesii* is one of the most handsome of all viburnums, with showy white flowers in spring and lovely leaf colour in the autumn. You can see how attractively it can be used with flowers of the Snowball tree on Plate 17. The wild wayfarer, *V. lanata*, is lovely to pick in the flower stage, but almost more welcome for its berries in the autumn. Many of the viburnums have good autumn colour and I like to use the turning leaves. The arching sprays of the Guelder Rose, *V. opulus*, last better than almost any autumn foliage I know: it holds its leaves so well that they remain on the branches even when they are quite dry.

CONDITIONING Hammer the ends of the stems, or put the ends into boiling water for a few minutes, before giving a long drink.

Viburnum tinus (Laurustinus)

Hardy evergreen with small rounded leaves and clusters of pink flowers in midwinter. Attractive used with or without its foliage. I like to remove the leaves to get the full colour from the flowers, using these in a vase of very early pink tulips and perhaps a few narcissi. A very useful shrub to grow, and excellent for picking well into the spring.

CONDITIONING Hammer ends of stems well, before giving a long drink.

Vinca (Periwinkle)

Hardy evergreen trailing plant used mainly as

Viburnum opulus sterile, the Snowball Tree

good ground-cover, but the green and white variegated variety has become popular for flower arrangement. These trails, if well conditioned, are a great asset for drooping down from a tall vase of either mixed shades of green or of flowers, now that plants with naturally drooping stems are more and more in demand.

CONDITIONING Put ends of stems into boiling water, then give a long drink (and in the case of variegated varieties, submerge completely) for several hours.

Viola (Pansy, Violet, Hearts-ease)

Hardy perennials with a sprawling habit and of many types, including the violet. Violets are nice to have in a small vase surrounded by their own leaves; always try to leave a stem or two out of water so that you get the benefit of the scent — in water they quickly lose it. Pansies can be arranged alone or in a mixed vase (see Colour Plate VII).

CONDITIONING No special treatment for pansies, but violets last better if their heads are dipped into water for a few minutes.

Viscum album (Mistletoe)

Traditionally a Christmas decoration, and connected with 'kissing under the Mistletoe', and so it has become a custom to hang up a sprig in every home at this time. I love to make a mistletoe ball with a round of Oasis; I stick in the stems until they make a rounded effect and then hang it up with scarlet ribbons. Or it is pretty in small pieces arranged for a table centre with Christmas roses and white candles.

Vitis coignetiae

Vitis (Vine)

Hardy perennial climbing plants with brilliant autumn colouring. *V. coignetiae*, with handsome spade-shaped leaves, is one of the most valuable from my point of view. A few of these leaves at the base of an autumn group are a great asset. The purple-leaved vine has useful foliage and charming little bunches of purple grapes. I grow a small vine called the strawberry vine because the grapes are thought to taste of strawberries, but I rarely eat them as I find it so useful to cut the small bunches of fruit and let them hang from the front of a vase.

CONDITIONING The sprays of leaves should be put into boiling water for a few minutes, before being given a long drink. The fruit needs no special treatment.

TO PRESERVE Odd leaves of good autumn colour may be pressed between sheets of newspaper. It is then advisable to put a florist's wire right up the back of the leaf and stick it with Sellotape to make a false stem.

Water Lily *see* NYMPHAEA

Willow *see* SALIX

Winter Aconite *see* ERANTHIS

Winter Cherry *see* SOLANUM and PHYSALIS

Winter Daffodil *see* STERNBERGIA

Winter Sweet *see* CHIMONANTHUS

Wisteria sinensis
Hardy deciduous climbing shrub with very sweet-scented trailing mauve or white blossom in May. It can be grown as a standard, though it is generally seen on walls or against houses. It is beautiful as a cut flower, but does not last very long in water. Used for the glory of one night is looks splendid alone in a vase, or with mauve lilac and mauve and pink tulips.
CONDITIONING   The method used in Japan is to put the stems into pure alcohol as soon as they are cut, and then to give a long drink.

Yucca gloriosa

Some of the finest specimens were those growing round the White House in Washington (alas, no longer there). I have used these elegant flowers for many special occasions; they are wonderful for a really large arrangement.
CONDITIONING   It is most important to put the ends of the stems into boiling water before giving a long drink.

Yulan *see* MAGNOLIA

Wisteria sinensis

Yarrow *see* ACHILLEA

Yucca (Adam's Needle, Spanish Bayonet)
Hardy and half-hardy evergreen shrubs with stiff tall spikes of creamy white bell-shaped flowers, growing out of a tuft of sword-like green leaves.

Zantedeschia aethiopica (Arum Lily, Calla Lily)
Generally a hothouse plant. There is a good hardy variety of *Z. aethiopica*, the white Arum Lily, but I have only seen it flourishing in warm corners of Ireland and Cornwall. Beautiful pure white flowers

and spade-shaped leaves — but too often considered funereal. It is ideal for large groups and for church flowers to be seen from a distance. *Z. elliottiana*, the yellow species, is also very handsome (see Colour Plate V). All these lilies have a texture that is almost like chamois leather and they show up better from a distance than perhaps any flower I can name. For a line arrangement in early spring, three blooms and a well-shaped branch give a vase a simple beauty and outlive a bunch of daffodils by days.

Zebrina pendula (facing page)

Zantedeschia aethiopica

CONDITIONING Give a long drink in a bucket of warm water up to their necks after picking. The leaves can be made to last much longer, for large groups especially, if submerged in a weak solution of starch water for twenty-four hours; this gives a slightly shiny appearance, but is worth doing for church festivals, when it is helpful to have groups that last well without much attention.

Zea mays (Maize, Indian Corn)

Z. mays japonica variegata is a half-hardy annual with truly beautiful cream and green striped leaves. There is also a pink and yellow strain which when mature goes a rich reddish purple. Both of these are great assets for the flower arranger. The seed heads are good in a fruit and flower group in autumn, or in a dried group. Suttons list an ornamental sugar corn with mature cobs ranging in colour from golden to purple, and this is particularly good.

CONDITIONING Do not pick until the plant is mature and fully grown, as before this the foliage is very tender and will not last well. Burn the ends of the stems and then allow a long drink in really deep water for at least twelve hours.

TO PRESERVE All corn can be preserved by hanging the heads upside down in a warm place. The husks turn a lovely golden colour and can be turned back to expose the cob, and used with fruits, or mounted on a wire and put in the centre of a dried group.

Zebrina pendula (Wandering Jew)
Greenhouse plant easily confused with trades-cantias, but it has slightly larger leaves, about three inches long, striped with silver and backed with purple.

Zenobia pulverulenta
Half-hardy evergreen shrub, liking peat and sandy loam and a moist sheltered position. The foliage is a delightful bluish-grey and the small bell-like flowers appear in pendulous clusters in June. The

Zinnias

Zenobia pulverulenta

flowers will show more clearly if a very few leaves are removed, and then sprays of all lengths are of great value.
CONDITIONING   Hammer the ends of the stems before giving a long drink.

Zinnia
Half-hardy annuals. There are many varieties that

vary in both height and colour, from the really large daisy-flowered head to the dwarf doubles. They have most lovely vivid colouring and give the much desired focal point for the flower arranger. Coming in every shade of red, pink, orange and cream, also white and even green, they are in constant use in the late summer and autumn for all kinds of mixed flower groups.
CONDITIONING   Cut and allow a long drink. If the blooms are exceptionally fine, it is advisable to put a thin stick up the hollow stem to prevent it from breaking.

Zygocactus truncatus (Christmas Cactus)
Greenhouse or house plant with cerise fuchsia-like flowers at Christmas-time. Good to use as a cut flower and effective with cerise anemones and small pieces of evergreen.

One of the new varieties of green zinnia makes a wonderful centre for a collection of autumn foliages and berries, including a leaf of a bi-coloured pelargonium and a hanging spray of cherry tomatoes. On the left are two stems of *Prunella grandiflora* in its dried seed-head state

Bibliography

The R.H.S. Dictionary of Gardening, edited by F. J. Chittenden, Oxford, Clarendon
    Press, 1951, 4 vols. *Supplement*, edited by P. M. Synge, 1956

W. Robinson, *The English Flower Garden*, 16th edition revised by Roy Hay.
    Murray, 1956

Alan Bloom, *Hardy Perennials*. Faber, 1957

Percy Thrower's *Encyclopaedia of Gardening*. Collingridge, 1962

T. Rochford & R. Gorer, *The Rochford Book of Flowering Pot Plants*. Faber, 1965

Patrick M. Synge, *Collins' Guide to Bulbs*. Collins, 1961

A. P. Balfour, *Annual and Biennial Flowers*. Penguin, 1959

C. Lucas Phillips, *The Small Garden*. Pan Books, 1965

Sybil C. Emberton, *Shrub Gardening for the Flower Arranger*. Faber, 1965

Margery Fish, *Gardening in the Shade*. Collingridge, 1964

Graham Stuart Thomas, *The Old Shrub Roses*. Phoenix House, 1956

T. C. Mansfield, *Annuals in Colour and Cultivation*. Collins, 1949

Index

Note: Varietal names in the Encyclopaedia section are not indexed here, since they are easily found when referring to generic and specific names. Also, as conditioning and preserving methods are appended in the Encyclopaedia section for quick reference, they are not re-indexed here.